AF361201

BLANK SPLENDOUR

Blank Splendour

Mere Existence in British Romanticism

DAVID COLLINGS

UNIVERSITY OF TORONTO PRESS
Toronto Buffalo London

© University of Toronto Press 2024
Toronto Buffalo London
utorontopress.com
Printed in the USA

ISBN 978-1-4875-5604-4 (cloth)   ISBN 978-1-4875-5606-8 (EPUB)
                                   ISBN 978-1-4875-5605-1 (PDF)

Library and Archives Canada Cataloguing in Publication

Title: Blank splendour : mere existence in British romanticism / David Collings.
Names: Collings, David, 1959– author.
Description: Includes bibliographical references and index.
Identifiers: Canadiana (print) 20230562868 | Canadiana (ebook) 20230562922 |
    ISBN 9781487556044 (cloth) | ISBN 9781487556051 (PDF) |
    ISBN 9781487556068 (EPUB)
Subjects: LCSH: English poetry – 19th century – History and criticism. |
    LCSH: Romanticism – Great Britain. | LCSH: Painting, British – 19th
    century. | LCSH: Romanticism in art.
Classification: LCC PR590 .C65 2024 | DDC 821/.709145 – dc23

Cover design: John Beadle
Cover image: Art Collection 2 / Alamy Stock Photo

We wish to acknowledge the land on which the University of Toronto Press
operates. This land is the traditional territory of the Wendat, the Anishnaabeg,
the Haudenosaunee, the Métis, and the Mississaugas of the Credit First Nation.

This book has been published with the assistance of Bowdoin College.

University of Toronto Press acknowledges the financial support of the Government
of Canada, the Canada Council for the Arts, and the Ontario Arts Council, an
agency of the Government of Ontario, for its publishing activities.

Canada Council   Conseil des Arts
for the Arts   du Canada

ONTARIO ARTS COUNCIL
CONSEIL DES ARTS DE L'ONTARIO
an Ontario government agency
un organisme du gouvernement de l'Ontario

Funded by the   Financé par le
Government   gouvernement   Canadä
of Canada   du Canada

Contents

Acknowledgments

This project had its inception when I came across John Clare's sonnet "Obscurity" in an Adam Phillips essay about the poet. That poem haunted me for several decades until conceptual frameworks suitable for highlighting by contrast what made that poem distinctive began to arrive a few years ago. Along the way, it inspired me to explore similar ventures in a range of further poems and paintings in the period; eventually, I realized that each instance revolved around a blank feature and that as a result I had unwittingly been writing a book on a consistent theme. What this book was truly addressing, however, continued to elude me for many years.

I would never have discovered the argument of this book and reworked the various chapters into suitable shape without the comments and suggestions of many colleagues all along the way. I thank Tilottama Rajan for her invitation to present a version of what is now chapter one (on Wordsworth) at the University of Western Ontario, to Nancy Yousef for inviting me to present a revised version at a CUNY Graduate Centre colloquium, and to Richard Sha and Joel Faflak for including a further rendition in their co-edited collection on emotion. Moreover, I am grateful to Jacques Khalip for inviting me to present an initial attempt at chapter four (on Clare) in a seminar at Brown, to Julie Murray and Lauren Gillingham for inviting me to present a revised version in a seminar at the North American Society for the Study of Romanticism (NASSR) conference in Ottawa, Canada, and to Chris Washington and Anne McCarthy for their invitation to include a version of that chapter in an essay collection they co-edited – and especially to Chris for his remarkably insightful comments on that piece as editor. The comments and responses on all these occasions – as well as at NASSR panels where I presented early versions of chapters two (on Coleridge) and three (on Keats) – have been pivotal to my work on this book, and I acknowledge specific suggestions in notes throughout.

Needless to say, the above occasions arose within the most definitive context for my work on this book, the extraordinary community of scholars on

Romanticism, one of the most lively, collegial, and inspiring cohorts in the humanities today. It is difficult to convey how wonderful it has been to spend my entire career working alongside colleagues like these in a field this rewarding. I especially thank all those who have served with me on the Board or in leadership positions with NASSR, doing their part to make the field into a flourishing, collegial environment for our collective work, especially Tilottama Rajan, Angela Esterhammer, Chris Bundock, Michelle Faubert, Kir Kuiken, and John Savarese, among many others; I am grateful as well to the many colleagues who have been willing to put in an immense effort to host annual NASSR conferences, where so much of our common work takes place. Among the many colleagues whose brilliance and enthusiasm shape the field, I especially wish to acknowledge those who have shared their encouragement and solidarity in relation to this project and to my work in these recent years, including (in addition to those mentioned above) Colin Jager, Alan Vardy, Nick Halmi, Rei Terada, Libby Fay, Billy Galperin, David Clark, Joan Steigerwald, Alexander Schlutz, Josh Wilner, David Sigler, Katey Castellano, Ian Balfour, Andrew Warren, Scott Juengel, Soelve Curdts, Kate Singer, Jamison Kantor, Andy Burkett, Allison Dushane, Taylor Schey, Hannah Markley, Armando Mastrogiovanni, Marc Mazur, and Isaac Cowell.

Once again, my work on this book could not have taken place without those who, at my home institution of Bowdoin College, have provided a lively intellectual community – most especially Liz Muther and Mark Foster, whose friendships have sustained me through thick and thin. I am grateful as well that many senior staff managed the College's affairs so well during these Covid years, making them far less onerous than they otherwise would have been. I thank the Faculty Research Committee for their support of this project through a Faculty Leave Supplement that made it possible for me to devote a portion of a recent sabbatical to drafting this book, a grant that allowed me to conduct research on Turner at the Fine Arts Library at Harvard, and funding that is enabling this book to reach publication.

Although the comments of many respondents provoked me to deepen the argument of specific chapters, something about the book's themes continued to elude me even as I submitted the initial draft. I thank the two readers for the University of Toronto Press – including Tilottama Rajan – for pushing me hard to craft more explicit and consistent claims; in response to their demands I have discovered quite a bit more about what this book has been saying all along. I am immensely grateful to Mark Thompson, my editor, for recognizing this project's potential and for enabling me to publish at the Press once again.

I am delighted to acknowledge my debt to the staff at the University of Toronto Press, which once again have demonstrated their outstanding professionalism. I especially wish to thank the production and publicity staff, including Deborah Kopka, Stephanie Mazza, and Sathya Shree Kumar, for handling the key phases of this book's publication with remarkable efficiency and grace.

I give my most immense thanks to Terri Nickel, whose profound love makes this shared life truly joyous. She has been the partner of my heart, editor, and colleague throughout my career, from start to finish, patiently abiding with my work even on this culminating book. The delight of her presence and the ridiculous antics of Jeremy cat lend magic to each day, reminding me at once and always of the incalculable bliss of existence.

A version of chapter one appeared as "Emotion without Content: Primary Affect and Pure Potentiality in Wordsworth," in Richard Sha and Joel Faflak, editors, *Romanticism and the Emotions* (Cambridge: Cambridge University Press, 2014), 171–91. A preliminary version of chapter two, a few sentences of which survive below, was published as "Positive Negation: On Coleridge's 'Human Life'" (*Romantic Circles Praxis*, 2017). An earlier version of chapter four appeared in Chris Washington and Anne C. McCarthy, editors, *Romanticism and Speculative Realism* (New York: Bloomsbury, 2019), 75–91. I thank these publishers for permission to include revised versions of these essays in this book.

BLANK SPLENDOUR

Introduction

Consider three moments within British Romantic poetry and art. In the first, William Wordsworth's 1798–9 *Prelude* features a child who, after the death of his mother and the ensuing loss of his secure grasp of the world, gains an orientation to it by feeling "whate'er there is of power in sound / To breathe an elevated mood by form / Or image unprofaned" as he listens to "sounds that are / The ghostly language of the ancient earth."[1] Suddenly incapable of finding himself in the world, this child has recourse to the primordial sound of the earth, through which he can absorb a mood without form or figure and thereby enter into existence – albeit one that precedes any content, any positive features. In the second, the narrator of John Keats's *Fall of Hyperion*, bearing with the motionless silence of the fallen gods Saturn and Thea, witnesses the condition of what has been utterly dispossessed, coming to share in the blank affect of stone. Finally, J.M.W. Turner fills the upper two-thirds of one of his last paintings, *Sunrise with Sea Monsters*, with a light that, originating in no sun, showing no phenomenal world, illuminates only itself – and thus displays the radiance of an appearing that makes nothing but itself appear. These instances capture a radically reduced, bare state by evoking the moodless mood of pure sound, impassive stone, or empty light, in these ways conveying the tone of a blank existence.

Consider as well two further moments that evoke this state with even greater severity. In "Human Life: On the Denial of Immortality," Samuel Taylor Coleridge, faithful to an eternity that cannot appear within the limits of time or space, conceives of human life within them as so denuded of significance, so absolutely without substance, that even an attempt to register this condition emotionally is futile. For his part, John Clare, in the sonnet "Obscurity," depicts an old tree over which sweeps a summer wind that leaves no record, no trace – a wind whose anonymous, indifferent force condemns all living things to oblivion. In these passages, bare existence transpires in a domain beyond affect, eradicating the import even of an emotional response.

What condition do these various moments capture? All of them speak of a state from which the ordinary attributes of existence – time and space, subject and object, articulation and differentiation – have fallen away, leaving a domain without attributes, outside the world and thought. In this state a supposedly substantial, grounded condition of being gives way to a mode without origin, justification, explanation, destination, or guarantee – a condition that I will call "mere existence."

This condition shares much with what Emmanuel Levinas names the *there is*.[2] In a pivotal chapter of *Existence & Existents*, he imagines the situation of a mind at night, when all appearances dissolve in the dark, and argues that in this nothingness, "[s]omething would happen, if only night and the silence of nothingness." Such a state "transcends inwardness as well as exteriority; it does not even make it possible to distinguish these. The anonymous current of being invades, submerges every subject, person or thing." Furthermore, "[w]e could say that the night is the very experience of the *there is*, if the term experience were not inapplicable to a situation which involves the total exclusion of light." In this night, "we are not dealing with anything. But this nothing is not that of pure nothingness," for "this universal absence is in its turn a presence, an absolutely unavoidable presence." This state "is no longer a world. What we call the I is itself submerged by the night, invaded, depersonalized, stifled by it. The disappearance of all things and of the I leaves what cannot disappear, the sheer fact of being in which *one* participates, whether one wants to or not, without having taken the initiative, anonymously."[3] Insofar as this sheer fact of being cannot disappear, engulfing all things with its implacable persistence, the *there is* "has 'no exits.' It is, if we may say so, the impossibility of death, the universality of existence even in its annihilation."[4]

Levinas's deployment of night to elucidate the *there is* goes far towards clarifying its features. But insofar as several instances in Romantic works depict that state without reference to night, one must consider that element in his argument as a metaphor for the more definitive concern, the disappearance of world, however conceived. (I use the term "works" here advisedly, not to give poems or paintings a grandiose status but to find a neutral term that can apply to them both.) Taking his argument in this way, one can regard it as a useful depiction of how the erasure of the positive features of the world – of objects, things, persons – leads not to utter disappearance but rather to an anonymous, bare being, or what I am calling, so as to avoid the ontological confidence of the word "being," mere existence. Setting aside the metaphor of night, however, has a further consequence: one must now argue that this condition eludes direct experience not because it takes place without light but rather because it occurs in a situation logically prior to experience as such, outside the security of either subject or world; strictly speaking, then, it transpires for a nonsubject in a nonworld, a receptivity that one cannot assign to any differentiated entity and that is intrinsic to the insistence of the *there is* in its own right.[5] This argument reinforces Levinas's suggestion that one caught in this state endures in a condition outside mortality – not in immortality or eternity, which is a state beyond time, but rather in what I will call nonmortality, that is, in an existence that "cannot disappear," that persists without limit in a perpetual, futile continuity. The import of this state remains open: while the vacuity of the *there is* might give rise to a certain horror, as Levinas suggests, much as its implacable flow may inspire a "horror of immortality," it may just as well inspire a bliss of pure existence, an astonishment at the sheer, endless persistence of the world.[6] Arising at the very limits of what one can grasp or conceive, it has no definitive import, no proper form: it repudiates every effort to determine its precise significance.

Because mere existence persists without world or subject, it occupies a difficult status. As Levinas argues, one cannot say that something is there, yet this is not a condition of sheer nothingness. How might one capture its elusive character? In experiencing that state, does one enter a domain beyond the world? Maurice Blanchot provides a useful approach to this question. On the opening page of *Le Pas Au-Dela*, translated as *The Step Not Beyond* – where the French word *pas* denotes at once *step* and *not*, indicating that this is simultaneously a step, and yet not, into the beyond – he writes, "Time, time: the step not beyond that is not accomplished in time would lead outside of time, without this outside being intemporal."[7] A certain state is beyond, and yet not beyond, outside of time, and yet not intemporal. One could adapt this formulation to capture the state of mere existence: it is outside of existence without ceasing to exist.

What strategies do Romantic works pursue to capture that elusive condition? Like this passage in Blanchot, they deploy fundamental aspects of existence while also erasing them, unworking basic dimensions of representation, figuration, or narration as they do so. They display remarkable skills in this effort, for they create situations that are at the limits of comprehension while still remaining accessible. They share a number of strategies in this regard. Each artist in this book invokes motions that can never be reduced to objects or subjects, such as winds, breezes, tides, or waves, tracing the effects of a process that never becomes secure enough to provide an ontological grounding. Levinas calls upon a similar figure to make this suggestion when he writes, as we have seen, that "[t]he anonymous current of being invades, submerges every subject, person or thing." In this context, the wind is especially apt, for even though it has effects on objects and subjects alike, it is difficult to fix in a secure form; accordingly, it readily figures a movement that, like Levinas's current, submerges every subject, person, or thing without becoming yet another entity in its own right. While it may be tempting to argue that these works suggest what one might call, in a parody of the term "object-oriented ontology," a process-oriented metaphysics, in fact they deploy process not to highlight process itself but rather to indicate how it brings into view a groundless condition. As these winds sweep across phenomena, as these waves drown all finite things, they exemplify a force that, while evading reification, hollows out everything in the world we know.

Bearing out this pattern, these works also take up the crucial theme of temporality, anticipating Blanchot as they conceive of an inoperative time, a time outside of time. But one who endures in a time without time also persists in nonmortality, in a life outside of the ordinary assurances of life. Variations on this theme appear across all the instances in this book. Coleridge defines mortal human life as transpiring without reason or purpose – thereby constituting a form of life that is as vacuous and senseless as death. The narrator of *The Fall of Hyperion*, given the opportunity to witness the suffering of the fallen gods, suffers the pain not so much of immortality but rather its loss, its slide into a stasis that nevertheless forever persists.

A state that eludes more familiar understandings of time is equally difficult to place in the visible world. The old man of Coleridge's "Limbo" presumably seeks a sign of eternity in the light of the moon in order to fix his existence in a knowable world, but he blindly gazes at what cannot gaze at him, seeing nothing that can secure his position. Moneta's eyes, which emanate a mild glow like the light of the moon, see no external things and thus cannot respond to those who seek comfort from them; in her face the blindness of the old man and the light of the moon fuse into a single image, a blind light that cannot give the world significance. Turner's sun, blazing too brightly for human eyes to bear, obliterates the visible world, dissolving at once the viewing subject and the domain of phenomenal appearances. In all these instances, something cancels sight and visibility alike, as if a form of blindness has befallen both the subject and the world.

While one might fear that such evocations verge on erasing the political, flirting with a depoliticizing ideology, in fact these works evoke a state of supreme fragility that underlies the urgency of political response. Beginning with his visceral horror at the prospect of war between England and France, which he regards as dismembering the cultural formation he knows best, Wordsworth gradually works through a series of more and more reduced evocations of that violated state, and after moving into the context of his own life, ultimately suggests that through the loss of his mother, he loses the world – suffering a loss that comes not simply to him but through relationship itself. Here the condition of the nonsubject within an utterly denuded world marks not the erasure of the political but the insistence of its most ineradicable dimension, a primordial alterity. In his unfinished epic, Keats cuts through the assurances of narration to capture what narrative excludes, the situation of those who have been cast aside by the imperative to recount historical change and forgotten by those focused on the actions of agents and subjects. In effect, he lingers over those who have been abjected by narrative, jettisoned from the world of visible and knowable politics, and thus suffer from the politics of the political itself, the exclusions that make it possible. Finally, in a corpus preoccupied with the dispossession of the commons and the perilous situation of nonhuman creatures, Clare delves further into those concerns in his sonnet, revealing a vulnerability that the old tree and human beings share under the flow of oblivion, thereby conceiving of a new understanding of commonality: a politics of severe fragility, a solidarity in oblivion. Each of these instances, then, outlines a version of the political that, outside its ordinary conceptions, insists in an even more implacable form.

I

The fact that these works share this range of strategies, despite their many differences of genre, medium, or emphasis, is perhaps best revealed by the fact that each relies on the word *blank* – or its corollaries in a blank region of a painting – as it depicts the contours of mere existence. This usage is the most pivotal indication of what is at stake. Although other passages invoke the word *blank* at key moments (as students of British Romanticism can easily attest), it is crucial for our present purposes that this usage appear within an exploration of the state of mere existence, that it reveal a concerted engagement with that condition. Thus it is telling that all of the literary instances in these works deploy the word *blank*, that is, an adjectival form rather than a substantive noun such as *blankness*, indicating that they do not wish to use the term to establish any systematic figurative or conceptual schema. Moreover, the fact that such a modifier is attached to a wide range of nouns – from misgivings to splendour, from accident to oblivion – indicates that it never appears in any proper form, any fixed scene, but rather, as Levinas suggests, invades all possible regions of existence. In effect, this variety of usages gestures towards an evacuated state without attempting to claim that it can be contained in any conceptual architecture.

The status of that blank condition, then, remains elusive, just out of view from what one can grasp. But its elusiveness is borne out even further in the divergence of attitudes manifested towards it in these works. Because it transpires in a state logically prior to the delimited experience of any given subject, it has no specific affect or tone in its own right, not even or necessarily the horror to which Levinas refers; accordingly, as we have seen, some works depict it in part as an instance of minimal affect, while others subtract even this feature from their accounts. Moreover, in some cases, as we have seen, authors elicit it in a mode of stunning austerity: one cannot go much further in this direction than Clare in his sonnet on oblivion. But that sonnet also shows that the movement of oblivion provides shelter and indeed a form of hospitality, making possible the mode of mere existence that various modes of life share. Even over the brief course of that sonnet, the tone modulates. Wordsworth's approach undergoes even more changes. In his initial treatment of that state, he regards it as the inception of his relation to existence, the first step of his entering a possible world. In further lines of the same poem, he suggests that as a result of such developments he could sense the bliss of mere existence. But in the Intimations Ode, he adds a further twist: he remembers how the child in that evacuated state suffers "blank misgivings" when aspects of the phenomenal world, less definitive than that state, cannot attain the status of reality and in consequence fall away from him. What affords bliss can also lead to crisis. Keats, for his part, includes divergent tones in a single image: in a key passage, the narrator of his unfinished epic looks into the "blank splendour" of Moneta's eyes, which are at once splendid in their mild glow, comforting those on whom they cast light, but also blank, providing no guidance, no response to anyone who may see them. This phrase fuses splendour with futility, comfort with radical indifference, indicating that mere existence is at once radiant and barren.

This variety of tones suggests that it is too hasty to assume that one must discuss mere existence in a tone of despair, for it is accessible to positive and ambivalent depictions, as well as to responses that can evolve and transform. I have chosen to indicate the complexity of these responses in the title of this book, which follows Keats in encapsulating contrasting features in a single phrase. Moreover, although this condition can be evoked in many figures and scenarios, it is not linked primarily to any one of them and thus cannot be mastered through any definitive trope. This array of instances makes clear that it is neither a referent nor an idea; it belongs to no philosophical system, no discipline, no institution, no single figural strategy. For all these reasons, I have chosen to refer to it as "mere existence," resisting the temptation to rely on conceptual determinations or figural elements (in a phrase such as "bare existence") so as to hold closely to its absolutely minimal profile. Of course, even the word "mere" brings its own overtones. As Rodolphe Gasché points out, Kant relies on the German equivalent, *bloss*, in his third critique to accentuate the autonomy of reflective judgment, to set it apart from other faculties; in a somewhat analogous fashion, I will use the word to draw attention to a mode of existence without attributes, excluding every feature aside from existence itself.[8]

The merits of this approach may only become evident if one ponders alternative strategies for designating this state. A fascinating array of attempts beckon to us here: the moment when Levinas, as we have seen, refers to "this universal absence" as "a presence, an absolutely unavoidable presence," or when Denis Hollier, attempting to capture Georges Bataille's notion of the sacred, describes it not as the "*absence of* [God's] *presence*" but the "*presence of* [his] *absence*."[9] Such moments reveal the attempt to refuse the nostalgia implicit in speaking of the absence of presence – as if absence still retains the imprint of what has been lost – and emphasize instead the palpable force of the opposite, the imprint of the absence. Yet this very gesture risks making absence itself into a positive presence. A similar fate befalls Jacques Lacan's term "the Real," which while designating what destabilizes the symbolic is nevertheless an apparent term within the symbolic in its own right – and moreover, a term that, in its commonsensical denotation, seems to refer to reality, the most exemplary reification of all. Thus it is no wonder that Derrida attempts to escape this impasse by creating a neologism that mangles existing terms, claiming that *différance* "is neither a word nor a concept," even though despite this claim he still finds himself using the term as a noun in suitably grammatical sentences – that is, as a word – and as a concept of what undermines the concept; despite his best efforts he finds himself in a somewhat more elusive difficulty than that of Lacan.[10] In the light of these later adventures, the Romantic strategy of relying on the adjective is compelling in its efficient refusal of such failures; it suggests that a gesture is more astute than a name – even the name that I am using here, "mere existence" – and that an evocation goes further than a concept.

These difficulties point us towards a crucial feature of mere existence: outside of Romanticism itself, it becomes most apparent in the work of thinkers who belong to a generation after the emergence of Heideggerian thought but before the arrival of Derrida. They thus belong to the complex trajectory that Tilottama Rajan has examined in *Deconstruction and the Remainders of Phenomenology*, arising at a particular phase within a genealogy extending from Husserl, Heidegger, Sartre, and others through Derrida, Foucault, and Baudrillard.[11] As Rajan demonstrates, in his notion of the *there is* Levinas attempts to rework several themes in the work of Jean-Paul Sartre – such as his thematics of nausea and of nothingness – and move beyond Heidegger's metonyms for the subject as well as his thematics of light.[12] For his part, the early Blanchot, also engaging with Sartre, displaces Heideggerian themes so consistently that, as Rajan writes, "Blanchot is Heidegger with a minus sign."[13] The resonances between these two thinkers is no accident; indeed, Blanchot relies upon Levinas's writing on the *there is* as he elucidates his own concerns, incorporating that depiction of a denuded state into his account of the literary work.[14] Although the two thinkers take divergent approaches – one by means of a remarkable shift within and against the phenomenological tradition, another through a severely negated theory of literature – they both depict a state where the world, having fallen away, leaves a worldless state that, bereft of every feature, endlessly persists. The severity of these contributions is so striking that Rajan places them both within what she calls "an earlier deconstruction" that arrives well before the emergence of Derrida, much as, throughout that book, she argues that deconstruction cannot be reduced to a specifically poststructuralist mode of thought.[15] This analysis suggests, then, that a certain deconstruction begins with the radicalization of what French thinkers inherit from Heidegger and Sartre, with a more astringent refusal of the ontological legacy.

In that case, it may be well to pause here to examine what procedures or approaches are distinctive to this early deconstruction, for doing so may clarify what is at stake in Romantic evocations of mere existence as well. Blanchot's response to Heidegger's notion of being-towards-death provides a useful example. In *The Space of Literature*, a discussion of Stéphane Mallarmé leads Blanchot to propose that death establishes the preconditions for dying, "as though death had first to be anonymous in order to occur with certainty in someone's name." Since in this mode, death precedes its event, in some sense "the event could never happen," for it takes place in that "hour which has never yet come, which never comes, the pure, ungraspable future, the hour eternally past."[16] Accordingly, death "comes either too soon or too late, prematurely and as if after the fact, never coming until after its arrival. It is the abyss of present time, the reign of a time without a present."[17] Such reflections lead him, in his later reading of Rainer Maria Rilke, to challenge Heidegger directly, for he argues that death is "the extreme of power, as my most proper possibility, but also the death which never comes to me, to which I can never say yes, with which there is no authentic relation possible. Indeed, I elude it when I think I master it through a resolute acceptance, for then I turn away from what makes it the essentially inauthentic and the essentially inessential." In consequence, "death admits of no 'being *for* death'; it does not have the solidity which would sustain such a relation."[18] Here Blanchot, in articulating his understanding of literature, at the same time hollows out Heidegger and accentuates the radical negativity of existence *tout court*. Later, responding in part to the ethical philosophy of Levinas, Blanchot enlarges on these concerns, writing in *Step Not Beyond* that this dying that "does not concern me … puts me in play in all my dying, by way of a relation that does not arrive through me" – that is, as John D. Caputo comments, "in relation with, in play with, the other's dying," in which case the step not beyond is not my own but "the step of the other at my door."[19] The ravage of a dying that has already taken place does not single out the subject but rather befalls others, all others, so that this death befalls in a nonproper mode, through a certain alterity that one might recognize as what remains of the ethical or political. This broader reach of Blanchot's concern emerges even more visibly in *The Writing of the Disaster*, which deploys the above arguments regarding death on the much broader terrain of disaster. Here a terminal, nonempirical event has already befallen everyone and everything: "The disaster ruins everything, all the while leaving everything intact"; rather than arriving, it "has put a stop to every arrival," so that "[t]o think the disaster … is to have no longer any future in which to think it." Suggesting in the following pages that disaster cancels knowledge, power, mastery, and the value of experience, Blanchot declares that disaster produces a "[t]ime without present, I without I."[20]

In such passages, a version of deconstruction arises in the refusal to hypostasize death or disaster, to transform the inauthentic into the authentic, the inessential into the essential, the negative into an enterprise that bears the slightest traces of the positive. But what sort of negativity does Blanchot invoke? In his discussion of Blanchot's subtle renditions of *pas*, the neutral, and the border, Derrida points out that the formulation on which these renditions often depend – "X *without* X" – "neutralizes without negativity, while affecting the neutral with an absolute heterogeneity."[21] We have already encountered a version of this usage in Blanchot's reference to a time outside of time, but a version of that usage appears in Levinas as well in his discussion of an experience without experience. In effect, both thinkers delineate something that erases existence while leaving it intact, an existence without existence. But in arguing that Blanchot "neutralizes without negativity," Derrida writes another version of "X without X," for in effect he points to a negativity without negativity. This negativity, of course, is not an instance of the Hegelian negation of the negation, a productive negativity; on the contrary, as Blanchot maintains, it is an *unusable* negativity, one that cannot be sublated or metabolized.[22] In Levinas and Blanchot, then, one sees an awareness that the very concept of negativity must also be erased; to unwork the likes of Hegel and Heidegger requires what is ultimately a second-order negation, an even more severe erasure of erasure itself.

Taking up the mode of thought of this early deconstruction is especially relevant in the current critical climate, when reflection is considering questions that are not necessarily conceived in linguistic terms; doing so also highlights those features of Romantic works that remain radical even today, capable of challenging or displacing versions of contemporary posthuman critique. A good case in point is speculative realism, a philosophical movement quite relevant to this project. In *After Finitude: An Essay on the Necessity of Contingency*, Quentin Meillassoux attempts to fashion a mode of thought that can conceive of a world whose objects appear without reference to humanity. But just as Blanchot, confronting Heidegger's apparently severe notion of being-towards-death, finds in it an unwarranted confidence that one can thematize death, so also one can discern, in Meillassoux's emphasis on the arche-fossil, a mode of reflection that leans heavily on the apparent solidity and reality of the physical world, that eclipses the subject only to discover an alternative foundation in the domain of objects, and that as a result re-establishes a version of certitude, a positive presence, even in the absence of the human.[23] It may appear that Ray Brassier, another key theorist in this tradition, provides a better approach, for near the end of his study he emphasizes not an arche-fossil but rather the death of the sun – the *disappearance*, that is, of a particularly significant object – and argues, following a suggestion by Jean-François Lyotard, that "the solar catastrophe needs to be grasped as something that has *already happened*."[24] He thus brings about the temporal transposition proposed in Blanchot, showing how the eventual death of the sun already hollows out existence *tout court*. In such a moment, Brassier is the heir of early deconstruction, using speculative realist thought as a fulcrum to generate once again a sense of mere existence; indeed, as he elucidates this argument, he invokes those dimensions of Levinas's work that would allow one to "describe extinction as a traumatic seizure of phenomenology."[25] Yet insofar as this argument arises late in a book that is still focused on thinking a world apart from humanity, it continues to elevate the object-world and thus leaves in place key features familiar in Meillassoux.

A more rigorous thought, then, would insist that one need not take a detour through the object-world, even through the death of the sun, for as Brassier acknowledges, the death in question operates continuously through all phenomena, is evident at every moment, and is intrinsic to temporality itself. Nor would it take up a further strand of speculative realist or new materialist thought and rest content with emphasizing material process, however important it is, for doing so would, through its very emphasis on this subtler dimension of the domain of objects, evade its more crucial import, its capacity to erase objects and subjects alike.[26] The most rigorous approach, then, would take the form of Clare's astonishing sonnet, in which, by means of process, a traceless oblivion has already befallen the old tree, has already erased the significance of all finite things. As I argue in chapter four, that sonnet has absorbed what Brassier has to teach and gone much further, taking up themes that speculative realism, even at its most adventurous, has not contemplated.

This early deconstruction readily cuts through further theoretical trends in our moment; it is indeed strikingly contemporary. The emphasis on affect, for example, goes far towards displacing more traditional analyses of representational or conceptual strategies, moving past certain established understandings of the subject. But even in its more adventurous formulations, affect theory retains an encrypted reference to human emotion, however attenuated, unconscious, or displaced. Here again, even negative modes of thought still retain vestiges of what they attempt to erase. A negation to the second degree would argue instead that in mere existence there arises not only an I without I, a world without world, but also an emotion without emotion – an emotion without content, precisely the mode of affect that Wordsworth elicits in the passages I will discuss in chapter one. Or take historicism as a further example. Once again one may move from historicism per se, familiar to all students of British Romanticism, to a Heideggerian historicity, to a state of historical exposure; but this historicity, in turn, which carries with it the remainders of subjectivity encrypted within Dasein, would under the pressure of a further negation give way to a more denuded state, a historicity without history, a time without present – a sense of history that Keats explores in his Hyperion poems, the subject of chapter three.

One might well work through a similar sequence in response to still further theoretical approaches of our moment. But here it may be best to pause to consider an important aspect of this early form of deconstruction: thanks to its very procedure, it cannot address itself to any definitive feature. Although it need not take a detour through the object, nor indeed through a linguistically oriented deconstructive analysis, it does not designate an alternative object as its concern; indeed, it cannot directly capture what it attempts to evoke. The necessary indirection of this mode of thought has important implications. Because mere existence cannot be apprehended through any concept, figure, or emotion, it can emerge only through a subtle indication – an intuition, a surmise, a hint. Only a sophisticated *strategy* for eliciting it will do, only a careful approach that refuses to fix it in a direct or reductive representation. Accordingly, the works discussed in this book approach it by initially establishing a set of accessible terms, complicating them, and eventually stepping outside them without abandoning them altogether; they pass through mediating contexts that they eventually elude to make a specific evocation legible in a procedure very like the one I have just traced in relation to speculative realism. This pattern reveals that the attempt to elicit mere existence belongs to no specific commitment – neither to a politics of the commons, for example, nor to landscape painting – but can arise within them and many others.

For these reasons, to decipher this pattern one can rely neither on the resources of the history of ideas, for example, nor on the analytic tools of keyword analysis. Nor can one approach them through any particular contextual grid – a specific historical or political concern, a formally distinct aesthetic practice, or a coherent set of philosophical arguments. It eludes all such determinations. As a result, in the chapters that follow I will pursue a different strategy, examining five idiosyncratic renditions of mere existence, none of which necessarily shares details or terms with any other, and that together provide a disjunctive array surrounding a shared theme that can never become visible in its own right.

The divergence of contexts at stake in this book, however, does not imply that the abiding concern is free of context. On the contrary, the fact that such works appear across several regions of poetry and art in the same period suggests that historical developments not limited to those particular endeavours – but rather transformations in the conditions of Western culture as a whole – helped to generate this new concern. One can attribute the emergence of a sense of this state not to any particular context, then but rather to what one might call a metacontext, to a transformation in the premises attendant on virtually every mode of thought in the late eighteenth century.

To understand the rise of attempts to evoke mere existence, then, one must theorize this wholesale alteration in the conditions of thought. To do so, here I draw on and expand the historiography I proposed in *Disastrous Subjectivities: Romanticism, Modernity, and the Real*.[27] In that book, I suggested that in the late eighteenth century there emerged a widespread sense that empirical history had lost its ground in a divine origin or end. This sense, characteristic of modernity, appeared in what Reinhart Koselleck describes as the temporalization of history, its breach of the predictable patterns in which it was previously understood to move, and thus by implication its loss of any sustaining framework that gave it significance.[28] But the cancellation of a transcendental ground does not lead to its outright disappearance; instead, the mark of that cancellation endures as an intrusive obstacle, an unassimilable element. As Joan Copjec argues, "[I]f one wants to prevent the formation of an outside," of an origin or end, then one must "inscribe in the interior" of history "a negation that says 'no' precisely to the possibility of an outside." This negation perpetually destabilizes that history, for "if history has no outside," that is, "if history is without limit, then it must accommodate or be invaded by the infinite, the never-ending, by undying repetition, or the undead."[29] One can trace the inscription of that mark across many discourses in the Romantic period. If history is no longer anchored by divine creation or redemptive apocalypse, then it is vulnerable, for example, to the perpetual interruptions of natural disaster, which rather than speaking of any divine intention reveals the contingencies of a material existence shaped by the realities of astronomy, geology, and biology. By the same token, if the political order is no longer founded on a sacred principle but is subject to the vicissitudes of an ungrounded history, then it is vulnerable to unpredictable, disruptive events at every moment and without limit; as a result, no state can become immune to factors that perpetually elude its forms of governance, its styles of state-thought.[30] This shift does not produce a truly secular arrangement, a consistent, self-authorizing modernity, but rather a domain endlessly disrupted by that cancelled transcendence. It follows that modernity, in its very attempt to supersede tradition, becomes subject to a deadlock that is part of its own functioning – an internal limit – being forever susceptible to being disturbed by what Copjec, following Lacan, calls the Real.

In the context of the present work, one must complicate this reading of modernity. For one thing, one must immediately note that the transposition that Copjec traces – the shift of a cancelled origin or end into an internally displacing component of a limitless, ungrounded history – is precisely the one that Blanchot puts into play as, suspending a future death or disaster, he maintains that they have already taken place and have as a result disabled time. The transposition Copjec renders through the Lacanian Real, then, finds its counterpart in Blanchot's disaster, as both accounts bring a future negativity into the present, inscribing a certain nonphenomenal, nonempirical devastation into the phenomenal world itself. Yet these theorists pursue alternative strategies for designating that inscription. Terms such as the Real or the internal limit treat it as a singular element, an uncanny Thing, whereas the notion of a time without present conceives of it as a feature one can scarcely locate or discern, a nonevent that ruins everything but which one cannot apprehend. One might well find here an instance of what Žižek calls the parallax, "the confrontation of two closely linked perspectives between which no neutral common ground is possible," for although they attempt to bring into view a single problematic, they rely on divergent strategies for doing so.[31]

These contrasting ways of eliciting that concern point us back to a similar parallax operating within Romanticism itself. On the one hand, the Real often takes shape in Romantic works as a spectacularly visible intrusion into the phenomenal world – an impossible ghost, a catastrophic experience, an immortal act. The works I discuss in this book, however, abandon these figures of the uncanny to elicit a barren, ungrounded condition. In effect, they evoke an alternative version of the Real, one that is purified of event or visible form, one that inheres in the very erasure of the ground. To arrive at this alternative, they cancel even the mark of cancellation, bringing about a negativity to the second degree; in doing so, however, they do not enter a state that follows after this second move but rather bring into view a blank state that obtained all along, the erased space beneath that mark. For them, as for Blanchot, the "'phantom' is meant to hide, to appease the phantom night. Those who think they see ghosts are those who do not want to see the night."[32] Those who are spellbound by the spectacular Real, these works suggest, do not wish to endure the mere *there is*, to survive in a worldless world.

Consider in this context two contrasting pairs. In Matthew Lewis's Gothic novel *The Monk*, the reader encounters a fictional ghost that spectacularly violates the realistic premises of the world in which she appears.[33] But in Coleridge's "Human Life," the ghost gives way to the summer-gust, to the status of mortality as a puff of wind, to a life that is indistinguishable from its disappearance. The endless activity that unfolds simultaneously as the creation and destruction of the earth's surface in Wordsworth's account of his descent through the Gorge of Gondo becomes, in Clare's sonnet, an invisible process that consigns all forms, human and nonhuman, as well as any memory of creation or destruction, to oblivion.[34] As Leslie Hill puts it, capturing an aspect of Derrida's reflection on Blanchot, this catastrophe takes place as "an apocalypse without apocalypse, an apocalypse of apocalypse."[35] The intrusion of natural, political, or ethical disaster becomes the more subtle disaster that, in the words of Blanchot, "does not come." In this blank poetics, disaster undoes its spectacular form, erasing any such arrival in favour of a time without event. The idea of a singular, catastrophic interruption of reality gives way, in short, to a dislocation already inscribed within reality itself.

While the shift from a marked, uncanny version of the Real to a more subtle Real of erasure is consistent across these works, one should not attempt to stabilize it too greatly, for that unmarked feature can emerge in strikingly divergent ways. Consider in this respect a pair of instances that appear in this book – instances that reveal alternative modes of grasping an erased transcendence. As I will argue in chapter five, for Turner in several paintings before his final phase, the sun at times ceases to be an unquestioned force that, from a place above the world, illuminates it – and becomes instead a visible feature in its own right, in which case it enters the visual field with so violent a light that it threatens to annihilate the domain of the visible. In contrast, as I will argue in chapter two, at times in his later decades, strangely working against his own attempt to defy modernity and sustain a coherent theological stance, Coleridge ponders the consequences of maintaining, in a post-Kantian vein, that divine transcendence could never appear in phenomena. Accordingly, in "Limbo" he ponders a world in which no imprint of the divine can appear, forcing one to seek in the visible world for what is not there, to suffer a radical blindness. Here an attempt to provide a poetics of faith coincides with a scenario that anticipates aspects of deconstruction, creating a strikingly a/theological articulation. In Turner and Coleridge, then, one can see contrasting renditions of what follows when transcendence is dislodged from its position of grounding the world without appearing as such within it: that transcendence either enters the phenomenal domain, immersing it in a brilliance so great that it blinds the world, or retreats too far from that domain and thus makes the very attempt to see anything futile. In either case, the world is blanked out, evacuated, ruined. In their divergent ways, these instances confirm that modernity emerges through a disorder in transcendence, but they do so by discerning the imprint of that disorder not in an uncanny apparition but rather in the blanking-out of phenomena themselves, in an erasure of experience.

Given the impressive divergences between the works I discuss in this book, perhaps their most consistent feature is that they emerge in a mode of inscription that is perpetually incomplete or undone. In nearly every case, the works that elicit this elusive condition are inscribed in tentative articulations – in notebooks, fragments, drafts, or at times completed works that are left unpublished or unexhibited at the artist's death. Consider the drafts of poems Wordsworth writes early in his career and publishes only in multiply revised versions much later; the notebook passages and unpublished drafts that provide crucial contexts for Coleridge's late lyrics, as well as the notebook passage from which the not entirely coherent "Limbo" is extracted; the unfinished Hyperion epics, the second of which remained unpublished until thirty-five years after Keats's death; the sonnet Clare writes for a collection that failed to appear in print in his lifetime; and the stunning paintings of Turner's last phase, left abandoned in his final years.

What can explain the cryptic status of these works? They appear in such a variety of contexts, in early and late stages of the career, in notes not crafted for the public and poems or paintings intended for eventual publication but failing to reach that status, that no specific pattern applies to them all. Nevertheless, the fact that these works so often remain in notes or drafts – and disclose even in published or exhibited form a certain insufficiency in language or visuality – indicates that the attempt to evoke mere existence sustains a relation to what cannot belong to any secure form of articulation. Yet the preservation of these works in an unpublished or incomplete state shows that artists valued not only those works but more crucially a certain activity that exceeded the apparent goal of publication or exhibition per se. As Donald H. Reiman argues, the cultural practice of preserving unpublished manuscripts, emerging around the late seventeenth century, increased over time and reached its maturity in the Romantic period.[36] This is not simply a background factor in the study of Romanticism; on the contrary, because scholars in the field have for many years been recovering and publishing these texts – and giving them increasing critical attention as well – one may now discern the constitutive relation of Romanticism to what the preservation of these works reveals: the endless, incomplete activity intrinsic to the work. Drawing on Blanchot's pivotal essay "The Essential Solitude," Marc D. Mazur thus argues that Romantic works often exemplify what he calls "the (un)published" – the "incessant and demanding materiality," the "textual instability," that arises from this process.[37] Within this (un)published Romanticism, "the work is never done and never becomes whole," for as Blanchot maintains, every work participates in its own unworking and is thus an instance of worklessness.[38] Most of the works I discuss in this book exemplify this kind of textual instability, then, because they attempt to evoke what can never be incorporated into any complete statement, a condition that unworks not only literary and artistic works but existence itself.

How does the subtle but unmistakeable imprint of mere existence on British Romantic works alter our sense of Romanticism overall? To be sure, the fact that such an imprint may be found only in a small set of works tells us that Romanticism does not everywhere speak of this concern. Nevertheless, these widely scattered instances suggest that this concern is symptomatic of how Romanticism bears the new metacontext that bears upon thought in that era. Although they are few in number, they nevertheless reveal what remains implicit throughout the period, a problem that in moments of distinctive import comes to the surface. These works thus make it possible to discern, within a Romanticism that so often seems to radiate an ontological confidence, what one might call (to borrow from Rajan's description of Blanchot) a Romanticism with a minus sign, in which one encounters not transcendence but its erasure; not the absorption of the sacred into history, nature, or mind, as the secularization narrative would have it, but the inscription of its disorder into these nonsecular domains; not a poetics of an abundant, effusive subjectivity but of a radically evacuated non-subject; not the triumph of the aesthetic but (as we will see below) its eclipse; not a nature that everywhere registers human concerns but a domain across which flow the winds of oblivion; not a history that speaks of progress or modernity but an evacuated historicity that reveals what such scenarios cast aside; not a set of masterful artefacts but works that perpetually inhabit the impossibility of their completion; and not a poetics of an affirmative community but of an unworked community that endures in the shared fragility of its devastated remainders.[39] What one sees, in short, is a Romanticism that, perhaps thanks to its apparent confidence, managed also to elicit the fragile, unworked, blank state that underlies the modern world.

II

One crucial aspect of the above argument still needs further elucidation: the reliance of Romantic works on a strategy of figural indirection, that is, on a particular feature of the aesthetic. So far I have suggested that they use this strategy because they explore the limits of articulation: they deploy not the concept *blankness* but the adjective *blank*; they rely on a range of figures to evoke a condition that they never attempt to name directly; and they lay bare the insufficiency of their modes of articulation, the incapacity of the aesthetic itself. But these characteristics lead to several further questions. What precisely is the status of the figural, and indeed of the aesthetic, in relation to that of the concept, especially since philosophers and theorists, even while addressing it, do so in a figural mode, as if to indicate that while it lies outside philosophical conceptualization, it is still in some way articulable? Furthermore, why do such articulations reveal the limits of their respective domains, philosophy and the aesthetic alike? Why must thought conduct itself in these regions through such a frayed version of the aesthetic, this unworked version of the aesthetic work?

Here the contemporary thought of Novalis (the pseudonym of Friedrich von Hardenburg) is remarkably useful. The destabilizations of the late eighteenth century took shape for him and others, especially in Germany, through the panoply of provocations in Kant's critical philosophy. In the wake of those provocations, Johann Gottlieb Fichte sought to follow up on problems that in his view Kant had left unresolved, in his *Science of Knowledge* positing a system that builds on the initiating, transcendental act whereby the absolute subject posits itself. Responding to Fichte's system in certain notebooks eventually published under the title *Fichte Studies* – in a further instance of the (un)published mentioned above – Novalis makes a contribution pivotal to this book, for as he contests Fichte's fundamental propositions, he not only theorizes a version of mere existence but also argues that it cannot be approached directly through philosophical thought.

Taking on Fichte's version of the transcendental act, Novalis writes, "The essence of identity can only be presented in an *illusory* proposition. We abandon the *identical* in order to present it."[40] In his account, one cannot argue that the act of positing the I comes first; insofar as that act presents an identity, it reflects upon it in a distinct movement. The original act "occurs in feeling," prior to reflection; moreover, because "[i]t is not possible to present the pure form of feeling," every presentation of it must take place from a position in reflection.[41]

Thus a gap opens up between the initial state and reflection upon it, undoing the unity of the transcendental act on which Fichte relies. As Jane Kneller explains, "Because self-consciousness is a reflective act, an attempt to reach an intuition (feeling) in thought, the best it can accomplish is only a reflection of this feeling. It is the feeling grasped in thought – the thought of the feeling – but this grasping is not identical to the feeling itself."[42] Since for Novalis, the subject only comes into being after self-consciousness begins, and the object only in relation to the subject, in that initial state one finds neither subject nor object.[43] Accordingly, in his account, "No modification – no concept – clings to mere-being."[44] Prior to the opposition between an I and not-I, as well as the differentiation between signs intrinsic to concepts, there is only what he calls "mere-being" – a rather exact analogue to "mere existence." But because that initial state appears to reflection only retrospectively, Novalis suggests that one must rely not on conceptual argument but rather on the resources of literature, which can evoke feeling through a number of figural strategies. In his analysis of Novalis, Thomas Pfau points out that Novalis, turning away from Fichte's attempt to establish a ground through a conceptually enclosed system, proposes that through literature one can "simulate the 'ground' of subjectivity … now reconceived as the object of aesthetic surmise."[45]

A similar treatment arises in Heidegger as well. In *Fundamental Concepts of Metaphysics*, Heidegger theorizes a preconceptual, or quasiconceptual, arena of feeling, a mood prior to conscious emotion. Attending to the elusive status of this mood, he writes that every attempt to ascertain it, to bring it to consciousness, will destroy it, "whereas in awakening mood we are concerned to let this mood be as it is, as this mood. Awakening means letting a mood be, one that, prior to this, has evidently been sleeping, if we may employ this image."[46] As Pfau comments, "Heidegger's shift toward an overtly metaphoric register hints that, methodologically speaking, the desired awakening can only ever be realized in the figural, virtual domain of the aesthetic."[47] On one level, Heidegger follows through on the insight of Novalis, extending the thesis that only the figural can elicit mood as mood. But Pfau's comment hints at a further dimension: the reliance on metaphor here shows that Heidegger, too, calls upon its resources even within his philosophical discourse.

These moments in Novalis and Heidegger leave marked traces in Levinas's account. Working within the legacy of Heideggerian phenomenology, Levinas does not explicitly provide an analogous argument regarding mood, in part because Heidegger already broaches that theme in his own work. Yet as we have seen, in the passages in which he radicalizes Heidegger, he too relies on the figural to evoke mere existence. Moreover, it turns out that for him, as for Novalis, a certain pure state of emotion – what one might call an emotion without content – is a constitutive aspect of mere existence. In his elaboration of the *there is*, Levinas argues that the dissolution of the I in that state is "announced in emotion," which "puts into question not the existence, but the subjectivity of the subject; it prevents the subject from gathering itself up, reacting, being someone." Moreover, much as Novalis maintains that this initial state precedes any act of reflection, any claim to identity, Levinas emphasizes that one must sharply contrast it with the "transmutation" of it into a "substantive," into the "hypostasis" of the subject.[48] Following through on these reflections, he uses the metaphor of night to encapsulate the encounter with *there is*, effectively deploying a literary strategy to elicit a state that in his own account necessarily eludes conceptual analysis. Thus the passages that appear across this genealogy from Novalis to Levinas outline a condition that, outside the domain defined by the subject and phenomena, can be presented not through an identity or hypostasis, but only through the resources of the figure.

This emphasis on the figural has still further import. It suggests that in this context, the aesthetic is not simply the aesthetic, for it is doing what is properly philosophical work – except that in this regard philosophy as such cannot do what it is called upon to do. As a result, the situation familiar to students of British Romanticism arises – that in which the figural perpetually sustains philosophical weight. That situation makes possible the critical practice of interweaving literary texts with philosophical arguments, of using each to elucidate the other; in effect, each is internal to the other within a field that is larger than them both, a realization borne out in the practice of many thinkers who blend theory and the practice of reading. But it also suggests that pivotal developments within Romantic aesthetics bear on more than narrowly aesthetic terms. As scholarship has demonstrated for a generation or two, Romanticism's explorations of the preconditions of subjectivity provide the space for more adventurous and wide-ranging dispossessions of the subject, often via alterity, anonymity, and the nonhuman. They can do so, as Kate Singer argues in *Romantic Vacancy*, by taking affect beyond the gendered body into a nonsubjective, figural mobility, into a mode of vacancy best captured in the speculative dimensions of the aesthetic.[49]

But it is also crucial to recognize that the lyric can take such gestures so far that it implodes lyricism itself. As Forest Pyle argues in *Art's Undoing: In the Wake of a Radical Aestheticism*, at its highest pitch the lyric encounters what it registers "as undoing, as evaporation, as combustion," achieving a figural magnitude so great that it consumes the world and itself alike. "At certain moments in certain texts," he writes, "we encounter a radical aestheticism, one that undoes the claims made in the name of the aesthetic – as redemptive, restorative, liberating, compensatory, humanizing, healing," becoming "a kind of black hole from which no illumination is possible."[50] But insofar as the aesthetic speaks of more than itself, as I am suggesting, then its evaporation has an import beyond the aesthetic as such: it brings about more than art's undoing. When the aesthetic evacuates itself, it simultaneously annihilates what it bears of the philosophical and indeed of the discursive overall. What appears at this point is a *blank* intensity in which all articulations have disappeared, leaving only a state of stunning dispossession. Thus it is not surprising that, as far as I can determine after an extensive search, evocations of that condition appear within Romanticism exclusively in certain intense, distinctive moments in poetry or painting.[51] But rather than confirming once again a certain privilege of the aesthetic, as Romantic works are so often said to do, these moments point towards what disables aesthetic, philosophical, and empirical discourses alike.

The genealogy I traced above across moments that mark out the limits of the philosophical raises a further question: Why does this delimitation arise at this specific moment alongside the emergence of Romanticism? Perhaps my account of modernity, broached earlier, will provide a useful approach to this question. With the erasure of a transcendental ground for thought, philosophy can no longer start from given premises but must begin without a foundation. In its most symptomatic attempts to do so, it seeks to convert the absence of ground into the very basis for reflection. In an exemplary instance of this strategy, in his *Science of Logic* Hegel argues for the unity of undetermined nothingness and being, sublating both into becoming; in this move he attempts to establish as well the necessity of the dialectical procedure thanks to which he can account for a beginning and thus start the work itself.[52] In *Being and Time*, Heidegger responds to the difficulty of making a beginning in philosophy by describing Dasein as "distinguished by the fact that, in its very Being, that Being is an *issue* for it," and argues that as a result the analysis of Being must be sought in "the *existential analytic of Dasein.*"[53] In doing so he makes Dasein's existential vulnerability into the core problematic on which he can elaborate throughout the rest of that work. In both cases, however, the attempt to transform the absence of ground into the framework for thought leaps over the task of demonstrating the necessity of grounding one's argument in this *specific* thematization of groundlessness. As Frank Ruda remarks on Hegel's text, "The only thing to begin with is beginning itself, the beginning of thought in decision, grounded in the absence of a beginning (i.e. not grounded at all)."[54] Both cases, then, make visible how within modernity there can be no secure place from which to begin.

The works of Novalis and Levinas, indirectly contesting attempts to find a basis for philosophy in such beginnings, reveal that a truly coherent philosophy is impossible in the modern era. Rather than overcoming that impasse, they outline what arises within it, tracing the contours of an encounter with that groundlessness, that state without any familiar substances or entities, that world without a world. Their works, then, cut through the conceptual frameworks familiar in Hegel and Heidegger alike to elicit the blank state beneath them, the region that can never be mobilized in any conceptual regime. At least two key strategies arise from the encounter with this erasure of ground: on the one hand, one might elucidate aspects of literary writing, a self-consciously figural practice (*écrire*), and become Blanchot, or one might return to philosophy anew and expose how that groundlessness perpetually unworks every mode of artic-ulation, of writing as such (*écriture*), and thus become Derrida.[55]

This affinity between Novalis and Levinas has still further implications. It reminds us once again that Romanticism considers in its own moment a prob-lematic that emerges with renewed force in the twentieth century and beyond – a situation that confirms once again that the modernity broached in the Roman-tic period remains in the centuries since. This problematic endures not only in the speculative domain, as we have seen in our discussions of early deconstruc-tion, but also in the aesthetic domain as well, where one can easily trace a series of permutations on the question of how to elicit mere existence through the affordances of the visual arts. Here it is especially relevant that the modernist avant-garde, in another version of aesthetic implosion, strips away representa-tion to focus on the nonphenomenal preconditions of art, the premises that make aesthetic representation itself possible. One of the first major interven-tions in this mode is *Black Square* (1915), in which Kazimir Malevich presents a square of black paint without any modification or feature, in effect proclaiming that an artwork need contain nothing at all to be a work of art, that it consists of the very space in which it is presented. Works like this announce the onset of an aesthetic mode that extends from modernism through mid-century abstract expressionism and beyond. As Craig Dworkin details in *No Medium*, many artworks in the avant-garde tradition are composed of blank sheets of paper, erased versions of artworks or of published books, musical compositions that transpire in silence, and paintings composed of white surfaces. For Dworkin, all such gestures draw attention not only to the materiality of the medium but also to the "material interaction[s]" in which they are received, including the "conventions on which they silently rely."[56]

What follows from these blank presentations? As Slavoj Žižek points out, *Black Square* presents the abstract space within which an object must appear for it to be regarded as an artwork, whereas Marcel Duchamp's *Fountain* (1917), an inverted urinal signed "R. Mutt," exemplifies the status of how any object becomes art once it is inserted into that conceptual space. Accordingly, he argues, "What Malevich's minimalist disposition does is simply render – or isolate – this place as such, an empty place (or frame) with the proto-magic property of transforming any object that finds itself within its scope into a work of art. In short, there is no Duchamp without Malevich: only after art practice isolates the frame/place as such, emptied of all its content, can one indulge in the readymade procedure." This conjunction foregrounds the relation between two versions of the Real: the structurally empty space that is "never actual or experienced as such but can only be retroactively constructed and has to be presupposed as such," and a "fascinating/captivating presence" that "masks the structural Real."[57] In these two artworks, then, one encounters an instance of the parallax in renditions of the Real – the fascinating and the empty, the spectacular event and the blank space beneath it – as if to make that parallax concrete and visible. Here again, the aesthetic, in exceeding itself, in exploding the very medium of figuration, speaks of two versions of the Real that obtain well beyond the limits of the aesthetic itself.

This modernist or postmodern aesthetics of the blank surface has inspired further reflections that are highly relevant to this project. In his book *The Inhuman: Reflections on Time*, Jean-François Lyotard argues that the avant-garde can take up the aesthetics of the sublime, inherited from Romanticism, to contest the categories of philosophical and aesthetic abstraction and delve into a condition where they no longer apply. From a perspective rooted in his analyses of the avant-garde, Lyotard rereads Edmund Burke to emphasize that a version of the sublime can arise in a world stripped bare. This process goes very far; in his view, it contests even the basic categories of interest to Kant, for "what is hit first of all … in our modernity, or our postmodernity, is perhaps space and time."[58] In a world reduced to that degree, one confronts what he calls matter, that is, "a mindless state of mind, which is required … *so that there be* something," a matter that designates "this '*that there is*,' this *quod*, because this presence in the absence of the active mind is and is never other than timbre, tone, nuance in one or other of the dispositions of sensibility."[59] This sublime cannot buttress the claims of the subject; on the contrary, Lyotard suggests that the *now* of certain avant-garde works "is a stranger to consciousness and cannot be constituted by it. Rather, it is what dismantles consciousness, what deposes consciousness, it is what consciousness cannot formulate, and even what consciousness forgets in order to constitute itself."[60] In that version of the *now*, he suggests, arises a condition of sublime privation in which one of the "dispositions of sensibility" in something prior to the subject registers pure facticity through timbre or tone. In this analysis, art moves past the attempt to body forth the preconditions of its medium, as mentioned above, and provides instead a certain timbre or tone through which that sublime privation can make itself felt.

This passage thus contributes, at still another phase of speculative and aesthetic history, to a theory of mere existence. Indeed, Lyotard adds new details to the evocation of that state, contributing features that will be relevant throughout this study. What is perhaps most surprising in Lyotard's account is that a region of sensibility might survive the dissolution of time and space – that the apprehension of the *there is* may take place through the senses even when the subject and object have disappeared. Much as other thinkers sustain an affectivity without affect, a time without time, or a world without world, here one sees a sensibility that operates even without a subject or world. Moreover, much as others retain certain figures (the night, death), Lyotard sustains timbre and tone, revealing in his own way that even where the aesthetic erases itself, certain minimal elements remain. For a work to gesture towards mere existence, one might say, it must retain minimal features of this kind, even if in doing so it only beckons towards the condition that ultimately eludes it.

III

What I am attempting to elicit in this book, then, is a version of Romanticism that locates it in an especially elusive genealogy of modernity in a number of registers – a blank Romanticism, as it were, that lurks within its more familiar forms. But what emerges in this book is not at all foreign to recent work in the field; on the contrary, this book may make more visible, and extend, aspects of Romantic scholarship that have been especially salient in recent decades. In several works, Rajan has demonstrated how Romantic works deploy renditions of unusable negativity, one that neither texts nor history can assimilate productively.[61] Sara Guyer has revisited Levinas's scene of insomnia, discerning how in that scene one lives on alongside the useless persistence of the world.[62] Anne-Lise François has explored a literature of "uncounted experience" that features an attenuated subject, a withdrawn action, a turning aside from assertion.[63] Jacques Khalip has foregrounded an anonymous feature of Romanticism, one that dispossesses and depersonalizes the ostensible subject.[64] Across several key essays, David Clark has delineated a philosophy and aesthetics of radical scarcity that emerges in encounters with war and disaster.[65] All these studies approach the problematic of that early deconstruction, articulating a precise constellation of concerns through which Romanticism is attuned to an anonymous, superlatively negative movement that dispossesses the subject and the world.

Khalip's most recent book, *Last Things*, takes this tendency further, and in doing so draws very near the concerns of this study. In that book, he discerns in Romantic works the prospect of what he calls, borrowing from Wordsworth, a *now no more* that does not grieve for what has been eclipsed, that "does not desire anything else, either before, after, then, or soon," an aesthetics that "derealiz[es] humanistic investments in futurity, endurance, life, and expressiveness."[66] Within such an aesthetics, an image of ruins does not "protest against things as they are" as much as "demolish the very notion of 'world'"; it moves past the world without attempting to recover or replace it.[67] Photographic images that emanate from this mode "abide in just this nonplace, the infinite lastness that emanates *after* but also *to the side of* the death of the subject – a lastness that is something other than mortality"; such images "errantly sleepwalk out of time."[68] In such passages one can discern a further figure for evoking mere existence, for eliciting a state without subject, world, mortality, space, or time. One need only take Khalip's figure slightly further to enter the problematic of this book, to note that, while what he identifies may come after, it may also transpire to the side of mortality, as he indicates, or indeed may emerge before any delimited version of mortal life begins. What such an aesthetics evokes thus has no proper moment before, during, or after, for in logically preceding temporality it hollows out the entire sweep of time, creating a depleted time – the nontime, that is, of mere existence.

The nonredemptive feature of the aesthetic, especially important in what Rajan, Pyle, and Khalip have taught us, speaks to art's place within the overall contours of modernity. This feature ultimately suggests that the mere existence this aesthetic evokes cannot be superseded from within the conditions of modernity, for it reveals what remains intrinsic to that supposed settlement, what is constitutive to its cancellation of transcendence. A full-fledged encounter with that state, then, cannot help but erase promises that art can redeem, heal, or even console. Nevertheless, it can, with a certain intransigence, disclose a condition that unsettles every aspect of that modernity, making palpable what virtually every other modern discourse tacitly attempts to disguise or eclipse. The fact that Keats's narrator paradoxically bears with an anguish so endless it is unbearable, for example, reveals that if one takes seriously the commitment to a poetics of soul-making, the project that inspires the poet in the later phases of his career, it goes beyond humanism into a practice that can linger alongside what is lost beyond all hope most especially because it does not attempt to thematize that oblivion in anything like a being-towards-death. A poetics that seeks to look into the human heart, in short, can enter those regions where the heart is lost, where the human, now abandoned, takes on the contours of stone, where redemption falls away in a time without time. In such moments art hints at a nonmortal condition that persists alongside or within what seems to be the realm of experience.

So far I have emphasized how the evocation of mere existence, arising within the Romantic era, speaks to the constitutive impasses of modernity in a range of speculative texts and aesthetic works in that era and since. But the fact that criticism has approached this problematic more and more closely in recent years suggests that a metacontext of our own moment may be making itself felt: the arrival of what some call the Anthropocene, the era in which humanity is leaving its imprint on geological strata and on the activity of the biosphere, or more severely, the emergence of the possibility that humanity as a whole might become extinct in the coming decades or century. This latter prospect constitutes still another instance of the logic of transposition that, as we have seen, informs the arguments of Copjec and Blanchot. Here I will move through that transposition one last time to illuminate what may be this book's most pressing contemporary reach of concern.

As I argue in a book written alongside this one, *The Rubble of Culture: Debris of an Extinct Thought*, the term "Anthropocene" is meant to follow the terminological practices of geology, a discipline in which, if the term is adopted, it would refer to a unit of geological time discernible in Earth's strata.[69] But that definition implies the existence of a future observer, a geologist to come. The fact that today we can no longer be certain that humanity will still exist a few decades hence casts the very idea of the Anthropocene into question. Furthermore, when one attempts to imagine a world that would persist after the death of humanity, one in effect attempts to view that world in anticipation, despite the absence of any subject who could in fact view such a world. To conceive of that world, then, one must consider instead the erasure of the viewer, the undoing of thought itself.[70] Under the sign of the terminus – the possible disappearance of humanity – thought must think its *own* disappearance, confront its *own* extinction.[71] But this potential future event also undoes the premises for thought; it cracks the assumptions inscribed into the political, cultural, religious, literary, and social traditions of the West, those from which the current global trajectory has most obviously emerged. As a result, the emergence of that possibility shatters the field that the heirs of Romanticism inhabit, leaving in its wake a vast scene of debris, the battered and incoherent remnants of the tradition.

This argument – the sense that a future cessation reveals that a catastrophe has befallen the entire tradition – once again relies on the transposition that Blanchot invokes as he moves from a future disaster to one that has already taken place. To theorize the extinction of thought is to participate in the writing of the disaster. Indeed, one might argue that the encounter with the notion of deep time in the Romantic era – along with a series of closely associated developments, such as the awareness that the sun, like other stars, came into being through natural processes and will disappear for the same reasons in due course, or that humanity itself appeared and will disappear thanks to purely biological causes – already inscribes within the scientific understanding of the material preconditions of human existence a counterpart to Blanchot's disaster. In that case, some might argue that the awareness emerging in the Romantic era already encompasses the prospect of extinction that humanity faces today. Such is not the case, however, for the latter arises not only from material causes but also from the actions, indeed the increasingly knowing and deliberate actions, of certain human beings, whose impact on those material circumstances is having and will have an immense effect on the biosphere and humanity itself. As a result, virtually nothing in the Western tradition directly anticipates the situation thought faces today.

Yet the difficult task that thought now faces – that of thinking its own erasure, its own disappearance – nevertheless belongs to the problematic I sketch in this book, for that task confronts us once again with the strange condition of mere existence, though now in a new form. The condition of the subject without subject, time without time, or world without world is now also of a thought without thought. While previous treatments of that problematic do not directly anticipate the dilemma of our moment, then, we who face that dilemma discover that we, too, find ourselves in that blank condition. Today one must once again attempt to think, to write, to figure, to paint that world without world, that experience without experience, that thought without thought. While the Romantic works I trace here do not attempt to speak of a human disappearance shortly to come, we who read or view them may find in their evocations of that state suggestions that they could not suspect, and recognize once again, even in this terminal moment, that we still live within a Romantic problematic broadly conceived, still endure a certain erasure of the world.

Thus in their various ways, the works I discuss in this book reveal how an extraordinarily subtle event, the arrival of mere existence, hollows out a range of seemingly coherent and enduring arenas, such as subjectivity, history, time, space, faith, affect, the political, the object world, and the visual field. If we take them seriously, they suggest that none of the features of modernity, including attempts to repudiate it (as in the case of Coleridge), are immune from the intrusions of mere existence. This pattern puts its impress even on adventurous modes of thought influential in our own moment. Accordingly, mere existence, in cutting through these approaches – in revealing the prospect of a moodless mood or a process that dissolves even nonhuman things – makes palpable the gap that unsettles every scenario of thought, no matter how recent or compelling it may be.

After such a recognition, how may we respond? Perhaps we may dissolve into another version of Turner's surrealist assemblage, into a condition that no longer enjoys the integrity of a body that can see. Perhaps we might discern how the mere sound of the world and the mere light of light engulf us with a blank splendour, so that we behold a nameless disaster that nevertheless affords us the shelter of its hospitality. Should we, in the wake of such realizations, participate in a nonhuman, featureless joy? Or should we, to borrow from a suggestion in the sonnet by Clare, leave this encounter as nothing all behind, close this book, and live on?

1 Blank Misgivings: Primary Affect in Wordsworth

From many accounts of the state of blank existence, one might conclude that because it is so utterly denuded of subjectivity and conscious emotion, as well as of time, space, and indeed the world itself, it is a state of sheer horror. But this conclusion is premature, for in that state one might also discover that the world, after its disappearance, does not vanish but gives way to the sheer *there is* – and thus might instead be entranced by the ineradicable persistence of existence as such. One might well be transported by the enjoyment of existence at its very limits, where without any positive feature it takes on the purity of a nearly absolute state. Such, at least, is the possibility that Wordsworth identifies when, upon entering this state, he discovers that while listening to the sound of the earth he feels a primary affect, a moodless mood, with great intensity. In Part Two of the 1798–9 *Prelude*, he celebrates the ur-experience of the nonsubject, which absorbs and participates in the bare, primordial affect of pure existence.

The import of that state fascinates the poet so greatly that one can well discern in his writing before that poem a drive to work through a series of delimited emotions as he approaches, then finally elicits, that affect. But a further phase awaits him: although the poet celebrates what he is able to evoke in that brief *Prelude*, in the years that follow he discovers that his memory of that state brings with it a range of difficult complications. The embrace of primary affect, it turns out, has strikingly ironic effects. Because mere existence exceeds the conditions of finitude, temporality, and mortality while also in this account shaping the mind at its beginnings, the mind retains within its very precondition – within its most enduring feature – a capacity that it can never assimilate into the finitude that otherwise defines it. As a result, that nearly absolute condition is too featureless to be borne, too boundless for one who also faces the prospect of living within time.

Thus while the poet can call upon that condition to respond to the crisis outlined in the opening stanzas of the Intimations Ode, reminding himself that he is not entirely subject to the constraints of mortality, he does so at the hazard of bringing into play an unassimilable vastness. In certain moments in the Ode, then, he suggests that his memory of that state deprives him of his purchase on finitude; to be charmed by mere existence is to be lost without a world. In resolving one crisis, the Ode discovers a second – a difficulty in moving from immortality, as it were, into the conditions of mortality. In its final stanzas, it explores subtle resolutions to this second difficulty, attempting to align aspects of primary affect with the sympathies that obtain within embodied, mortal life and thus to salvage aspects of its initial resolution for a stance that can encompass and affirm finitude. But this refigured response, however generous, nevertheless retains the hazard it is meant to overcome, for in viewing mortality from the vantage of primary affect, it leaves in place the contrast between what forever endures and what falls away. Within the poem's final stance, a certain unassimilable excess remains.

This sequence from the early career through the Ode, then, shows that in celebrating mere existence, Wordsworth articulates the impress of the Real on him as a child and adult. His ur-experience of mere existence does not give him access to transcendence; on the contrary, it reveals the wholesale cancellation of all guarantees, erasing rather than grounding the world, unworking subjectivity rather than authorizing it. His celebration of mere existence is rather unexpected, for it acclaims a state that, however vast, is a mode of utter dispossession. When this state persists within the temporality of consciousness, it disrupts the latter with a nonmortal intensity and scope, bringing into its noise a nonphenomenal silence, revealing a gap within the contours of modern subjectivity. Yet while Wordsworth retains this constitutive deadlock, he nevertheless discloses what one might not expect, the sheer entrancements of primary affect, the bliss of listening to the mere turning of the world – or, as the final stanzas of the Ode propose, of embracing the fragility of human beings and the dissolution of worlds.

Wordsworth may maintain such a distinctive rendition of and response to mere existence because he approaches it step by step with deliberate care over the course of several years and across many ambitious poems. His treatment of this question is embedded in his longstanding interest in how to capture the various moods that arise as a consequence of cultural dismemberment. As he works through a series of carefully wrought figural structures, each of which attempts to depict the characteristics of a dissolving world, he anticipates accounts of exposure and abandonment that appear later in Heidegger and Freud, bringing aspects of phenomenology and psychoanalysis into these more capacious scenarios. Over the course of several poems, he becomes more adept at revealing that every such depiction relies on suspect fictions, that each continues to elude a mood that remains in force on a less explicit level. Accordingly, he pushes further towards that state not to jettison his social and political engagements or to dismiss these anticipations but to sharpen them, to isolate what he senses may be their most definitive feature, an utterly dispossessed condition.

To grasp the initial sequence of poems through which Wordsworth arrives at his formulation of primary affect, it would be helpful to build on Pfau's work in *Romantic Moods*, where he provides a subtle guide to the question of affect. Drawing on the work of Martha Nussbaum, he argues that while mood is prior to thought itself, and indeed to conscious emotion per se, it nevertheless is "quasi-cognitive" – that is, cognitive without becoming fully conscious – and through it "communities establish a sustained, quasi-intentional and tacitly evaluative relation to their experiential world."[1] For Pfau, as for Heidegger, mood is "the horizon wherein all conscious practice … is being transacted, a horizon that therefore can never come into view as such," much less be fixed in "representational form." Accordingly, following Heidegger's suggestion that mood should be awakened, rather than represented, Pfau argues – as we saw in the introduction – that this "desired awakening can only ever be realized in the figural, virtual domain of the aesthetic."[2] In his account, this understanding of affect is already broached in Kant as well as Novalis, Hölderlin, and Hegel, who "progressively conceived 'mood' as an aesthetic phenomenon," something best captured "in the modality of virtual, figural constructions."[3] Pursuing a rigorously nonreductive mode of reading, Pfau argues that such constructions evoke no specific empirical history but rather a certain historicity, a "perilous historical situatedness" endlessly thematized and falsified by history's actual events.[4]

In pointing to an aspect of mood that shapes emotion while lying beyond what is consciously experienced or represented directly, Pfau maps out an approach that is strikingly congruent with Wordsworth's practice and indeed useful for discussions of Romantic texts more generally. Moreover, while his book considers paranoia, trauma, and melancholy as distinctive moods, each deserving separate treatment, his readings of key texts in the period of central concern, especially those written in the mid-1790s by Wordsworth, Blake, and Godwin, make it possible to discern what he does not explicitly indicate, that at times a given emotion can modulate into another, that the formulation of paranoia, for example, can transform into that of trauma. Moreover, insofar as mood occupies a space prior to conscious differentiation, any given version of mood can never be defined clearly in contrast to others. A capacious and flexible account of mood, then, affords one the opportunity to trace how Wordsworth moves through a series of evocations, capitalizing on a certain affective and discursive mobility in a sequence that in the poet's account eventually arrives at the depiction of an originary state.

Such an approach is especially useful as one traces Wordsworth's movement in the early and mid-1790s across moods that, following Pfau, I will call paranoia and trauma.[5] In the early 1790s, Wordsworth writes poems marked by a revolutionary passion, one that readily accepts the polarizing terms we could align with a certain paranoia. This mood is evident in the poem *Salisbury Plain*, written when the poet anticipated the incipient horror of a war between England and revolutionary France, which responds to what it depicts as a total violence by celebrating a violent enlightenment in its final lines. The revision to that poem, *Adventures on Salisbury Plain*, written largely between 1795 and 1797, moves from paranoia to another mood as the polarizing scenario of the initial draft changes remarkably: the wanderer on the plain, once a victim of dismembering violence, becomes an involuntary participant in it as well when he commits murder. In this way the revised poem outlines with exemplary force the dense affect of what we might now call trauma, in which one becomes implicated in horror or violence against one's will and involuntarily suffers or replicates on the most intimate level the very thing one most intensely resists. The shift marked by the revision of this poem hints that the transformation in literary figuration registers the collective's process of reconsidering its mood and finding its way towards an affect more attuned to its historical exposure, especially as that exposure alters over time. The collective sense of historicity moves; literature's task in part is to articulate this shift, doing so in this case through an unusually clear instance of autocritique.

But the value of these poems goes further. Insofar as both of them feature a solitary figure setting forth in a barren landscape, they depict the situation of Dasein, that figure of abandonment familiar in Heidegger's *Being and Time*. Indeed, with rare exceptions, it is difficult to find so clear a poetic exemplar of Dasein before these poems, a possibility that confirms Pfau's argument that the sense of exposure to historicity familiar in the past two centuries first becomes paramount in this period.[6] Because this is also the moment Koselleck identifies as that when the sense of history's temporalization – its breach of any enduring, predictable framework for collective experience and thus its encounter with an open, unknown future – begins to affect the discourses of the West, one can align temporalization, historicity, the mood of exposure, and Dasein's abandoned state as various refractions of the same overall predicament. This sense of that moment is confirmed by the fact that for post-Kantian thinkers, Wordsworth, and other authors writing in the 1790s this situation constituted a novel problematic calling out for sustained treatment.[7] In Wordsworth's case that treatment takes the form of a careful exploration of scenarios surprisingly akin to those that appear in Heidegger. Yet the Salisbury Plain poems suggest that the anguish of Dasein can be evoked variously as the situation of being exposed to an alien force, bearing the guilt of having violated the world, or both; abandonment, as it were, does not speak for itself, for its articulation seems to require a broader scenario and an attendant figural logic.

Within these poems, the exact significance of Dasein's implication in such scenarios remains unclear. While one could propose that these scenarios are not intrinsic to the fundamental situation of Dasein, arising instead as elaborations of it, it is also clear that without such renderings one cannot evoke that situation at all, for they are attempts to awaken what is primary, what pre-exists articulation. No figural logic can articulate that exposure with authority, simply because the historicity of Dasein has no proper form, no objective existence. As a result, even Heidegger's own terms must be taken as evocative rather than definitive: they insistently rely on a spatial rhetoric (being-there, thrownness, fallenness, being "not-at-home") although the dilemma they depict is not spatial but existential: even Heidegger must rely on what are ultimately literary figures. Given the difficulty of capturing that exposed condition in language, one could argue that evoking it now in one figural logic and now in another takes the measure of its elusive status, conveying the latter precisely through the movement from one tonality to another. The very movement of trope, in this view, may be the most adequate language for evoking Dasein's perilous historicity, its ultimately unrepresentable situation.[8]

Although the Salisbury Plain poems broach these questions, shifting from one articulation of mood to another, they do not yet meditate on the implications of what they achieve. Wordsworth takes this step soon thereafter in a series of poems written in 1797 and 1798. In one sequence of poems, he muses on the transformation of the anguished sailor into the untroubled old men of "Old Man Travelling," "The Discharged Soldier," and "The Old Cumberland Beggar."[9] These poems explore how pain, endured long enough, may undergo a figurative transformation by turning into an insensitivity to pain and accordingly how exposure to existence and historicity can take on the tone of a numbed peacefulness. The initial mood, pursued to its extreme, modulates into another, or perhaps into its own encrypted variant, into a more muted, but still palpable, evocation of pain. The poet goes further in his juxtaposition of *The Ruined Cottage* and "The Thorn," in the contrast between Margaret, who for the Pedlar is eventually transfigured in death, and Martha Ray, who remains rooted to the grave of her child forever chanting her misery.[10] In this sequence the poet moves from a narrator identified with apparent calm to one who speaks of a sensationalized distress, undercutting the reliability of narrative depiction overall. In doing so, he foregrounds the starkly figurative and reversible element of all virtual evocations of affect. But even these two poems may expand on the situation evoked in "Incipient Madness," a short draft that preceded them, in which the themes of the abandoned child, obsessive desire, and the ruined hut are already present. This possibility implies that one could cut through the elaborations of *The Ruined Cottage* and "The Thorn" by melting them down into a handful of stark terms prior, and perhaps ultimately resistant, to narrative. In that case, the relationship between these three texts is highly instructive: the two longer poems ramify the fundamental situation in mutually implicated but contrasting scenarios by elaborating on the potential narratives embedded in the original assemblage of bare figures. But given how the poet casts doubt on the rhetorical, fictive nature of those elaborations, one might value in retrospect the relatively minimal articulation he gives his themes in that initial fragment.

These three poems, taken together, emphasize the psychoanalytic, rather than strictly phenomenological, rendition of exposure, for they evoke a babe's search for the mother's breast, and as I argue elsewhere, anticipate Freud's account of the *fort-da* game as they enlarge upon infantile fantasies of revenge against the abandoning mother.[11] For Wordsworth, the abandoned child is embodied, caught in a world defined by gender, riven with desire, and pierced by a range of competing fantasies whereby to address the sense of abandonment. Moreover, the poet's focus on the Pedlar's manner of addressing his listener in *The Ruined Cottage* foregrounds the situation of narrating and receiving tales about such abandonment, making explicit the problem of how to encounter the basic dilemma through the dynamics of interpretive exchange, in this regard once again anticipating the concerns of psychoanalysis.[12] The fictive elaborations of these fantasies, in turn, are interwoven with the evocation of an impoverishment registered in *The Ruined Cottage* through the themes of unemployment and material distress. By swerving from a purely existential scenario, these three poems implicitly address a concern of interest to reflection over the past century or so: whether it is more rigorous to sustain a focus on the bare situation of existential thrownness, as in the work of Heidegger; to emphasize by contrast the implications of embodiment, as in Merleau-Ponty; to highlight the logic of fantasy that elaborates on the dilemmas of such embodiment, as in Freud; or to foreground the dimension of materiality and historicity, as in a range of recent interventions, including that of Pfau.[13]

Although mapping out various ways of capturing the experience of abandonment continues to interest Wordsworth in several further poems, his critique of narrative elaboration also inspires him to pursue another strategy of evoking mood more directly, of drawing nearer to the problematic that increasingly concerns him. This exploration is especially significant in the Two-Part *Prelude* of 1798–9, which assembles a series of key passages, later distributed across the epic-length versions of the poem, into a cluster on whose concerns the poem focuses intensively and whose import is thus more explicit in this version than in later revisions. In the First Part Wordsworth once again brings together solitary wandering; the experience of being out of place; the orientation to spots linked to abandonment, murder, and guilt; erotic fantasies circulating around signifiers of gender; and the retrospective feeding upon these charged scenes. But in this poem he invokes a broadly defined autobiographical framework to justify leaving these scenes in their cryptic, unelaborated state. In the spots of time, for example, a given scene's proximity to an affect too dense to articulate gives it a certain privilege, an unexplained power to nourish and repair the mind (1.294). The poet leaves that affect undefined, writing that one scene inspires "the workings of [his] spirit" without clarifying where those workings might lead or why they might be satisfying (1.374).[14] What's more, insofar as he narrates these episodes directly to his reader without staging the scene of storytelling as he does in *The Ruined Cottage* or "The Thorn," he suspends the interpretive dynamic, tacitly repudiating the endeavour to decipher whatever those episodes convey. Recovering the dense affect embedded in such moments matters to him more than any attempt to expand upon their import. In such passages, he moves to a new phase of his endeavour, resisting narrative elaboration to seize upon the sheer evocation of affect itself. But the implications of this strategy remain unclear: what precisely is at stake in recovering such an early affect without any further elaboration?

While the implications of this approach remain unstated in the poem for several pages, eventually they become explicit some distance into the Second Part. The recitation of the leading episodes founders when Wordsworth sets out to "tell / How nature, intervenient till this time / And secondary, now at length was sought / For her own sake" (2.239–42). Here the poet invokes the idea that a review of his affective education should eventually lead to a larger poetic argument about the contours of his adult emotional capacity, the disposition of mind that underlies his poetic vocation. But his resistance to this scenario, already evident in the spots of time passages, comes to the fore almost immediately, for he revolts against the prospect of attempting to capture the mind's overall affective disposition in this way; the very thought provokes him to attack any thinker's attempt to "parcel out / His intellect by geometric rules" or to propose interpretive "distinctions" while believing they are "things / Which we perceive and not which we have made" (2.242–3; 253–4). Here again, discursive elaborations are fictions which cannot actually represent or decipher what is at stake. On the contrary, he insists, each dimension of the "soul" – its "general habits and desires" and "each most obvious and particular thought" – "in the words of reason deeply weighed / Hath no beginning" (2.262, 263–5). What does have a beginning, he proposes in the Blest Babe passage that immediately follows, is the individual's affective life per se, which arises in the infant's capacity to "gather passion from the Mother's eye" (2.273) and to "combine / In one appearance all the elements / And parts of the same object" (2.277–9). This explicitly figural capacity to render parts into a whole, Wordsworth suggests, makes the mother available to the child, founds relationship, and makes possible the infant's orientation to "[a]ll objects through all intercourse of sense" (2.290). In effect, the poem now argues that the love of nature arises from the infant's initial response to the mother and thereafter to the world.

Yet this suggestion is not conclusive. The poet soon returns to an autobiographical mode as he offers up what many have read as an encrypted discussion of the consequences for him of surviving his mother's death at the age of eight. Suddenly it seems as if the speculations in the Blest Babe passage prepare the way for a more crucial discussion, the poet's reflections on how his mother's death intruded into that mode of responsiveness and transformed it into another. The passage that inaugurates this new movement returns to the problem of abandonment with an urgency and rigour not anticipated by any of the previous poems: "For now a trouble came into my mind / From obscure causes. I was left alone / Seeking this visible world, nor knowing why" (2.321–3). If we pursue the familiar reading, this passage refers to a child's inability to understand the mother's death *as* a death, and indeed in any terms at all: the mother's disappearance has causes he cannot understand. But if we attend to the passage's more daring indications, it seems to suggest that for the child this event is not understood with reference to the mother, a mode of understanding that assumes a prior capacity to treat her as a separate person, for instead it is rendered as an inexplicable trouble in the operations of the child's own mind – a construction thoroughly consistent with the theory sketched a few lines before in the Blest Babe passage.[15] It is as if the child, having derived passion, love, perception, world, and even his sense of himself from his mother's presence, in her absence loses his access to them all, loses even his secure sense of his own mind. In yet another move, the passage suggests that the child, now facing "this visible world," does not understand why he should seek it at all, for the world may have no significance outside the presence of the mother; the mere demand to deal with the world is felt as an imposition. Furthermore, when it describes the child seeking without knowing why, it raises the prospect of a seeking without desire, a yearning that seems not to be intrinsic to the subject but to existence as such.

This reading of the passage has still further implications. Because the poem does not explicitly refer to the mother's death, even though it does so elsewhere, one might rightly object that it refers not to that event but to another, perhaps more general condition. Every child raised by a mother must at some point discover that she is absent and thus confront an existence in which she is missing. The mother's loss and her death are structurally similar, for both lead the child to ponder how to sustain a mode of being despite that loss. One could thus surmise that even if the poem here refers to the mother's death, it treats that event as an instance of a general pattern, folding an autobiographical into a nearly universal experience.

In this passage, the poem complicates the earlier account of relation, suggesting that the lines on the Blest Babe tell only a part of a story that necessarily includes a much more difficult episode. The Blest Babe passage hinted for a moment that solitary exposure is not fundamental to affective experience, for on the contrary the infant enters the world in a richly affective interplay that shapes human life to the core. But in these later lines, Wordsworth suggests that this intimate relationship to the mother must eventually give way to the shock of her absence – and what is more, to the disappearance of the very figure through which the child previously secured its relation to the world. Thus the passage conceives of abandonment not through the figural logic familiar from

1795 through 1798 but radically *without* figuration, proposing that the absence of the mother is precisely the *loss* of all figure – of reality, world, motive, and indeed of conscious affect as well. The passage thus explores a prospect scarcely conceived in Heidegger; indeed, it implies that the child enters the state that Levinas calls "existence without a world," the bare *there is*, mere existence. In contrast to Levinas, however, who as we have seen describes that experience in terms of a nocturnal insomnia that oscillates with the daytime security of a world, Wordsworth depicts a crisis that puts even the latter in danger, evoking an erasure more devastating than night, one that apparently befalls the world in all its manifestations.[16] Furthermore, by suggesting that the absence of the mother is the loss of all figure, and thus of any stable subject as well, with Blanchot it proposes that death takes place not in a future event but already in an initial devastation of a subject that nevertheless persists in a worldless world. In effect, it suggests with Blanchot that this dying puts the child "in play … by way of a relation that does not arrive through" him, hinting that what is primary is not the subject, nor even relationship per se, but the disappearance inscribed in relationship itself.[17] Here the sequence that began with *Salisbury Plain* reaches its culmination, for the poet completes the process of stripping down the scenarios of cultural dismemberment to a primordial ravage that can never simply be one's own, bringing alterity into what might seem to be one's own most intimate regions. In doing so, the passage moves into the blank condition that underlies all subsequent modes of figuration and political articulation, the most reduced condition of "perilous historical situatedness": the state of mere existence.

The intricacies in this passage are so daunting that it is no wonder the poem introduces it with the warning, "Yet is a path / More difficult before me, and I fear / That in its broken windings we shall need / The chamois' sinews, and the eagle's wing" (2.317–20). This domain without figure, it seems, is like an Alpine peak where the chamois roams and the eagle soars: it represents the very pinnacle of difficulty. In this way, the poet rightly indicates that his project carries him into a zone that skirts along the edges of what he can articulate. With the loss of all figure, with the loss of reality itself, the child finds himself in an almost inaccessible domain.

Yet just as the poet describes the child's dilemma, he begins to outline a possible resolution: "The props of my affections were removed / And yet the building stood as if sustained / By its own spirit" (2.324–6). Here the sliding of one metaphor into another, the absorption of those props into the implied timbers of the child's building, suggests that the figural capacity that oriented the child to the mother may sustain him again, having become the very form of his spirit. In this initial account, the mother as figure returns in a new guise; what her absence erases is now restored to him: "All that I beheld / Was dear to me," he continues, "and from this cause it came / That now to Nature's finer influxes / My mind lay open" (2.326–9). Thanks to his relation to the mother, the world is dear to him, and accordingly he can treat the world as a single figure, as "Nature," in a mode of intense receptivity; the mother's loss makes more evident what her presence made possible for him, a relation to the world of sense. As Geoffrey Hartman writes of this passage, "The fixated or literally animistic mind feels that if nature remains alive when what gave it life (the mother) is dead [or absent], then the mother is not dead but invisibly contained in nature."[18] But in that case, the child relies on an instance of figuration, whereby one vivid psychic reality stands in for another. Insofar as the substitution of Nature for the mother makes a relationship to reality possible, this figural substitution constitutes a primordial event that conserves the possibility of world as such. For the poet, at least, it is a kind of *ur*-figure, a pre-figural figure, without which the building's entire superstructure would collapse.

Exploring this possible solution, the poem identifies what may be a precondition of the child's survival in the world of sense. In these lines, the child can respond to the world by extending the terms of relationship with a person, orienting himself precisely through an "intercourse of sense." One might object that by transferring the figural dynamics of relationship to the world, the child treats the world as other than it is. But for the moment it seems that this primordial conception of the world as a counterpart in relationship brings it into existence for the child; no domain of literal objects pre-exists this gesture, for it is only through such a gesture that the phenomenal world becomes available to the child in the first place. In this account, relationship founds the world, rather than vice versa. This portion of the poem, from the Blest Babe through the lines on loss and recovery, forcefully challenges what Nancy Yousef has called the "isolated cases" of Enlightenment epistemological speculation, those figures of consciousness that seem to emerge in utter solitude, as well as proleptically the isolated case of Dasein, in favour of a relational epistemology.[19] Here Wordsworth provides, as does Coleridge some decades later in his *Opus Maximum*, a theory of the person as an alternative to the post-Cartesian, abstract, philosophical subject – a person who, in Pfau's description in another work, is intrinsically active, dynamic, transformative, and relational, initially emerging in relation to the mother.[20] By depicting how a child may enter the mother–infant bond, suffer its loss, and restore it in a new key, the poem suggests that the child may discover a capacity to apply the dynamism of relationship to a domain where no person is explicitly evident and thus respond to an apparently faceless world in affective and potentially ethical terms.[21]

Yet the poem's gestures in this regard are tentative; they do not provide a definitive conclusion to these concerns. The poem hints as much when, a few lines later in the same verse paragraph, it proposes an alternative outline of the origins of affect. This further passage does not flow directly from the lines that precede it and has no introduction; it intrudes upon its context, delving into this problematic in an even more surprising fashion, and for that reason deserves unusually close scrutiny:[22]

> [F]or I would walk alone
> In storm and tempest or in starlight nights
> Beneath the quiet heavens, and at that time
> Would feel whate'er there is of power in sound
> To breathe an elevated mood by form
> Or image unprofaned: and I would stand
> Beneath some rock listening to sounds that are
> The ghostly language of the ancient earth
> Or make their dim abode in distant winds.
> Thence did I drink the visionary power.
> I deem not profitless these fleeting moods
> Of shadowy exultation, not for this,
> That they are kindred to our purer mind
> And intellectual life, but that the soul
> Remembering how she felt, but what she felt
> Remembering not, retains an obscure sense
> Of possible sublimity to which
> With growing faculties she doth aspire,
> With faculties still growing, feeling still
> That whatsoever point they gain, they still
> Have something to pursue. (2.351–71)

This passage's references to elevated places and dim sounds imply that here at last the poet is attempting to trace some length of those broken windings he mentioned earlier. Indeed, it is no easy matter to construe these lines. Given its phrasing regarding the soul's "[r]emembering how she felt, but what she felt / Remembering not," one could read this passage as depicting the adult's difficulty in reconstructing what the child felt in this scene. But the passage overall disallows this reading, for it tacitly equates the "elevated mood" the child experiences with the "fleeting moods / Of shadowy exultation" one feels in the mode of such an odd remembering and thus suggests that the suspension of all form and image in that sound suspends any particular emotion as well. The child himself, it seems, does not know *what* he feels: he feels with great intensity no specific emotion. This passage is thus a meditation on what I will call *primary affect*, that is, an affect that arises in the utter loss of a world, in the erasure of form, image, motive, thought, or feeling. *This* is what it is like, the passage seems to say, to find oneself in a mode logically prior to any particular emotion, before it can be rendered in the figures of exposure, wandering, pain, or abandonment, situated in any narrative, or even placed within a substantial, visible world.

While the passage in context seems to be provided as an illustration of how the child felt after finding a positive orientation to the world, following on lines that explore that theme, one must conclude instead that it evokes an emotion that transpired not after that event but near its beginning, when the child finds a way to sense the world in its blank entirety. As a result, it provides an alternative to the previous account of the child's mode of surviving the loss of a world. A few lines earlier, the poem suggests that the child can endure by regarding the world as a domain with which he might sustain an "intimate communion," but here something else takes place, for he survives instead through a primary affect he discovers when he is awakened by the "power of sound." In the earlier passage, the infant enters into feeling as he "gather[s] passion from his Mother's eye," from "one appearance" in which he combines the "parts of the same object"; here, however, the child absorbs emotion from what is *without* form or image, however cryptic, and thus without articulation or appearance. Without referring to the suggestion a few lines earlier that the child can substitute the world for the mother and thus leaving that resolution in abeyance, here the poem insists that the world can arise as a possibility for the child precisely as what can arise in a domain without figure. Moreover, the world takes shape here not as a substantial domain of visible, rooted, and enduring phenomena, not as a landscape or as Nature, but as one that eludes any such condition.

Thus these lines, setting aside figuration, in effect delve into that aspect of mood that articulation attempts to evoke – hoping to present that unrepresentable state. Whereas Heidegger argues that mood can be awakened after the fact through its virtual articulations, Wordsworth attempts to outline bare mood as such, writing of it as something that arises through a response to a pure virtuality in the world of sense. In doing so, the poet suggests that the mood of this child is not intrinsic, as if awaiting in his depths, but is brought forth by his attending to an expressive capacity outside himself. If we find an instance of that capacity in the passage's reference to distant winds, then these lines are quite close to the possibility outlined by Lyotard, who as we have seen suggests that there is a "mindless state of mind" required not to grasp matter but "*so that there be* some something," a "presence in the absence of the active mind" which "is never other than timbre, tone, nuance in one or other of the dispositions of sensibility" – in this case, in the sound of the wind – "a singular, incomparable quality – unforgettable and immediately forgotten," of which the mind "conserves only the feeling – anguish and jubilation – of an obscure debt."[23] What the mind discerns in such an instant, Lyotard speculates, is a matter that "has no need" of the mind, insisting "'before' questioning and answer, 'outside' them," in a zone, Wordsworth would add, that is ancient and ghostly, that pre-exists the child's apprehension.[24] In that case, the child comes into being this time not through "mute dialogues," as in the Blest Babe passage, but through attending to something that, as Adam Potkay notes in another context, is "not answerable to human life or logic."[25] Rather than enjoying an autonomous state of consciousness, the child emerges through a profound receptivity to this nonhuman, external sound, a receptivity that remains in the form of a half-forgotten, obscure debt.

At first one might conclude from the passage's final lines that this primary affect is a struggle to find a specific mood and thereby a figurable world. But the thought of a specific affect does not appear, even in the distance; the sound breathes a mood that refers to no particular feeling, much as it speaks a language without form or figure. The passage takes these suggestions further in referring to "sounds that are / The ghostly language of the ancient earth / *Or* make their dim abode in distant winds" (emphasis added): this *or* hints that these sounds of the earth can arise apart from the movement of any winds, that they inhere in nothing more than the silent movement of the planet itself. But this *or* also hints that there is no real distinction between the sound of the planet as it revolves and the dim, indecipherable movement of the air; neither is the definitive figure, neither is the ultimate sound of the world. The indecipherable emptiness of this sound and the formlessness of this affect spill over into the child's entirely intransitive aspiration. This pursuit is another version of what the earlier passage marked out as a seeking without motive, a seeking embedded in the situation itself, prior to subjectivity – a pure potentiality of the "soul" to feel emotion as such, to exist as a pure affect of growing intensity. Following the hints in the passage, one might attempt to read this formless aspiration as an instance of the sublime. But the parallel with the instant described by Lyotard suggests that he might place it instead in a zone "after the sublime," for it arises in response to matter without finality or destination – or, in Wordsworth's terms, in a zone before the sublime, before the thought of destination has arisen.[26] Indeed, the passage suggests that the mind's faculties aspire only to an "obscure sense / Of possible sublimity," for they are oriented not to any formal structure of aesthetic response but to the possibility of responsiveness as such.

The passage suspends familiar determinations in yet another respect. It is virtually unique in *The Prelude* for not locating a moment of affect in a particular time or place, perhaps because it speaks of an emotion free of form and image. The child experiences this moodless mood at times "in storm or tempest" and at other times "in starlight nights / Beneath the quiet heavens." This contrast between storm and calm evokes a similar contrast between distressed and peaceful wanderers, between the misery of Martha Ray and the peace of the dead Margaret; in effect, it points to the divergence between two ways this poet evokes the experience of abandonment. One would think that the mood of exultation would take place in the midst of calm rather than storm, for it seems to register the crossing from anxiety to reassurance. Yet the equivocation indicates on the contrary that this shadowy mood exceeds features of *both* possibilities, calm *and* storm, and thus implicitly exceeds either figure of maternal disturbance or care as well. It does so not by reducing these two modes to the same content but rather by treating both as instances of mood as such, whatever its features may be. But then primary affect is more fundamental than anything the poet explored in the earlier poems of storm or calm; by invoking both of those latter modes he makes clear that he now wishes to take a further step, to outline an understanding of affect more capacious than any single location or episode can evoke. In these and other ways, then, the passage insists on the priority of mere existence to any figure, location, or mood that would attempt to capture it, locating that state in a region that eludes articulation of any kind.[27]

On the basis of this passage the poet returns to the previous question and explains how he came to love nature as a whole for its own sake. In the following verse paragraph, he insists on the continuing power of his affective apprehension of the world, suggesting that in certain moments "what I saw / Appeared like something in myself – a dream, / A prospect in my mind" (2.399–401) or, conversely, that his mind was "Subservient strictly to the external things / With which it communed" (2.416–17), as if to suggest simultaneously that the world was in his mind and his mind in the world. Such a suggestion bears out features of the "power of sound" passage, in which the child's primary affect arises from the similarly primordial affect of the world, a mood revealed in the "ghostly language" uttered before language itself comes into being, before the differentiations of form and image take shape. Not long after, the poem claims that at the age of seventeen, he was only "[c]ontented when with bliss ineffable / [He] felt the sentiment of being spread / O'er all that moves, and all that seemeth still," for "in all things / [He] saw one life, and felt that it was joy" (2.449–51; 459–60). In effect, the poem argues, because he gained access to earthly existence in response to a formless expressiveness, he apprehends being not as the field of objects or actual perceptions but rather as an affect that contains no specific feature, as what Novalis would call "the pure form of feeling" of "mere-being."[28] Thus one must take the phrase "sentiment of being" in its full grammatical complexity as a sentiment that being feels and a sentiment that he feels in the presence of being, or more rigorously still, in its suspension of either attribution, its hint that this sentiment pre-exists the distinction between mind and world.[29] Having absorbed the world's ancient mood into himself, what he now feels is an instance of that primordial, impersonal affect, giving this phrase a truly uncanny significance. Moreover, since this apprehension of being must subtend the experience of all specific phenomena, it follows that this primary affect tacitly accompanies the child's sense of any aspect of the natural world (see 2. 448–60) not as a feature of positive experience but as the primal, empty sentiment intrinsic to his sense of the mere existence that underlies and permeates that world.

One result of the persistence of primary affect in this sentiment is that it enables a stunningly affirmative response to the world it makes possible and potentially an ethical disposition to the life of things.[30] Here again the poem proleptically revises Heidegger, linking speculations that the philosopher never definitively conjoined, suggesting that only through the experience of absolute deprivation can one attain what Heidegger elsewhere describes as the astonishment of being, the pathos in response to the fact that the world exists at all, for only if the world seems to be entirely lost can one experience a "bliss ineffable" in the prospect that it endures.[31]

Certain remarkable implications of what Wordsworth outlines in the passage on the power of sound become evident in "A slumber did my spirit seal," a poem that, written in late 1798, is roughly contemporaneous with the Two-Part *Prelude*:

> A slumber did my spirit seal;
>   I had no human fears;
> She seemed a thing that could not feel
>   The touch of earthly years.
>
> No motion has she now, no force;
>   She neither hears nor sees,
> Rolled round in earth's diurnal course
>   With rocks and stones and trees.[32]

This poem blends several motifs from the passages just discussed above. Here a female figure helps the speaker establish a relation to what is left to him after a great loss, enabling him to enter an intimate communion with the earth. But in this case her posthumous survival in the earth is now explicit, in contrast to the suggestions of the relevant passage in *The Prelude*, and what is more, occurs through her disappearance into the blank affect inherent in things, drawing on motifs from the "power of sound" passage. This blend of the two figural strategies outlined in the adjacent passages discussed above leads to more daring formulations of certain themes. She has "[n]o motion" and "no force," yet she is nevertheless "Roll'd round in earth's diurnal course / With rocks and stones and trees" (5, 7–8): she dissolves into the revolution of the earth, into a repetitive motion at once agitated and calm. What she evokes is beyond either tempest or quiet, a state that is closely akin to primary affect, the mood of mood. But the tonality of this affect receives a highly specific accent here. This poem's speaker has awakened, it seems, to the knowledge that she *could* feel "the touch of earthly years" (4), those revolutions in which she is now "roll'd round." If so, then this speaker, too, can feel those years: he has now been tutored in affect, in such things as "human fears" (2) or human calm.

But how human are these fears, or this fearful calm, if she feels those years in her being "roll'd round" with the earth? The speaker seems to discover affect not by discerning a human state but by finding it in the mood of the posthumous or nonhuman; though to him she once seemed to be a "thing that could not feel" (3), she is now for him apparently a "thing" that paradoxically *can* feel what it is like to be "roll'd round ... / With rocks and stones and trees." While the poem can still refer to her as "she," then, it also conceives of her as an instance of inanimate affect, the mood of rocks and stones and trees. Bereft of sight or hearing, she can nevertheless share in the sentiment of being, in the mood of the world that one can apprehend in a manner other than phenomenal perception. Sensing her, the poem's speaker participates in the ghostly affect of the ancient earth, which moves here not in distant winds but in the cycling of the planet itself, in its endless, restless peace. In this poem, primary affect arises from a capacity to participate in the nonhuman, or what Lyotard would designate as the inhuman – in the "life of things," as the poet puts it in another moment of posthumous apprehension – that is, from a responsiveness to the earth's resonant, empty turning.

In the power of sound passage and "A slumber," the exploration of primary affect brings about something altogether more subtle than a poetics of transcendence. These poems accentuate a mode of vulnerability that underlies and ultimately shapes the perilous situatedness of historicity, carrying onto new terrain what Wordsworth explored in his renditions of cultural shattering. Furthermore, they also outline a state in which the nonsubject emerges through its absorption of a pre-phenomenal aspect of the world. Far from idealizing the fullness of an autonomous self, they depict a condition without ground or figure, a stunningly denuded state in which the mind endures only thanks to its capacity to absorb a pure resonance outside itself, to enter a specific form of alterity. When Wordsworth finds his way towards these depictions of primary affect, taking one thread of his work over several years to its apparent destination, he arrives not at a Romantic ideology of an ahistorical subject but rather a strikingly anti-ideological depiction of a nonsubject that is fragile through and through, that at least initially is nothing more than a receptivity to the timbre it finds in the silent sound of the world.

Once the poet works through resonances of primary affect in these poems, he feels confident in writing several further lyrics in ensuing years on how his adult poetic persona participates in inanimate affect. "These chairs they have no words to utter," for example, contemplates the possibility that one might lie in bed as "Happy as they who are dead" while yet drawing breath (12), and "Personal Talk" (initially titled "I am not One who much or oft delight") celebrates the ability to "sit without emotion, hope, or aim" by the fireside (11).[33] In these instances, a certain bare affect arises in a moment of absolute rest, without emotion or apparent life, in which one can share in the inanimate mood of the world. These lyrics innovate on the core theme in several respects; they locate primary affect within an adult's experience in a quotidian, domestic space, in familiar aspects of everyday life, even as they consider various ironies, such as the prospect of being as happy as the dead while remaining alive.[34]

Yet soon Wordsworth moves to a further phase in his thinking about primary affect. Perhaps only at this point can he begin to complicate his understanding of its import by placing it within a more difficult interplay of imperatives. The poet gives this phase of his exploration a singular urgency, embedding it in the Intimations Ode, the first version of which he completed in 1804 and which he thereafter regards as the most definitive poem of his career – as an especially urgent version, as it were, of the truly published, albeit in a form that continues to elude comprehension. By placing his new consideration of primary affect at the crux of the poem, at the hinge of what transforms crisis into triumph, and drawing on it in its concluding stanzas, he gives it an even more pivotal role. Were it not for the passages and poems examined above, it would be difficult to decipher what is at stake in the key lines. But with the help of the discussion above, one can follow Wordsworth through this specific thread in the poem (a thread to which I will adhere closely at the expense of many other aspects of this extraordinarily complex poem) as he draws upon and alters his previous suggestions, providing a more vexed and ambivalent rendition of a primordial, blank bliss.

At the turning point of the Ode in stanza nine, the poet reworks the initial bewilderment of "seeking the visible world, nor knowing why" of *The Prelude* into the "Obstinate questionings / Of sense and outward things, / Fallings from us, vanishings" (144–6), transforming a motiveless seeking into interroga-tion.[35] In these elusive lines, which unlike virtually all the other passages in the poem have no counterparts elsewhere within it and thus remain challeng-ing to interpret even within its own terms, Wordsworth finds in that seeking of the external a suspicion that the phenomenal world cannot measure up to the sentiment of mere existence.[36] If the mind can be founded in a state that precedes mere phenomena, then it is susceptible to what the Ode depicts as the "[b]lank misgivings of a Creature / Moving about in worlds not realized" (147–8). Here it seems possible that because primary affect arises in a situation prior to positive experience, it renders the phenomena of the world inferior, weak, evanescent, unreal.[37] This possibility bears a strong affinity with the lines earlier in the 1804 Ode, eventually deleted under pressure from Coleridge, on how for the child "the grave / Is but a lonely bed without the sense or sight / Of day or the warm light, / A place of thought where we in waiting lie" (120–3): the questioning child sustains what can also take the form of a posthumous state of mind, a mode in which thought persists without the perception of a world in a counterpart of the Levinasian night. (That passage suggests, in retrospect, that the child of the Second Part enters primary affect after severe loss by listening while "[b]eneath some rock," as if already under a gravestone in a posthumous or inhuman state of his own; it also hints that the figure in "A slumber" rolls round with rocks and stones and trees because she lies in the grave and is thus physically located within the earth.)[38] Such hints indicate that the primary state endures apart from one's participation in the circumstances of ordinary, mortal life, at once preceding them, surviving them, and by implication abiding throughout them as well. Accordingly, even though that initial state creates the preconditions for one to enter into a quotidian mortality, it remains distinct from the latter, for it is a mode that can persist through life or death without belonging to either. On this basis, the poet can claim that those "first affections" still endure as the "fountain light of all our day" (151, 154), that primary affect – which he virtually names outright here – underlies every dimension of actual experience throughout an adult's life, which in consequence retains the traces of a nonmortality that persists despite and within it. This intimation at the poem's turning point suggests that nonhuman, anonymous, primary affect *is* what the poet calls immortality, for as a state logically prior to all specific experience it can never be cancelled by that experience nor by the birth, life, or death of any persona that operates in the world, even if it underlies that experience as its fundamental precondition.

In all these ways, the poem accentuates how primary affect is indeed a *blank* state, a supremely evacuated condition in which the mind persists without a world, without entering the quotidian conditions of mortal life. This condition is so pivotal in the poem that one is tempted to argue that the memory of this blank, nonmortal affect is sufficient for the poet to overcome the crisis that inspired the poem. But in fact, the key lines emphasize instead the memory of those blank *misgivings*. In a bold gesture, Wordsworth displaces his focus from primary affect itself to the difficult position in which it places the mind, in effect revising the movement of his early career, his celebration of the bliss of being in the Two-Part *Prelude*, and indeed the apparent movement of the Ode itself up to stanza nine.

Because of this surprising emphasis, one must pause to examine the import of those misgivings closely. As I suggested above, that phrase seems to indicate that the bliss of being can imply a disaffection towards positive phenomena, a distrust of anything that is not being itself. Because primary affect is blank, these misgivings follow from a mood without content; seized by that empty affect, the child may prefer it to any alternative and thus regard the object-world with suspicion. This prospect is consistent with the suggestion that these misgivings are akin to those "[h]igh instincts, before which our mortal Nature / Did tremble like a guilty Thing surprized" (149–50); those misgivings about the vanishings of phenomena may arise from the instincts that make mortality itself tremble. But the child may also feel misgivings because phenomena vanish under the pressure of being; he may be stunned that those worlds vanish so easily precisely because he wishes they *were* realized, that they *could* endure. He may be in distress because the worlds have left him in a blank domain, without phenomena to grasp, lost without refuge in a primordial state. Moreover, it is not as if the child, seeking an alternative, can take refuge in eternity; after all, as these lines indicate, that state militates against his "mortal Nature," much as in the previous stanza it is capable of haunting and enslaving him (113, 118). Thus one must recognize, with Simon Jarvis, that the "difficulty of 'holding' or containing bliss, the difficulty of bearing bliss, stands over the whole poem as much as the sorrow of losing it."[39] The child has nowhere to turn, neither towards a being too vast for him nor the worlds that perpetually vanish. He is caught between infinity and finitude, eternity and time. This is no contingent difficulty; on the contrary, as the use of the first-person plural indicates, the lines on blank misgivings depict an impasse constitutive of consciousness as such, when, barely capable of distinguishing itself from the nullity of sheer being, it finds itself between that domain and the affordances of mortal existence.

One must pause here to note the extraordinary fact that the poet evokes the difficulty of this state not by describing what it feels like to *encounter* something blank but rather to be caught *within* a blank condition, to participate in an affect that has no content and no definition. The emphasis in this poem is not on how the child senses a blank region outside of himself – neither a mother invisibly contained in nature nor the ghostly language of the ancient earth – but rather on how he suffers his *own* blank state. By daring to present the confusion of one who suffers ontological placelessness in one's actual state of consciousness, the poet is especially bold. A useful contrast may be the Kantian mathematical sublime, which culminates in the realization that the sublime must reside in the mind, not in the world. That realization follows on the mind's shift from an overwhelming phenomenal experience to the idea of the infinite, to an infinity that remains in some sense abstract.[40] In this passage, however, as in stanza eight, the child suffers from a difficulty that is the inverse of the one Kant captures, for as he partakes in an infinity that overwhelms him, he cannot catch hold of the finite phenomena that are perpetually falling away.

The impress of what these lines convey is so great that it partially displaces the emphasis of the Ode's opening stanzas. The poem has added to its initial emphasis on the loss of the world's radiance in childhood the further problem of how to respond to primary affect; these questions play out together in an especially complex sequence as the poem proceeds. As we have seen, near the end of stanza nine the poem suggests that those "first affections" never disappear, a dimension of nonmortal life persisting as the basis for all further experience, including that of mortality. As stanza ten suggests in closely associated phrasing, one can thus find strength "[i]n the primal sympathy / Which having been must ever be" (184–5). Here the poem suggests that primary affect is also "primal sympathy," an eager absorption of an external expressiveness, creating the template for sympathetic affect in response to the lives and deaths of others and enabling those "soothing thoughts that spring / Out of human suffering"

(186–7): the capacity to grieve for and with others belongs to a pattern already created by that "primal sympathy." Here the disappointment that those worlds are not realized – and the implicit wish that they might endure – modulates into an ability to cherish those worlds even in their evanescence; the poem revises the distrust of phenomena into a cherishing of what can be lost. But it does so while also holding that this remains a *primal* sympathy, one that primary affect shows towards what vanishes. This response to suffering and mortality emerges from within nonmortality. Indeed, because the nonmortal is already in part posthumous, as we have seen, it can provide a surprising framework for the seemingly orthodox "faith that looks through death" (188). But it is precisely because it can look *through* death, because it is nonmortal, that it sustains a *primal* sympathy with what vanishes, an enduring capacity to cherish all that passes away.

But the poem does not stop here. It also suggests that this response is rooted in "years that bring the philosophic mind," that living within a vulnerable condition over decades or a lifetime can deepen that primal sympathy into an even greater responsiveness. As Helen Vendler argues, the movement from childhood to adulthood, while distancing one from the child's sense of the world's radiance, can give the adult a much greater sense of the metaphorical resonances of the world's appearances, as the final lines of the poem suggest: thanks to this development, the "Clouds that gather round the setting sun / Do take a sober colouring from an eye / That hath kept watch o'er man's mortality" (199–201).[41] But these resonances go even further; they do not come to rest on the sunset as a figure of mortality, crucial as that figure may be for the poem's response to its opening four stanzas, for they also enlarge on the import of primary affect. If one takes the context of stanza nine into account, as well as its allusions to prior passages in the poet's work, then one must acknowledge that the setting of the sun is also a metaphor for the vanishing of unrealized worlds, the falling away of what is impermanent; it stands in for what is even more severe than death, the seemingly absolute loss that makes possible the entry into primary affect. The poem hints as much in its final lines, where "the meanest flower that blows can give / Thoughts that do often lie too deep for tears" (205–6): the fragility of that flower, a metaphor for the evanescence of all things, can take one not into a deeper inwardness but more radically into a receptivity beyond grief, into a mood without mood.

This complex sequence in the Ode subtly reconceives of the poet's political engagements. As we have seen, in his earlier work Wordsworth gradually strips away various scenarios to capture the nonsubject's stunning vulnerability in a groundless world. But because primary affect can lead the child to enjoy the bliss of being, this sense of vulnerability can modulate into shock at the vulnerability of phenomena themselves – and into a demand that they provide something other, something more. Accordingly, the lines on the child's blank misgivings in the face of what vanishes speak of what Rei Terada has described as dissatisfaction with phenomena, which she reads as implicitly political in its gesture towards possibilities as yet unrealized.[42] Thus the Ode, which has often been read as a sign that the poet abandons his earlier politics, through this feature retains it in a new key, in the demand that things be otherwise.[43] Yet those lines on blank misgivings, as well as the stanzas that follow, bring further orientations into play. The child's wish that phenomena not vanish reveals a yearning for them to stay. This longing, in turn, leads him towards the attachments of mortal life and grief at its losses; it also opens up the way for primal sympathy to deepen. These latter features are also implicitly political, for they speak of the poet's attachments to those who are fated to vanish, and thus of a sense of solidarity with all those who retain, like the poet, a mortal nature. They hint at a regard of the fragile for the fragile, or rather, to pursue suggestions provided by Part Two of *The Prelude*, as well as by Blanchot, a regard of what is fragile because, in its primary orientation to alterity, it suffers the fragility of others, because its own dying takes place through the loss implicit in relationship itself. Yet this fragility takes shape paradoxically in the domain of the nonmortal, of what, in the wake of that dying, cannot vanish. The poet's orientation to others inheres in the blank state of the nonsubject that endures through all scenarios, and thus in a perspective that never relinquishes its misgivings with regard to the world as it is. The demand that the world be otherwise, then, is embedded in the love for the vanishing, for those who are still subject to the world as it is.

The impact of these responses remains paramount even as the poem closes. Nevertheless, this modulation of one response to another, from dissatisfaction to solidarity, is possible because each refers back to aspects of primary affect itself. The poem thus relies on that more definitive state even as it outlines a range of orientations that follow from it. Thus it is not surprising that at a key moment in its final lines, the Ode evokes that state once again, this time reconceiving of primary affect even more capaciously so that it can now accommodate new concerns. As we have seen, in its late stanzas the Ode suggests that beyond the question of nature's metaphorical depth for the adult lies the prospect that the fragility of any form of life is a metaphor for that of phenomena in general. If one discerns in the poem's final sunset hints of the earth's movement, to which any sunset must refer, and which is evoked with such eerie force in the power of sound passage and "A slumber did my spirit seal," then the poem leaves us in the position of one who, having survived the loss of worlds, can still discern them from within a pre-mortal or posthumous state and can abide with the turning of the day, and of the earth, in a mode of endless receptivity. In doing so, it revises stanza nine in a key respect, for it recasts vanishing as perpetual turning, as the endless arising and falling of worlds, suggesting that the nonsubject, rather than being disappointed at what falls away, may abide alongside the perpetuity of this process, the endlessness of this disappearance.

The *there is*, Wordsworth seems to say, does not simply persist endlessly; as it does so, it *revolves*, in which case one might say, to parody Levinas, *it turns*. Here evanescence morphs into a version of the earth's ghostly language, an instance of the wind's movement. As a result, the Ode suggests that beneath dissatisfaction and solidarity lies another mode that, to follow Khalip, "does not desire anything else" – a receptivity that is endlessly absorbed in the *it turns*.[44] Coming to rest on no specific figure, it invokes figuration *in toto*, the perpetual turning of the earth and of trope. Despite our expectations, then, the poem does not merely invoke intimations of immortality; on one of its levels, it evokes the state within which the nonsubject attends forever to the language of the earth, to a nonmortality that bears the impress of that ceaseless movement.

Terada has outlined for us the shape of emotion after the death of the subject, opening up a space, we can now see, that Wordsworth explores in these poems.[45] Initially, he moves past various figures of dispossession, whether from phenomenology, psychoanalysis, or materialist critique, and problematizes a theory of the origin of personhood in relationship as he arrives at his depiction of primary affect. That condition, as we have seen, is not transcendent but rather exemplifies what remains after the erasure of transcendence, after the removal of any ground for the world: the domain of mere existence, the sheer fact of the *there is*, which this primary nonsubject absorbs while listening to the sound of the world. What initially removes the world from him, however, eventually restores it to him, leading to his feeling a "bliss ineffable" at the prospect of its endurance: the erasure of the world ushers in an astonishment at its endurance, a bliss in mere being. This bliss, however, creates the extraordinary, surprising complications of the Intimations Ode, placing the child between the unendurable bliss of eternity and the vanishings of time. Yet by its end, in still another surprising move, the poem suggests that the affect embedded in the utterly denuded state of the *there is* can carry over into all the emotions of the "human heart," "its tenderness, its joys and fears" (202, 203), so that what is primal can remain in what is also mature, the nonsubject in the subject.

This resolution nevertheless bears the imprint of what it has ostensibly overcome. By showing how that primary state initially arrives through the devastating loss of the world, Wordsworth articulates the trauma of modernity, its encounter with the mere existence that arises with the erasure of transcendence. While the culmination of the Ode depicts nonmortality's primal sympathy with time, indeed a certain solidarity with the vulnerability of finitude, greatly shifting the poem's tone on these matters, in the very act of doing so it retains its prior contrast between the endurance of the primary state and the evanescence of mortality. In that way, it reminds us that rather than grounding the phenomenal domain, as transcendence once did, mere existence reveals its fragility without providing an alternative. Primary affect, then, exemplifies the impact of modernity, the unassimilable Real that renders all historicity, temporality, and affect stunningly vulnerable. In the final stanzas of the Ode, the poet conceives of primary affect as a receptivity to the domain it unsettles, absorbed in what it now considers the permanent condition of evanescence. But this very blessing arises from an unaccountable place, from a position that is already to some degree posthumous; it exceeds the world it attempts to embrace, and indeed any world, for it remains the very experience of the worldless. Even in the mode of its tender affirmation of evanescence, then, the nonsubject intrudes upon the assurances of subjectivity, perpetually sustaining the thoroughgoing erasure that underlies the historicity of the modern world.

Yet even as it articulates this structural impasse, along the way Wordsworth's poetics articulates with unusual subtlety the moodless transport embedded in that primary state. In those passages when the poet conveys how a preconscious or posthumous figure listens to the silent movement of the earth or rolls round with rocks and stones and trees, he evokes a nonhuman, inanimate ecstasy. If modernity is haunted by a silent and scarcely traceable cancellation of any ground, Wordsworth proposes that the ur-experience of that empty domain is utterly transporting. In the even more daring suggestions encrypted in the Ode, he takes these hints further, proposing that the experiences of mortal life can deepen that primal sympathy: now the vanishings of all things prompt feelings even deeper than bliss. Those blank misgivings at moving about in worlds not realized, it seems, can modulate into the blank absorption in the passing of all mortal things, the ecstasy of abiding with the frailty of worlds.

2 Blank Accident: Nothing's Anomaly in the Late Coleridge

Any critic approaching Coleridge faces a unique challenge. One who attempts to interpret his poetry confronts the unusual arrangement whereby, as Tilottama Rajan demonstrates, he simultaneously participates in the construction of Romantic subjectivity and abjects himself from it. A similar pattern extends across his work in other modes, where he posits a certain affirmative self-presence while denying his own access to it, creating a bifurcated discourse that in a variety of ways he sustains throughout much of his career.[1] In its later phases, Coleridge's writing perpetually invokes the dominant institutions of the modern writerly subject – authorship, the work, the career, the completed philosophical system – while also subverting them, presenting their realization as impossible, their premises (whether discursive, institutional, or conceptual) undone from the start.

Such a procedure does not prevent his friend and collaborator Wordsworth from taking up aspects of Coleridge's construction of Romantic subjectivity and working with them in his own right, nor does it prohibit the heirs of Romanticism from conceiving of that subjectivity as intrinsic to the formation of modern literary and cultural practice.[2] Yet because of his distance from what he helped invent, Coleridge remains at once central and marginal to that legacy, a figure necessary in any account of its formation yet inexplicable within its terms. In consequence, when a mode of criticism invested in that mode of subjectivity confronts Coleridge's work it often falls prey to the assumption it must describe his career as failing to accord with received definitions of the writerly life. Yet one cannot surpass that approach by arguing that the work, resisting such definitions, relies on an anti-normative framework; while the writing undermines traditional claims, it does not openly repudiate the ideologies from which it excludes itself. Indeed, insofar as it contests them, it requires them as well; as Rajan points out, "the textual abject is intimately and symbiotically related to the discourse of subjectivity."[3] Neither officializing nor dissident, this writing entwines both approaches into an apparently contradictory ensemble, demanding of its readers the ability to follow its project of maintaining what it cancels. As a result, that work invites a reading that interprets it as interrogating the very assumptions according to which a modern *oeuvre* has typically been read, for it ultimately consists of a sustained problematization of the discourses and institutions of subjectivity.

As Rajan demonstrates, the poems written after the composition of the Dejection Ode stand out as especially revealing. Half-canonic and lyrically thwarted, statements of apparent failure or despair, these poems are situated within a practice of divided articulation that Coleridge takes very far indeed. But one must expand this approach to decipher an even broader range of statements in which Coleridge deployed this practice. In this regard, the Ode marks the initial phase of the poet's turn away from the attempt to find a correspondence between the poetic subject and nature towards a search for an eternal principle beyond the phenomenal world. This turn is consistent with a shift, especially marked in the later decades, from a Unitarian to a Trinitarian Christianity, a development in his thinking that eventually leads him to embark upon what he considered to be his capstone work, *Opus Maximum*, left incomplete at his death.[4] This conjunction of faith in transcendence and poetic despair might confuse us were we not already aware of the pattern that shapes Coleridge's writing; it is not a contradiction but rather a symbiosis that makes it possible for each feature of the later thought to appear.

While in this late phase of his career Coleridge crafts a sophisticated theological stance, his discourse of abjection invites him simultaneously to compose poems of astonishing spiritual desolation. In the most telling moments, he writes the two poems I will discuss below, poems that reveal a yearning for a transcendence that is excluded from the domain of time and space in which he finds himself: "Limbo" (1811) and "Human Life: On the Denial of Immortality" (c. 1811–15). These poems suggest that the very prospect of addressing an extra-phenomenal transcendence places him within the radically depleted state one can recognize as mere existence; in effect, they depict the latter as a desolation intrinsic to faith.

The implications of these two poems are so astonishing that they raise the stakes of interpreting Coleridge's career. As I argue in the introduction, when modernity cancels a transcendental ground for the world, that erasure henceforth dislocates the world from itself. During the later decades of his career, Coleridge sets out to resist modernity, to maintain the best features of the theological tradition and thus avoid falling into this depleted state. Indeed, in the latter half of *Minding the Modern: Human Agency, Intellectual Traditions, and Responsible Knowledge*, which carefully examines the failures that underpin the modern intellectual tradition, Pfau considers Coleridge as the figure in the Romantic era who best advocates for the concepts of person and relationship, as well as for an overall normative framework, that the West inherits from

Aristotle, Augustine, Aquinas, and others but has forsaken in the modern era.[5] This treatment of Coleridge's late thought, particularly of *Opus Maximum*, is often quite revealing and useful. But these two poems suggest that at least in certain respects, despite his very resistance to modernity, Coleridge produces a further instance of it.

What can explain this surprising development? At certain moments, his stance is not so far removed in its consequences from the gesture whereby Kant, in his critique of the teleological power of judgment, places a transcendental order of the world beyond the terrain that reason can reach, acknowledging the gap that must obtain between rational apprehension and faith.[6] This gap, in turn, accentuates the divergence between the major faculties through which Kant organizes his thought, faculties that never completely align and that no superior faculty can subordinate to its own ends, making his work an instance of a philosophy of the aporia, as Howard Caygill has argued, or an exploration of the differend, as Lyotard has rigorously demonstrated.[7] Inheriting aspects of this Kantian legacy, Coleridge finds it impossible to find any means within reason to close the gap between natural metaphor and transcendence. For both Kant and Coleridge, reason can neither secure its own domain nor anchor itself in a divine order; the architecture of thought never becomes complete. That gap has signal consequences in the Kantian legacy and in Coleridge's thought, for it leads Coleridge to ponder what must result if time and space are permanently alienated from an ontological grounding. By incorporating aspects of Kantian rigour into his own thought, Coleridge struggles to secure a relation to the divine either through signs in the empirical world or through the affordances of thought itself. Although he maintains these Kantian teachings to distinguish the divine from the vicissitudes of finitude, this very attempt ultimately constitutes still another disorder in transcendence and thus produces an alternative version of the modernity he sought to overcome.

It does not follow that Coleridge sets out to undercut his faith in these poems. Indeed, in each case he stands back from what he depicts as if to suggest he merely depicts an abject spiritual state (in "Limbo") or mocks what he describes ("Human Life"). Yet as I will argue below, these poems articulate his stance with far greater fidelity than this attempt at distancing would suggest: they are symptoms of the aporia in his work. In consequence, his poems suggest that the contrast between faith and the secular on which so many accounts of modernity rely conceals what can be a far closer relation between them than we might suspect, an intimacy between an orientation to the divine and a confrontation with the "blank accident" of mortal life.[8] The intensity of Coleridge's search for redemption lends these poems an extraordinary urgency, motivating him to suggest that without a link to transcendence, every possible trace of the positive necessarily disappears from existence. But in that case, one encounters in these texts a procedure not unlike what appears later in atheological works from Nietzsche through Derrida, which so often attempt to expunge even the subtlest remnants of the divine. To interrogate the import of a finitude without transcendence is not so far, it seems, from exposing the consequences of God's death; in either case, one ultimately sketches the contours of the mere *there is*, the scene of a blank existence.

I

While certain implications of this bifurcation between the phenomenal world and the divine await the late phases of Coleridge's career, its preconditions begin to appear even in the earlier, more canonic work. In several of the most familiar texts, the speaker imagines the possibility of an immediate relationship between consciousness and world but can do so only at a distance from that prospect. The impossibility of joining in the experience of a monistic immediacy is registered in various ways, such as self-rebuke, generosity to another, joyous witnessing, or anguished desire. This orientation to an imaginary lyrical state from a condition deprived of it produces a Romanticism at a remove. Here one may discern a fractured stance that simultaneously yearns for a certain subjectivity and depicts it as an experience that the speaker cannot share. Although the obstacle to participating in that immediacy is intrinsic to the speaker's position within the mediation of the poem itself, these texts nevertheless dramatize the speaker's exile from lyrical fulfilment, depicting a subject yearning for what it lacks and can never have. In effect, because these poems suggest that this deprivation is intrinsic to poetic articulation while they still yearn for immediacy, they ultimately convey a disappointment with what is structurally necessary, depicting it as a form of dispossession. While such poems do not yet articulate a full-blown discourse of abjection, they put into place dissonant elements that will become more dominant in the later work.

One might note, for example, how the speaker of "Eolian Harp" muses on the possibility that the interplay of an "intellectual breeze" and the world of "organic harps" causes the world to hum into existence, inviting him to partake in a single, vast divine life, but distances himself from this prospect in a central passage where he imagines himself leaning back on "yonder hill" to allow the breeze of his thoughts to traverse the instrument of his brain (45, 47, 35).[9] The imagined subject in the distance, rather than the speaker, participates in the monistic universe. Evidently, the prospect of blending a divine subject with "all of animated nature" foregrounds the speaker's separateness all the more (44). The poem returns to its sense of this separateness in the final verse paragraph, which in an accusatory tone proposes that the speaker is unworthy even to ponder joining in such a union with the divine. In a similar disjunction, the speaker of "The Nightingale," struck by the birds' extravagant receptivity to the moon on its sudden appearance – and the equally bright-eyed delight of his child in the poem's final passage – attributes that responsiveness to those who live outside or before language, hinting that the adult male poet lives in a mode alienated from such an un-self-conscious form of transport.[10] Repeatedly bidding farewell to the bird and his friends without reaching home, the speaker ends the poem without the security that either can give him, finding himself in the space of representation instead. Finally, the preface to "Kubla Khan" describes it not as a poem but as the residue of a process whereby a text appeared without the mediation of composition, in images that are also words, as an emanation of the part of the mind activated by an external agency – an event that at once ostensibly reveals that the poet can receive a secular instance of divine inspiration and subjects him to the torment of being unable to revive it by an act of will. The fantasy that a poem-image flowed through him in this instance reinforces all the more the idea that without such a visitation he must suffer the condition of awaiting an event that will never recur. Evidently, adhering to the norms of social life (by receiving the visit of the man from Porlock or writing to an audience) excludes him from reawakening a divine creativity, even as it makes it possible for him to share his experience with the public; in effect, the capacity to partake in a merely human form of articulation forces him into a yearning for the impossible.

Despite the disjunctions in these works, they remain within the orbit of a lyricism whose affective appeal remains powerful and compelling. Insofar as the early canonic poems imagine a state that the speaker witnesses and in which he can participate indirectly, as in the final verse paragraph of "This Lime-Tree Bower My Prison," or attributes to the poet himself a condition of transport that took place in the past, as in the preface to "Kubla Khan," they hint that the speaker can share in some aspect of the condition he must nevertheless mediate through representation, as if dispossession can participate in the very state it cannot have. After 1802, however, what was once a structural impediment against blending the space of articulation with what it represents now modulates into a discourse that undercuts that representation itself, dismantling the lyricism on which the poet once relied. The later poems present themselves almost as anti-poems, relying on thwarted, truncated, or otherwise diminished forms. As Rajan argues, quite often that poetry consists of interactions of allegorical fragments ("The Pang More Sharp Than All"), abstract and impersonal statements ("Ne Plus Ultra"), or texts that blend poetry and prose ("The Blossoming of the Solitary Date Tree"). In these ways the poetics of abjection "protects the private as an emptiness that keeps a space for another self that has not yet emerged" and "preserves the empty form of creativity, discarded but also put away for future use," effacing a lyrical possibility that it nevertheless holds in abeyance.[11]

What can account for the transition from a poetics of mediated transport to one of abjection? Although the revisions to the Dejection Ode from the initial drafts through the completed version give it the polish of a canonic work, it initiates the practice that dominates in the later poetry.[12] Early in the poem, the speaker laments his affectively bereft state, contending that nature's generative power must come from the observer, that "we receive but what we give" (47). Here the poet disclaims the idea of a monistic immediacy on which he previously relied; now the affective force of natural images is read as the projection of an emotionally empowered subject. In that case, the overriding endeavour is not to participate in a fusion of mind and nature but to sustain a self-generating creative power. Rather than allowing this shift in his thinking to authorize an autonomous subjectivity, however, Coleridge reads it as demanding a certain capacity that he now lacks, declaring that his preoccupation with metaphysics has deprived him of his imagination. The idea that one must rely on the empowered subject is not only a philosophical claim, for it bears upon his situation as a person who may fall short of the capacities attributed to him. Moreover, by constructing his poem as an address to a beloved woman with whom erotic consummation is prohibited, he excludes himself from a further metaphor of joyous satisfaction. This sequence of claims thus constructs a framework for the discourse of failure he now applies to himself: ostensibly bereft of imagination and satisfaction alike, he maps out the contours of a state that for him is at once necessary and impossible.

One might well pause to consider whether in the following years Coleridge dissents from the stance of the Ode to construct an alternative. The theory of the imagination at the end of chapter thirteen in the *Biographia* is an excellent case in point. Here, he proposes that a certain distance from the ongoing immediacy of divine creation enables an echo of that process in a fully linguistic imaginative power. This theory revises the earlier poetics, conceiving of a primary process while valorizing a subjectivity that is distinct from it. Accordingly, this new schema seems to represent a major advance, relieving the subject of the pressure to disappear into that primary state and suggesting that secondariness is not a failure but the site for poetic creation. Yet this formulation reveals intractable tensions, for it attempts to conjoin immediacy and mediation, divinity and humanity, endlessly generative being and punctuated creation. Its precariousness suggests that it is less an account of an actual practice than the sketch of a potential resolution to various impasses that remain in place. Furthermore, in the context of the *Biographia*, it provides Coleridge with the conceptual armature to interpret and canonize the writing of another. While this stance enables him to become what Jean-Pierre Mileur calls a "prophetic reader," to sustain a productively revisionary engagement with poetic creation, opening up to him the powers of critical commentary and reception and thus the surprising authority of the secondary, anticipating practices that are essential to many features of modern literary institutions, it does so by allowing him to assign successful imagination to another and thus to locate himself outside the domain he privileges.[13] Here again the subjectivity that his position makes possible eludes him because of what he regards as his personal incapacity. In this regard, the sequence from "Frost at Midnight" through *The Prelude* and "To William Wordsworth" continues into this text, which participates in the process whereby the two poets collaborate in constructing what Rajan shows is "a binary relationship of imagination and dejection," a symbiosis of subject and abject.[14] As a result, the theory of imagination, despite its promising features, ends up reinforcing Coleridge's belief that he is excluded from the poetics he wishes to celebrate.

The overall stance that the Dejection Ode initiates, then, applies even in contexts that promise to surpass it. Moreover, it has broad implications for the mode of discourse Coleridge mobilizes in domains beyond poetry and literary criticism. As we have seen, while in that poem he insists on the failure of his own subjectivity, he also preserves the idea of a successful subject, attributing it to others or holding it in abeyance. But as this position plays out more fully in the writing of the coming years, he comes to believe that to anchor himself in an absolutely enduring generative power he must overleap the limitations of the empirical world, finding a plenitude in a sphere beyond both objective and subjective experience, beyond nature or poetic creativity – that is, in transcendence. This position, however, remains in tension with the earlier disposition towards finding aspects of that power in natural or biblical symbols, a tension that produces many of the conceptual dissonances of the later philosophical writing. As Ben Brice demonstrates in *Coleridge and Scepticism*, at times Coleridge attempts to provide "a theory of symbolism" that can "connect human language and reason to the 'intelligible' language of divinity incarnate in the natural world."[15] After around 1805, however, and especially after 1815, he finds it difficult to sustain the relation between the finite and eternal, between the natural and the transcendent. "The understanding and the senses," Brice writes, "could never be fully rejected by Coleridge and never fully integrated within his own philosophical and religious project," leaving a gap between them that he struggled to close.[16] Accordingly, he is increasingly caught between a resistance to the materialist premises of natural theology, an emphasis on the Neoplatonic and symbolic resonances of Scripture, and a "cherished Kantian principle prohibiting the embodiment or representations of spiritual truths in images of space and time."[17] By adhering to the latter principle, he "posits the kind of intractable gulf between matter and spirit that his sacramental theory of symbolism had been designed to bridge and overcome."[18]

This principle, consistent with the refusal of projection appearing in the Ode, underlies key dimensions of Coleridge's later thought. As Edward Kessler argues, although Coleridge "required the modulating power of love objects" to illuminate "Being," as he "moved into his later years, traditional metaphor ... became inadequate as a means of expressing a Being that was steadily moving beyond the world's appearances."[19] Insofar as Coleridge finds himself living in a world that "provides no self-reflection," he suspects that "all objects, including himself, were without any transfiguring glory," leading him to write the despairing poetry of the later phase.[20] Moreover, insofar as he sought something not directly evident in those appearances, this transcendence was marked out not in positive signs but as a gap in the texture of experience. In a telling passage in his notebooks in June 1810, Coleridge writes that a certain happiness "secures Religion to Man, as long as anywhere in the partakers of human Nature there remains that instinctive craving, dim & blind tho' it may be, of the moral being after this unknown Bliss, or Blessedness – known only & anticipated by the Hollowness where it is."[21] The failure in his own subjectivity – the blank eye of the Ode – has expanded to become a blank space in existence itself. Thus the contours of the bifurcated discourse appear in the post-Kantian theological position, producing a scenario whereby Coleridge anticipates a divine blessedness known only through its absence in experience. Here one encounters the negative outline of theological faith, a confidence in divine agency established through suffering a condition where it is not evident.

One could trace the implications of this stance across a series of Coleridge's later poems. In "Constancy to an Ideal Object" (possibly 1806), for example, Coleridge depicts how the subject can continue to seek an object ostensibly in the world – a beloved woman, an aspect of the landscape – but that now subsists entirely in an image sent forth by the mind. This unstable scenario, however, gives way over the coming years to a starker position, whereby the outer world can no longer sustain even this mode of projection, forcing the subject to endure in a bleak isolation. In "Work Without Hope" (1825), the abundant renewal of life in spring, traditionally a metaphor for the revival of inner resources, instead accentuates how the subject, "the sole unbusy thing" (5), is utterly alienated from the life that flourishes around it. A subject oriented to transcendence has no counterpart in the world, placing its hope only in eternity, but as a result its alienation from natural metaphors seems to place even that hope in abeyance. After its initial disappearance from nature, the object Coleridge seeks endures for a time in an ideal sphere but eventually seems to disappear altogether, leaving him without resources in an estranged world.[22]

The pattern that emerges in the later writing, already clear enough, takes a different shape in the mode of argumentation that appears in his late theological work, the *Opus Maximum*, a set of drafts towards a mature statement that Coleridge never assembled into an integrated work. Murray Evans shows that this text often relies on negative demonstration, whereby in response to a key question Coleridge refutes a series of available answers except for the one most consistent with faith, assuming that this surviving answer must hold true even if he cannot defend it in a rational argument.[23] In effect, this procedure allows him to find indications of faith in the gaps that appear in speculative demonstration, deploying a version of the absence of visible evidence of the divine – the "Hollowness" in experience – in the activity of thought itself.

These two instances suggest that the transition towards a greater insistence on a divine presence that exceeds human experience provides the context within which Coleridge can evoke that presence negatively, in what cannot be sensed or known. These developments in Coleridge's conceptions of experience and of argument reveal that the overall framework that generates the formal features of the later poetry applies to both the content and procedures of the late metaphysical works as well. The poetics thematizes the concerns that over time become more evident in the metaphysics, and vice versa, so that each foregrounds what is at stake in the other. While developments in these areas are not coordinated in any precise way, the pattern that obtains across them suggests that the underlying framework exceeds the determinations we might find in any of them; the scenarios that Rajan and Evans describe point us to a more fundamental impasse.

On occasion, the resonances between these late developments make it possible for Coleridge to create texts that deploy several of these registers at once. In seeking an absolute presence beyond the phenomenal world, Coleridge shifts his focus to a transcendental God and thus moves beyond his prior investment in Romantic subjectivity. Moreover, as I indicated above, on at least two occasions – in "Limbo" and "Human Life: On the Denial of Immortality" – he writes explicitly theological poems that situate the subject in relation to a blessedness it cannot reach, melding a poetics of abjection with a negative metaphysics, making it possible for him to articulate aspects of an overall poetic-metaphysical stance in ways that are unique in his works. In these poems, he explores the contours of hollowness with a vengeance, as if only a supremely bleak statement can provide him refuge from hollowness itself, and in the process articulates some of the boldest evocations of useless negativity in the British canon.

While these poems undoubtedly emerge from the unique circumstances of Coleridge's career, the metaphysical impasse they articulate shows that they bear a much broader import. The theological abjection to which they give voice, while Coleridge's own, is also a state that a discourse of faith in the modern era cannot wholly exclude. Indeed, Coleridge's work from the start may reveal not his own personal incapacity but rather his lucid awareness that the promises of Romantic subjectivity and of theological certainty alike are untenable. His work may thus expose the fissures within them, not from a position outside or hostile to them but from within their very premises, foregrounding the possibility that those living in modernity suffer from a deadlock even more implacable than one might otherwise suspect.

II

What we have encountered so far of the late work suggests that Coleridge constructs a particularly telling rendition of these themes. If one could argue that in his early work he depicts spectacular versions of the Real in encounters with inexplicable events or traumatic intrusions – in such poems as *The Rime of the Ancient Mariner* and "Kubla Khan" – in his later writing he draws closer to Levinas or Blanchot, for he evokes instead the understated, blank version of the Real that undoes the phenomenal domain through and through. This version of the Real does not stand out in contrast to what surrounds it – in the mode of the Mariner, for example, or of a poem that arrives as if magically from an internal yet exotic domain – but rather insists as a severe effacement that pervades the *entirety* of experience.

Such, at least, is the possibility that arises in the opening lines of "Limbo":

'Tis a strange place, this Limbo! – not a Place,
Yet name it so; – where Time and weary Space
Fettered from flight, with night-mare sense of fleeing,
Strive for their last crepuscular half-being; –
Lank Space, and scytheless Time with branny hands
Barren and soundless as the measuring sands,
Not mark'd by flit of Shades, – unmeaning they
As moonlight on the dial of the day! (1–8)

These lines suggest that this poem is an experiment in imagining "half-being." This is no place, yet one can somehow name it so; this is no time, for it is "scytheless," incapable of enforcing the temporality of mortality, yet evidently the sands continue to flow. This is no substantial zone in which shadows may appear, for it persists instead in a crepuscular state, as if it is a sundial lit by the moon. But a time without death is beyond life and death in nonmortality, a time without present, just as a space without shadows belongs to a domain where the difference between light and darkness is effaced. This is a state that endures in the absence of being, having suffered the cancellation of whatever gives space and time their significance, an event akin to the disappearance of the sun. Without being or significance, this state somehow still exists, but only in experiencing the nightmare of seeking what is denied to it, what is promised by that absent being, that foreclosed sun. In the evacuation of any positive sign of transcendence, this version of finitude cannot cast a shadow and thus fails to find its own outline or discern its own contours; accordingly, it is not even finitude and has not even gained the dignity of mortality but subsists uselessly in a tedium measured merely by flowing sand.

One might think that this is the state set aside for those who have denied God and thus alienated themselves from the blessings of transcendence, in which case the poem is meant to represent the absurdity that follows from refusing faith. But the reference to a depleted time and space shows instead that in this poem Coleridge wishes to explore the implications of accepting a specific argument about finitude and transcendence.[24] The situation captured so far in this poem follows from strictly distinguishing between time and eternity, regarding the latter not as an infinitely prolonged version of time but as a temporality that transcends empirical experience. If one locates being in a transcendence that is opposed to the phenomenal world, as Coleridge does in one strand of his thought, then one empties out time and space alike, treating them as domains without substance, outside being. Accordingly, insofar as he was in some measure drawn to this very argument, then it is not surprising that he would eventually maintain that "true being is not contemplable in the forms of time and space."[25] Taking this aspect of his thinking to heart, in "Limbo" Coleridge explores what transpires when being may be found *only* in transcendence; all else leaves no shadow, has no significance, and never takes place. Yet the personifications of Time and Space can nevertheless *yearn* for that absent transcendence. One cannot leap across the gap between this empty domain and the zone of being, yet the wish to do so implies that one suffers something more than sheer nullity; one exists in defiance of that nullity, furiously seeking what is foreclosed, attempting to ground one's experience in a significance of which there is no sign.

The poem goes on to evoke that thwarted condition in this resonant scene:

> But that is lovely – looks like human Time, –
> An old man with a steady look sublime,
> That stops his earthly task to watch the skies;
> But he is blind – a statue hath such eyes; –
> Yet having moonward turn'd his face by chance,
> Gazes the orb with moon-like countenance,
> With scant white hairs, with foretop bald and high,
> He gazes still, – his eyeless face all eye; –
> As 'twere an organ full of silent sight,
> His whole face seemeth to rejoice in light! –
> Lip touching lip, all moveless, bust and limb –
> He seems to gaze at that which seems to gaze on him! (9–20)

Alluding to those episodes in "The Nightingale" in which the birds respond to the moon with bright, glistening eyes and joyous song, "As if some sudden gale had swept at once / A hundred airy harps!" (81–2), and the child "laughs most silently, / While his fair eyes, that swam with undropped tears, / Did glitter in the yellow moon-beam!" (103–5), this passage sharply revises them, cancelling not only a monistic immediacy but the very prospect of an encounter between subject and world. Where the child responds spontaneously to the brightness of the moon, the blind old man only "seems to gaze at that which seems to gaze on him," so that neither subject nor moon actually sees or responds. Instead of a moon whose beauty engenders a response prior to language, here it cannot gain any significance from human language or perception, shining from a domain that human beings cannot reach. Each is blank; neither can discern the other. Insofar as nature contains no human meaning, it becomes ontologically empty, without affect or significance, so that one who turns towards it sees nothing of import and is thus blind. By the same token, since nature has no significance, it has no gaze to bestow.

In effect, then, this passage conveys the shell of an earlier lyrical scenario, outlining what survives after a severe evacuation of its terms. Yet some elements survive: the old man suspends his task and looks towards the skies, after all, and his "eyeless face" is "all eye," as if even in his blindness he sees. In this moment, the passage transforms the moon into a metaphor of the transcendence that he seeks; while the old man cannot see that domain, he can still seek it. He thus becomes an emblem of a Coleridge who yearns for something he places beyond phenomena – an emblem, that is, of faith. The eagerness of his search is striking: his face is all eye, much as he watches "with steady look sublime," embodying the sublime condition of an ineradicable orientation to the beyond. The poem almost hints that he achieves a "silent" sight, a form of apprehension beyond the senses, and that he can "rejoice in light" he cannot see but can somehow feel upon his face, but in both cases it demotes such possibilities onto the level of mere seeming. The scene takes place only *as if* the old man apprehends something beyond, for in fact he does not, nor will he ever do so in phenomena – in what a notebook passage translated from Jean Paul and associated with this poem calls "the dark universe Chamber of the material world."[26] Everything here works as if the poem, in a proleptic gesture, reworks the notion of the *there is*, revising the nocturnal insomnia of Levinas into a radical blindness in an empty world. Indeed, the old man turns towards the moon "by chance," the poem suggests, because in such circumstances a blind man cannot know where to look for the very thing he cannot see. In this scene blindness is not only an inability to see; it is an incapacity to know where to look. But this latter incapacity befits his condition precisely, for the angle of his gaze is irrelevant as he seeks a transcendence that lies beyond every mode of appearance, every line of sight. There can be no proper direction for such a gaze, and accordingly, he does not gaze *at* the orb but "gazes" it, in a kind of directionless yearning, as if to absorb what can never have a location of any kind.

If all this is so, then what counts is his watching with a "steady look sublime." Precisely because his faith addresses something whose sign can never appear, it takes place as a look that need not see, a subjective orientation and nothing more. In effect, the poem suggests that the old man cannot know whether there is a moon at all; he merely maintains a steady look for something that may not be there – for something that apparently does not seem to be seeking him.[27] But if no moon is there, no transcendence, is this figure still human at all? Does he still live in a universe with even a hint of promise? If a "statue hath such eyes," then one cannot be sure that this is a human being who looks; perhaps this vignette features a statue that merely "looks like human Time." Here the poem hints that a person caught within an evacuated world is not in any essential respect unlike a statue, much as, in the earlier lines, it suggests that such a scene occurs not in time and space but in their erasure. Perhaps with the absence of transcendence there is no such thing as "human Time," and indeed no such thing as humanity at all. The old man is already a statue, already dead. Yet in the final Coleridgean irony, even in that state of death, he endures in his nullity, seeking the possibility of a life that is foreclosed to him. This specific attribute, the passage suggests, makes his figure "lovely," for in his posthumous and posthuman state, he still manages to be "human" through the persistence of his useless gaze.

This stunning passage shows that within the context of this poem, at least, Coleridge's orientation to a pure transcendence denudes the world. Depicting faith as a suspension of one's ordinary task, as a search for what one cannot find beyond or outside phenomena, these lines make clear that it suffers the erasure of any sign of transcendence and that it arrives as a catastrophe, hollowing out lived experience. Faith brings with it the evisceration of time and space, making even the search for transcendence into a useless yearning in a barren world.

This poem's concern with the nonbeing inscribed within being becomes even more visible in its final lines, though in this portion it reveals that it took shape in a notebook, in a particularly unsettled mode of discourse, for it gradually ceases to present a coherent scenario. Confusing various ontological states with a certain abandon, it compels the reader to read its various claims as figures for concerns it does not manage to present in so many terms. In those lines, it moves beyond the "Purgatory curse" of "dull Privation" that it associates with limbo to contemplate a darker alternative: "Hell knows a fate far worse / A fear – a future state; – 'tis positive Negation!" (25, 26, 27–8). As Morton Paley points out, in these lines Coleridge alludes to a notion in the third sermon of John Donne, an author central to the entire notebook entry in which the original version of this poem originally appeared, that hell is the privation of God.[28] By shifting from privation to negation, the state he explores in the poem that follows in that draft, "Ne Plus Ultra," Coleridge suggests in effect that hell is nothing other than a certain negation itself, or what in a later annotation to the anonymous book *Eternal Punishment Proved to Be Not Suffering, but Privation,* he calls the "positive State" of "Eternal Death." For Coleridge, because eternal life and eternal death must be contraries, as are love and hate, eternal death "must therefore be a positive State."[29] Yet by departing from Donne and accentuating the idea that hell is not merely privation but also a positive negation of God, he redefines his notion of evil and places limbo by contrast into what he depicts as the comparatively less horrifying zone of privation.

One wonders, however, what all these concerns have to do with the vignette regarding human time that we have just seen, for as the poem moves into these final lines, it states, "No such sweet sights doth Limbo den immure / Wall'd round, and made a spirit-jail secure / By the mere horror of blank Naught-at-all" (21–3). This disclaimer might well give one pause: where must one place the "sweet" sight of the old man? Evidently one must locate him neither in limbo nor in hell but on a defamiliarized version of earth. In stating that hell is "a future state," the poem implies that those in this so-called limbo still face the prospect of the afterlife, in which case they share an earthly condition. Yet because that version of earth is also characterized by privation, as we have seen, it is an instance of limbo and indeed of the hell conceived by Donne, a domain where one suffers the absence of any phenomenal sign of God.[30]

In these lines, one might find resources to argue that the poem speaks of what the faithless must suffer. But as we have seen, this privation arises from the ascription of transcendence to a position outside phenomena. Thus one must arrive instead at the apparently paradoxical sense that the poem depicts the experience of faith itself as a kind of torment, a condition of suffering from the absence of what one yearns to see. In the end, the poem suggests that privation is not merely a category for organizing one's interpretation of the afterlife but also bears directly on one's reading of the human situation – a state that, in its view, ultimately becomes nonhuman. The real limbo, the poem seems to suggest, is to be found in mere existence, caught as it is in a condition utterly evacuated by the absence of what it cannot have.

III

While the telling features of this poem inspire astute critics to remark that the state it describes provides the best metaphor for Coleridge's overall stance, it would not be difficult to make an even stronger case for a poem that follows not long thereafter, "Human Life: On the Denial of Immortality," for the latter draws upon the strategy of negative demonstration on which Coleridge relies in his late theology and thus foregrounds with unusual precision the overall framework that informs the late poetry and metaphysics alike.[31] At first sight, this poem sets out to explore a *reductio ad absurdum*, to conceive of the ludicrous implications of what its title marks as the denial of the immortality of the soul. As several scholars have suggested, the fact that the poem is written in the conditional mode signals that it takes up a contrary-to-fact scenario, a possibility excluded by the theology Coleridge articulates in many of his late writings. But insofar as the poem relies on the assumption that the absurdity of what it describes makes the alternative persuasive, it pursues a version of negative demonstration explored above.[32] Moreover, the absence of any positive sign of immortality in the phenomenal world leads directly to the shadowy existence it portrays. Once again, in a logic very like that we saw in "Limbo," the orientation to a state that exceeds time and space hollows them out.

The poem insists repeatedly on the futile nature of a mortal existence. Its opening lines initiate this approach with exemplary force:

> If dead, we cease to be; if total gloom
> Swallow up life's brief flash for aye, we fare
> As summer-gusts, of sudden birth and doom,
> Whose sound and motion not alone declare,
> But are their whole of being! (1–5)

A life without immortality, it claims, is a merely physical life, every trait of which can speak of nothing more than itself. Disappearing as readily as a summer gust, leaving no trace behind, it lacks being so utterly that it cannot even begin to have significance. Even further, the poem suggests a few lines below,

> If rootless thus, thus substanceless thy state,
> Go, weigh thy dreams, and be thy hopes, thy fears,
> The counter-weights! – Thy laughter and thy tears
> Mean but themselves, each fittest to create,
> And to repay the other! (15–19)

Like physical motions, emotions are without substance, each following from or leading to equally weightless others. To feel, it seems, is just as empty as to breathe. But it does no good to achieve consciousness of this state; as the poem suggests a few lines later, it would be futile to mourn this life, but just as useless *not* to mourn it:

> Why cowl thy face beneath the mourner's hood,
> Why waste thy sighs, and thy lamenting voices,
> Image of image, ghost of ghostly elf,
> That such a thing as thou feel'st warm or cold?
> Yet what and whence thy gain, if thou withhold
> These costless shadows of thy shadowy self?
> Be sad! be glad! be neither! seek, or shun!
> Thou hast no reason why! (22–9)

One who laments acts in vain, but so too does one who withholds from grief; to sigh, or not to sigh, are equally wasteful. Just as it would be vain for a mere image of an image to feel warm or cold, it would be absurd for such a one not to do so. This life is so utterly without substance that even responding to this state has no meaning; to become aware of one's nothingness is an instance of the same state. To live such a life, the poem implies, is already to suffer a kind of death, or to enter a state outside both life and death, to endure a useless, futile persistence.[33] Here Coleridge cultivates not a Wordsworthian emotion without content but suggests that emotion *as such* for any merely finite subject is *necessarily* without significance, as if to deduce from that subject's mortality the utterly useless status of affect.

On one level, the poem's argument is clear. Insofar as a merely mortal life is the image of image, it replicates the nullity of the nonhuman world. The absence of substance in human life reveals once again the absence of substance in nature. But such an argument assumes that because any natural event does not participate in eternity, and mortal intention is not immortal, it is necessarily evanescent and thus merely ghostly; only an immortal intention has any substance.[34] These claims make any act within time or space futile. Accordingly, the poem might better be subtitled "The Denial of Temporality"; it refuses to find significance in any phenomenon, natural or human, that is subject to time. Under the pressure of this stance, the entire physical world dissolves into a ghostly summer-gust, a mere puff of wind, leaving behind only what transcends time and space.[35] Here, as on occasion elsewhere in Coleridge, the valorization of eternity leads to the erasure of existence; in this poem, as in "Limbo," the absurdity of the phenomenal world is embedded in a metaphysics of faith. This is the world that follows not from a denial of immortality but from belief that it is life's only substance. What seems to refute a lack of faith thus becomes a consequence of faith itself.

As one might expect, the embedding of futility in transcendence has a number of further implications. One might revert here to the poem's invocation of Milton, its emblem of theological, political, and poetic immortality: "If even a soul like Milton's can know death; / O Man! thou vessel purposeless, unmeant[!]" (7–8). On one level, these lines invite us to repudiate the apparently ridiculous possibility that such a figure could "know death," could indeed cease to be. Yet until his correction to the poem's proofs, Coleridge wrote, "And *when* a soul like Milton's can know death" (emphasis added), gesturing towards the thought, which still lingers in the published version of the poem, that perhaps so great a soul as Milton's *could* know death after all, that even Milton might have been mortal. But the phrasing of this passage hints at a further possibility, that Milton could come to *know* death, could contend with the impossible task of grasping it – or that so great a poet, through his figure of Death, could create the template for later attempts, indeed for Coleridge's own effort in this poem.[36]

By suggesting, even in such a cryptic manner, that one might carry out such an act, the poem hints that attempting to achieve this knowledge is precisely the task it attempts to fulfil as it outlines humanity's lack of substance. One could protest that these lines speak of knowing death as a figure for actually experiencing it, of ceasing to be. But one who undergoes that experience cannot know it, for the event cancels the possibility of knowledge. This poem, however, seems to have embarked on the attempt to gain this knowledge in another way. It suggests that insofar as life itself is without substance, a summer-gust, one need only attend to the contours of this life to know death; actually undergoing the experience of death may be redundant, for the substanceless is already here, in the very act of drawing breath. In that case, this poem anticipates Blanchot's argument that death does not arrive as a future event but as "the abyss of present time, the reign of a time without present" – an arrival of what one can never know or master.[37] The tone of astonishment in the poem, its insistence that what it attempts to present does not make sense and can never make sense, foregrounds in another way the severe impasses on which Blanchot insists; in effect, it too sets out to stage an exemplary encounter with this impossibility, to know, as it were, that one can never come to know death.

In pursuing this task, however, the poem does not merely reiterate its insistence on life's futility. Although it often discerns human uselessness across a series of registers, relying on what one might call, borrowing at once from Levi Bryant and Jacques Derrida, a flat hauntology, in a key passage it interrupts that prospect as it depicts the moment in which nature produces humankind:[38]

> O Man! thou vessel purposeless, unmeant,
> Yet drove-hive strange of phantom purposes!
> Surplus of nature's dread activity,
> Which, as she gazed on some nigh-finished vase,
> Retreating slow, with meditative pause,
> She formed with restless hands unconsciously!
> Blank accident! nothing's anomaly! (8–14)

At first a reader might think that in these lines apostrophe, which may be taken as a trope that typically animates or gives life, instead *dis*animates "Man."[39] But insofar as the impulse that shapes humanity causes an artist meditatively to interrupt her task of shaping a "nigh-unfinished vase," it intrudes into the activity of positive creation to produce an unintended surplus. In that case, humanity gains a certain distinction as the product of an unconscious act. If nature can interrupt herself and create humankind with "restless hands unconsciously," then humankind is the result of a slip of the hand, something unmeant but potentially significant, much as the father's "unmeant" words in the Conclusion to Part II of *Christabel*, for example, still retain a certain import.[40] Here one can decipher a further instance of the poem's overall logic. On one level it suggests that a life this vain cannot be the product of a conscious intention, which would give it a reflected purpose and dignity; if a nature the poem regards as "nothing" meant to shape it, then humanity would at least gain the self-consistent and ontologically secure status of an object containing nothing, a finished nothingness. Repudiating this possibility, the poem insists that this vain existence must instead be the result of an unintended act that by its very nature cannot reach completion. Because significance can arise only in the context of eternity, making any temporal existence futile, one must also deny significance to the moment in which such a futile existence begins as well. Nothingness, it seems, is too positive an entity, too secure a starting point; the poem insists that not only the creator but also the moment of creation must be without substance.

Yet such a position has certain surprising implications. Because the poem regards humanity as "nothing's anomaly," it suggests that nullity, by disrupting itself, produces something other than bare absence. Just as the subject is self-subverting, capable of uttering words of unmeant bitterness, "nothing" bears within it a surplus that does not express the purposes of nothingness itself. In creating humanity, nothing veers from itself, exceeding itself, producing something abjected even from the kingdom of nothingness, the refuse of nonbeing. The blank eye of the Dejection Ode and the hollowness in the empirical world have now morphed into the even more difficult status of this "blank accident." Here the poem denies humanity even the stability that might be derived from a natural process, attributing its emergence not to any material operation but to an anomalous, unintended gesture.

How might one trace the contours of this anomaly? One might first note that this status is not an instance of what the final line of "Limbo" designates as "positive Negation." According to "Ne Plus Ultra," that state, "the one permitted opposite of God," is a "Substance that still casts the shadow Death!" and is the "Sole interdict of all-bedewing prayer" (4, 9, 16). As its designation of "positive" suggests, that state is an effective counterforce to God, possessing a genuinely oppositional substance. Since it can cast the shadow of death, one must assume that it, too, is immortal. In contrast, as the above passage makes clear, humanity has no share in such a countervailing substance, enduring instead in a condition that is not as positive as negation, nor even as cogent as a Hegelian negation of the negation that would sublate negation into a further positivity, but rather is evacuated through and through. A mortal humanity fails to sustain its opposition to the divine or indeed any substance whatsoever. In effect, then, "Human Life" maintains that interpreting human existence as an instance of that positive negation would give it too great a substance, would provide it with an undue metaphysical dignity. From its perspective, a poem like "Ne Plus Ultra," which seems to perform a nearly hysterical horror in the face of positive negation, in fact evades confronting a far more difficult condition, ultimately celebrating the positive state it seems to decry. "Human Life," by contrast, insists on a *negative* negation, a form of negativity that can never be reversed into a metaphysical principle, that can never transform even into a negative ontology. It thus attempts to exclude human mortality from *any* metaphysical refuge, from *any* conceptual rescue.

To sketch this stance, however, is no simple affair; it cannot take the form, for example, of merely relying on the apparent redundancy of a negative negation. On the contrary, this passage makes explicit that one must rely on fairly adventurous gestures to maintain this stance. One might at first assume that negative negation exemplifies a stunning instance of deprivation, insofar as it lacks not only God's phenomenal presence but also the capacity to oppose him. But the poem complicates such an inference, for in these lines humanity is a *surplus* in the order of things, an accidental excess – even if, in this state, it suffers a surplus of lack, lacking even the nothingness that lack may be said to possess. It thus disarranges the framework of positive, privative, and negative, making it impossible for one to assign it a clear place within any category of being. Neither possessing nor dispossessed, it slides out of a place within an ontological system into the nonplace of the unassimilable Real.

Accentuating these suggestions, the poem incorporates an anomalous excess into its very form. Already consisting of two sonnets – the first Petrarchan, the second Shakespearean – that both lack a traditional developmental structure as well as the resolution usually presented in a final couplet, the poem concludes with a surplus twenty-ninth line, which captures its sense of humanity's excessive condition in still another claim:[41]

> Be sad! be glad! be neither! seek, or shun!
> Thou hast no reason why! Thou canst have none;
> Thy being's being is contradiction. (27–9)

In the very act of attempting to respond to human existence, it seems, humanity contradicts the very thing to which it responds. One cannot have any reason to decipher that existence or consider the implications of its lack of substance or significance, for such a reason implies that there is, after all, substance or significance in that pursuit – and there can be no such thing. It follows that the very act of attempting to figure nonbeing contradicts itself; a poetics or metaphysics of that condition is vain. Even the act of composing this poem, then – or interpreting it – on this account contradicts its own purpose, for it reveals the structural impossibility that any such action can have purpose. It, too, pursues "phantom purposes," an activity that cannot reproduce itself or lead to anything outside of its labour. The absence of transcendence from mortal existence makes every discourse useless. Here poetry slides into a mode of the work that is intrinsically workless, and what is more, into a mode of thought that attempts to grasp its own disappearance.

Thus in certain passages, "Human Life" graduates from a stance of privation to one of severe erasure. Insofar as human life is a mere anomaly, exceeding any status within the categories of being, it cannot sustain any mode of affect, knowledge, or figuration; it is unrepresentable for emotion or for thought. Such an impasse applies with special force to any attempt to know death. Attaining such a knowledge is structurally impossible, for we can neither anticipate such a knowledge before death nor gain it in the moment of expiration itself. Thus what I earlier described as the cryptic project of this poem runs aground, leading only to an encounter with this contradiction. But this situation, captured well by a thinker such as Blanchot, stands in for what the poem depicts as a more general dilemma whereby the goal of any endeavour, the purpose of any emotion or concept, dissolves in much the same way as mortal life itself, creating a catastrophe for human existence as such. In this regard, the poem participates in what Blanchot renders as a writing of the disaster, articulating the devastation that befalls "human" life when it ceases to have the integrity even of the human or of finitude.

Yet Coleridge, inscribing that devastation, proceeds as well to explore how any response to it also becomes futile. Not only encountering a fissure within the phenomenal world, the subject also endures the Real as a blank feature within its own experience, an erasure intrinsic to the activity of apprehension or affectivity as such. As a result, at key moments in "Human Life," the modern subject ceases to be a subject at all, becoming what we might call a nonsubject, that is, a site in which virtually every feature of subjectivity is evacuated and undone. Here, as in "Limbo," the poet hints that the nonsubject may not be animate, may scarcely be said to exist at all. Thus Coleridge moves past a philosophy of finitude or of existence, past even theories of temporality or affect, into a mode where finitude itself fades away. In such moments, he gestures towards a condition he cannot name, one more anomalous than a gust of wind.

The import of these poems, then, speaks volumes about the overall contours of modernity. In these poems a bitter denunciation of a finitude without transcendence takes shape through an exploration that anticipates the atheological mode of deconstruction, setting forth with perhaps even greater rigour what follows when a transcendental ground for existence dissolves. But if a lamentation at God's absence and an exploration of what follows from it can resemble each other so closely – and in these poems directly coincide – then one cannot exclude the possibility that each of these stances is embedded in the other, that at least at certain moments a post-Kantian fidelity and a ruthless deconstruction are aspects of a single overall stance. Modern theology and atheology may belong together as heirs of a disordered transcendence, twin delineations of the shared condition of mere existence.

3 Blank Splendour: The Debris of History in Keats's *Hyperion* Poems

Readers who consider the narrative scenario of John Keats's *Hyperion* poems might be tempted to assume that the displacement of the Titans by the Olympians represents a historical sequence, a shift from the *ancient regime* to a new order. In one account, the Titan Hyperion is to be dethroned by Apollo, whose greater beauty indicates that he represents the superiority of a later mode. Yet as the truncated state of *Hyperion* demonstrates, the poem cannot accommodate the entry of Apollo into his divinity, for he suffers an event that severely interrupts the narrative, placing him in a condition towards which the poem gestures by abruptly coming to an end. *The Fall of Hyperion* takes this development further, featuring the metamorphosis of the narrator into a figure who can witness the past only from a temporal position sharply distinct from it. Rather than allegorizing a story of progress, these poems suggest that a certain event surpasses the framework within which history was once imagined to take place, pointing to a split between that framework and the context for an experience of another kind.

Instead of accounting for such an unqualified departure from the past, however, these poems display its effect without comment. In this regard, they are defined by an aporia characteristic of modernity – one so severe that, as Fredric Jameson argues, modernity is not a historical condition but a rhetorical move, a trope.[1] Because any discourse that locates itself within modernity necessarily conceives itself as a product of a break from the past, its interpretive procedures derive from the assumption that this break took place and thus cannot explain how it emerged. Modernity establishes its interpretation of history not on the basis of any cogent analysis but rather through this trope. By the same token, the shift from an apparently external narrative imitating a classical or Miltonic epic to an internal scene of memory relies on the notion of internalization, which as Joshua Wilner demonstrates consists of "a reading that would be possible only insofar as it was already guided by the rules it was seeking to enunciate."[2] Nevertheless, a text can foreground the impasses intrinsic to these notions by allowing them to emerge in a modernizing narrative's confrontation with its own incoherence. These poems dare to take this step, for they show how the displacement from Apollo to the narrator of *The Fall* makes it impossible for that poem to complete the story of Olympian triumph that the narrator might eventually witness. Once he slips out of a historical continuity and enters another condition, there is no way back for him, no return to the state that he once shared with the past. The very position of this narrator as witness to the past shatters the scenario of which that past is a part, dismantling the architecture from which the initial poem derived its authority.[3] In displaying these tropes with exemplary force, the *Hyperion* poems draw attention to the fact that the break out of the initial narrative remains so unassimilable in the scenario that follows that it becomes traumatic, even haunting. As a consequence, in these poems the modern formations that such a break is usually understood to authorize, such as humanism, the secular, the historical, and the literary, suffer from an unaccountable element they cannot absorb and from which they cannot recover.

While these poems expose the aporias embedded in the trope of modernity with unusual clarity, they go further still, for they depict what follows as a condition of nearly absolute loss. Where one expects them to depict the displacement from one set of gods to another, instead they conceive of how the Titans suffer a severe loss of sovereignty and become exposed to the ravages of historicity. In effect, they emphasize how with modernity divine power gives way to the imposition of anonymous processes, a theological transcendence to the material preconditions of existence. But it does not follow that the gods disappear; on the contrary, they endure under the sway of the limitless operations of temporality and materiality, in a historicity of unsettling, unpredictable change without end. Rather than providing a coherent tale regarding the sequence of sovereign agencies, then, the narrator of *The Fall of Hyperion* endures alongside the anonymous force of historicity to which even the gods are now subject. Abiding with the nonmortality of the gods, the night of a useless persistence, the *there is* of a depleted world, this speaker bears up under a weight that exceeds his capacities. Caught in this domain, he can only dwell with what he witnesses, absorbing its misery in a poetics that promises no cure. The "blank splendour" the narrator encounters in Moneta's eyes conveys no promise of refuge, no hint of resolution to the crises of modernity, but only the soft light of an intractable disaster.[4]

In what way should a reader grasp the displacement from the Titans to the Olympians in *Hyperion*? One possible resource that the poem provides is the speech of Oceanus at the council of the gods, a speech that captures a perspective that a European in 1818 might share. Where other Titans voice their refusal to accept defeat or lament their new condition, Oceanus advises them to accept their position within a much vaster history in which they are merely one generation amid an endless sequence, declaring, "Thou art not the beginning nor the end" (2.190). These lines make clear that the poem does not merely remain faithful to features of classical mythology; on the contrary, by invoking that mythology in the process of reworking the divine matter of *Paradise Lost*, where the contest between superhuman figures is resolved in favour of the lasting transcendence of the one true God, its depiction of the passing of sovereignty from one generation to another carries out in epic and theological contexts the temporalization of history that Reinhart Koselleck finds in European historical narrative around the late eighteenth century.[5] In effect, Oceanus's speech temporalizes the gods. Far from anchoring history at its origin and end, as does the biblical God, these figures are caught by the same forces that operate within it: they are agents within a contest for power, suffering an inherently political and permanently unstable condition. Thus while the poem apparently aspires towards recapturing the tone of Miltonic epic, the fact that unlike *Paradise Lost* it focuses exclusively on the predicament of the gods, as if to outdo the epic itself, ironically accentuates the prospect that their situation evokes what now appears within human affairs – a change that takes history outside of its previous, largely predictable boundaries into an open arena without destination and without guarantees.[6]

Within this context, other features of this speech look suspect. If indeed each generation must give way to the next, so that according to Oceanus "another race may drive / Our conquerors to mourn as we do now" (2.230–1), by what logic can one conclude that each generation must excel the last, that "on our heels a fresh perfection treads, / A power more strong in beauty, born of us / And fated to exceed us" (2.212–14)? Oceanus's claim to recognize the greater beauty of the new gods sustains his own framework for judgment and thus, despite his claims, incorporates the supersession of gods into his own viewpoint. Here the ideological features of this speech come to the fore: while Oceanus gestures towards temporalization, he also attempts to reassure the Titans that this more open history is nevertheless progressive and that as a result it is worth submitting to its imperious force. Furthermore, when he claims that "[w]e fall by course of Nature's law, not force / Of thunder, or of Jove" (2.181–2) and that the movement from one set of gods to another takes place according to "the eternal law / That first in beauty should be first in might" (2.228–9), he suggests that another sovereignty now appears in the law of history itself, naturalizing his confidence in progress and transforming the latter into its own transcendental principle.

In this regard, the speech of Oceanus begins to look suspiciously like an attempt to reinscribe history within safe and predictable bounds. Such an attempt has a strong resonance within the moment of the poem's composition. The defeat of the Titans by the Olympians gestures towards the defeat of Napoleon by the Allies, hinting at the shift from an imperial sovereignty towards a more liberal political order, a change that it evokes as well by linking the

Titans with Egypt (a cultural site strongly associated with Napoleon) and the Olympians with the greater beauty of Greece.[7] Through these associations, the poem hints at a narrative of progress that moves through the Napoleonic wars into the presumably more humane present. But this tale of liberalization shuts down the very history towards which it gestures. Terada shows that these poems evoke the impasse of the postwar settlement, which in such thinkers as Hegel sought to foreclose any sense of political possibility by describing the current arrangement as reality itself. In this vein, Oceanus's association of beauty and might assumes that "[p]ower is the manifestation of organic and progressive processes, so that its appearance is irresistible, even to the vanquished, as a kind of beauty," in which case "anyone who really looks at power will be persuaded of its legitimacy." But the assertion that a description of reality can double as an account of how to respond to it effectively detemporalizes time and dehistoricizes history.[8] The poem's treatment of this speech reveals its resistance to any depoliticizing gesture, implicitly aligning it with the demand for political transformation that emerged in the French Revolution. In these and other ways, then, the poem alludes to the remarkable transformations through which European culture passed in the previous few decades, engaging with the historical and political import of those changes, and in doing so signals its own investment in retaining literature's capacity to evoke the broad political implications of contemporary concerns.

But the poem does not remain entirely on this level. It extends this mode of engagement with history in a series of further steps to convey the import of recent changes in other registers. In a remarkable moment, it rebukes Oceanus, suggesting that while he urges calm, he does not take into account the traumatic charge of historical events. Oceanus's claim that the ability "to bear all naked truths / And to envisage circumstance, all calm, / That is the top of sovereignty" (2.203–5) promises that by accepting history *tout court* one can achieve the utmost serenity. But the poem's abrupt ending in the midst of Apollo's deification undercuts such a reassurance. The final lines show how Apollo's attempt to bear all circumstance, to incorporate what Marjorie Levinson describes as "an irreducible order of being," the "very *form* of irrecuperable otherness" that is history – "Names, deeds, gray legends, dire events, rebellions, / Majesties, sovran voices, agonies, / Creations and destroyings" (3.114–16) – forces him instead to undergo a metamorphosis that shatters the sequence on which Oceanus's sense of history relies.[9] Moreover, as Carol Bernstein argues, although Oceanus "prophesies the modernity that is to be incarnated in Apollo," the latter's entry into modernity "comes as no easy birth: rather it is represented as an agonized dying into life."[10] One cannot absorb the lessons of history in any sovereign fashion; on the contrary, a confrontation with it causes an anguish that pours forth in Apollo's shriek and in the asterisks that follow. Evidently Apollo experiences what Oceanus evades, the horror of a history whose outline can never be glimpsed and whose processes are unassimilable. Although this scene seems to provide Apollo a divine knowledge, it interrupts the arrival of any such thing, cancelling the deification he seeks and giving him a palpable sense of the unknowable. To bear all naked truths, it seems, is to suffer the unbearable intrusion of the Real.

The implications of this final scene go far; they ramify through the first two cantos as well. No matter which gods are in question, all of them are dispossessed by history, dethroned by a process that no longer recognizes the enduring power of any supervenient figure. Although it contrasts the Titans and Olympians throughout, the poem places both under the sign of trauma, suggesting that each in distinct ways encounters an alterity in history. Whereas the poem registers the imprint of trauma on Apollo by interrupting itself, it does so for the Titans by revealing how they suffer from an event that took place before the poem opens, once again placing it outside what its narrative can capture. Joel Faflak points out that the Titans are "unable to remember their defeat by the Olympians."[11] As in a classic psychoanalytic account, the Titans cannot recover the event that traumatizes them. But what they endure cannot be housed entirely within psychoanalytic terms. The coming of modernity has implications so severe that it traumatizes ostensible losers *and* winners, Titans and Olympians, shattering the narratives by which *any* figure in the poem once seemed to live; it inheres, as it were, not in the psyche per se but in the worldlessness of the world itself. Following a break that now defines it, modernity endures a violence against which it can have no defence. Yet if anything, the strange status of this violence only increases its traumatic effect, making its new status even more unassimilable. The gods find themselves in a world whose incoherence impresses itself on them through an even more devastating affect. In this regard, the poem strikingly exemplifies the pattern that Pfau traces in *Romantic Moods*, for it registers the impact of temporalization through its evocation of the affective imprint of what is now a "perilous historical situatedness."[12] Yet the poem does not attempt to shrink back from this affect. As Jonathan Mulrooney argues, instead it "embraces and indeed draws the reader into the experience of history's trauma," daring to abandon any thought of refuge in favour of entering unreservedly into the scene of this fall.[13]

These features of the poem register the sense of historicity that emerges in the decades shortly before its composition. But the poem goes further, for by placing this transformation within the realm of the gods, it imagines how the break takes place as well *for the gods*. Already deploying a wide range of themes, the poem raises the stakes even further when it reveals how a shift in the conception of history bears on theology and its associated domains. The decision to figure the impact of modernity on divine protagonists is especially daring, for it allows Keats to touch upon questions that even adventurous examinations of history or politics seldom address directly. Rather than simply depicting what takes place with what Nietzsche recognizes decades later as the death of God, Keats creates gods who endure that death in their own persons. It is not merely that in the wake of the modern break no protagonist may attain a comprehensive knowledge of history; in this poem that break can actively *dethrone* knowledge, eradicate sovereign privilege, and traumatize the gods themselves.

But the poem does not only exhibit how the break dispossesses the gods. Much as Nietzsche suggests that Western culture sustains its faith in God even after his death, Keats depicts how the gods survive their dispossession.[14] In exploring this possibility, he takes up a theme that modernity seldom addresses, suggesting that even after its cancellation, transcendence endures in its shattered form, constituting a perpetual embarrassment. In this poem, the mere survival of the gods in this altered scene is a significant problematic in its own right. Now that history is the supervenient force, mightier than the gods themselves, they do not simply disappear but live on in a particularly elusive condition. As Hartman suggests, this subjection of the gods to historicity transforms them into phantoms, rendering them all – Titans and Olympians – into shadows within a tale where power always passes on.[15] Lacan remarks that while God is dead, he does not know it; he survives, as it were, after his disappearance.[16] In this poem, however, the gods are fully aware of their newly disempowered status, even if they can do nothing to remedy it. Their endurance in this mode radicalizes Lacan's point; the gods live on, revealing that despite its claims, modernity cannot entirely move beyond what it regards as the pre-modern past, that the break which inaugurated it crosses out a prior transcendence without removing it from the world. In effect, the poem ponders the fate of transcendence after that event, those features whereby it survives in a new condition.

The poem explores a defining aspect of this new state when it considers how the gods react to their loss of control over the physical world. At one point, Hyperion "[f]ain would … have commanded, fain took throne / And bid the day begin," but "He might not: – no, though a primeval God: / The sacred seasons might not be disturb'd" (1.290–3).[17] Here the poem suggests that Hyperion cannot control the movements of the sun. Nature is now consistent with itself, no longer subject to divine intervention; it obeys imperatives intrinsic to itself rather than divine law. Hyperion is faced with the difference brought about by a scientific modernity, its shift from personal transcendence to natural law; the physical world now has its own intransigent order, immune from Hyperion's command, in which case the activity of the gods no longer has much import.[18] What role might the gods play in such a world? While Hyperion survives in a state of dreadful anxiety, stunned by his new condition, he hears the whispers of another divine revenant, a heavenly guide who can do nothing. Shortly after his failure to budge the sun, Hyperion bends "[h]is spirit to the sorrow of the time" (1.301), stretches himself out, and listens to Coelus, the god of the heavens, who reveals that he can witness all that transpires beneath him but cannot intervene: "I am but a voice," says Coelus; "My life is but the life of winds and tides, / No more than winds and tides can I avail" (1.340–2). In effect, he is incapable of doing anything more than keeping watch over the suffering of the world in a mode of pained attentiveness.[19] While listening to this whisper, Hyperion lifts his gaze to the stars; when it ceases, he keeps his eyelids wide: "And still they were the same bright, patient stars" (1.353).[20] The whisper of Coelus has already intimated what their indifferent light conveys. Taken as a whole, this passage suggests that the idea of natural law undercuts sovereignty twice over: it abandons those who would seek divine assistance, but it also prevents the gods from assisting those who were once under their care. Indeed, it is precisely where the gods are abandoned, incapable of exercising influence over physical bodies, that they are also fated to abandon others; suffering their own dispossession, they must dispossess all those subject to them, placing them under the sway of a process as anonymous and placeless as the winds and tides.

The fact that the gods have lost control over the processes of nature – and thus now suffer in their own right their abandonment by the stars – brings into play another key dimension. In attributing impotence to the stars, these lines propose that Hyperion has endured a disaster in the etymological sense, for that term is derived, via the French *désastré*, from the Italian *dis-astro*, which, as Marie-Hélène Huet points out, "designated the state of having been disowned by the stars that ensure a safe passage through life."[21] The stars have abandoned Hyperion. But while the consequences of that abandonment for Hyperion are still to come, inspiring his fits of acute anxiety, they have already arrived for Saturn, who in the poem's opening lines survives in a state far removed from any beneficent light, "[d]eep in the shady sadness of a vale / Far sunken from the healthy breath of morn, / Far from the fiery noon, and eve's one star" (1.1–3). Moreover, Saturn has been deprived not merely of a heavenly guide, for he has lost the ability to protect *himself*, having fallen from supremacy into abjection, and as a result has been reduced to such a bare state that time, space, speech, motion, and even personhood seem to have departed from him.[22] The loss of sovereignty bears on a host of further categories, concepts, and experiences, plunging one into a state of absolute dispossession. Moreover, by broaching this version of disaster in its opening lines, the poem signals that the entire poem takes place under its sign, that despite its title, which foregrounds the sole Titan who has not yet fallen, this is ultimately an epic focused on a severe, ontologically devastated condition.

In treating the arrival of modernity as an instance of disaster, the poem may surprise us. Yet in this respect it brings into play an alignment characteristic of the period. As I explored in *Disastrous Subjectivities*, a range of texts in the British Romantic era followed the lead of late eighteenth-century natural science, shifting from the authority of the gods to the material preconditions of human existence. In doing so, they articulated the emerging awareness that the geological processes that had produced the features of the earth's surface over the course of deep time did so in part through natural disasters, indicating that because the processes of creation are also destructive, the very forces that enable life can also decimate it.[23] While composing *The Prelude*, Wordsworth mobilized his sense that such knowledge cancelled the guarantees of the biblical rainbow covenant and thus brought into view the God who, not yet bound by the relation to humankind that it instituted, unleashed the Deluge. This disastrous transcendence, whose sway the poet encounters during his journey through the Gorge of Gondo in Book 6, triggers the traumatic sublime that fissures his epic poem and from which it cannot truly recover.[24]

In contrast, for Keats this awareness dispossesses the gods themselves; rather than devolving into instances of an alien, terrifying transcendence, they become emblems in their own right of those who have endured a catastrophe. Rather than appearing as spectacular instances of the undead, uncanny revenants of the divine, they live on in a sharply distinct condition. To unpack its suggestions in this regard, *Hyperion* goes far towards dismantling a series of fundamental properties that one might typically attribute to the gods. In one of its most adventurous suggestions, it depicts the Titans as statues or stones, seemingly inert presences in the landscape that persist without motion or speech – as instances of what one might call, in contrast to the undead, the nondead. Shahidha Bari suggests that the Saturn who endures as a bare figure in a depleted landscape seems to exemplify the state of Dasein, that is, not of Being but of being *there*, severely exposed, as if thrown into an alien universe. Yet the poem also hints that he has fallen into a condition so far removed from the ordinary operations of time or space that even the status of Dasein eludes him. As Bari herself notes, the "ground-zero state" at the beginning of the poem "acknowledges the earthly situation of a post-apocalyptic life," so that the "gods that inhabit it also present the stony steadiness of being where one endures *after* the ending."[25] Whereas Dasein, finding itself within a temporality marked by the prospect of death, can still cultivate being-towards-death, Saturn can do no such thing, for in a mode remarkably like that we have encountered in Blanchot, he has already endured his death, and accordingly he survives in the darkness and silence of Levinas's night. The disaster that has befallen him pushes him past even the situation of Dasein, reducing him almost to the condition of stone, into a condition without a world and without a subject, into mere existence. The poem hints that there are modes even more denuded than those Heidegger explores, outside anything that the conceptions of sovereignty or subjectivity can identify. *Hyperion* thus takes us far into new terrain, exploring the lineaments of an outright ontological disaster.

Given these considerations on the status of the Titans, when the poem approaches the question of Apollo's deification it cannot simply carry through on its narrative design. Insofar as Apollo must also confront the alterity of history and thus suffer from the impact of modernity, he must undergo a transformation beyond the terms afforded by prior notions of divinity. But in that case, the poem itself must evolve beyond its initial story to outline a new problematic, one whose contours may be defined most clearly by the reconceived version of the scene of metamorphosis. Initially, after the narrator of *The Fall of Hyperion* eats and drinks from a primordial meal, he finds himself beneath an "eternal domed monument" in a domain where "the moth could not corrupt," as if, having escaped the mortal world, he is now within eternity (FH 1.71, 75). But soon thereafter, this protagonist, like Apollo, must undergo a process that a key simile in the first poem compared to that of dying into life (3.127–30). This later, more definitive scene of transformation reverses the initial account, revealing much darker implications to the leap beyond mortality. After that event, the narrator must endure a condition that, while outside of human time, is by no means welcome to him: he must suffer the version of temporality that befalls Saturn and Thea as they wait motionlessly beneath four phases of the moon.[26] One who encounters this passage might well initially take for granted an enormous difference between the infinite time to which the gods belong and the finitude of mortality and thus assume that the speaker's task is unbearable. But in fact the poem says that he *bore* that weight, suggesting that the finite can endure the infinite: "Without stay or prop / But my own weak mortality, *I bore* / The load of this eternal quietude" (1.388–90, emphasis added). The poem's suggestion is quite surprising: somehow, frail mortality is strong enough to hold up under the weight of eternity, even without props to support it. Thus the metamorphosis takes the narrator into a condition outside of the traditional opposition between mortality and immortality, opening up an unsuspected, perhaps unprecedented, condition.

What are the contours of his new state? Here in *The Fall*, as in the Second Part of the 1798–9 *Prelude*, something in finitude has the capacity to endure a seemingly impossible burden without stay or prop, hinting that in such weakness is an unknown form of resilience. But the poem's suggestion that the speaker can sustain this eternal quietude without being eternal himself raises the prospect that he has entered a subtle temporality. In effect, he dies not into life but into a state just outside it, into a life other than life; in *The Fall*, as in Blanchot, "the step not beyond that is not accomplished in time [leads] outside of time, without this outside being intemporal."[27] The poem emphasizes the contours of this condition when the narrator finds that, having been spared an ordinary death, he is now like Moneta "deathwards progressing / To no death" (FH 1.260–1). Like the Titans, he has moved beyond the condition of Dasein, having exceeded any prospect of being-towards-death and taking on instead a being-towards-*no*-death. The poem thus anticipates Blanchot in yet another respect, for now the speaker lives on in a state of radical passivity in relation to a death that never arrives.[28] The erasure of the prospect of death, however, alters the very character of temporality, for as the narrator experiences the fallen state of Saturn and Thea, he bears the weight of a time that passes seemingly without passing, a "time without present."[29]

The poem provides another meditation on this elusive state when the speaker, hearing Saturn's complaint, remarks, "Methought I heard some old man of the *earth* / Bewailing *earthly* loss" (1.440–1, emphases added). In a redundancy unusual for Keats, the poem twice insists that Saturn is earthly. In that case, the poem suggests that immortality does not relieve Saturn of anxiety but rather exposes him to it without limit. As Bari remarks, for the Titans in their post-apocalyptic state, the world's "survival is obscene"; "the world, intolerably, persists."[30] In effect, the fallen gods, free of the anguish of death, face an even more dire state, for they live out a condition that exposes them infinitely to the condition of finitude. But this is precisely the condition of the speaker as well: he, too, endures an eternal process in his finitude, having leapt into a life without life, a time without time. This parallel between the gods and the narrator becomes nearly explicit in the interstices of the *Hyperion* poems: as Susan Wolfson points out, where in the first poem Hyperion "flared / From stately nave to nave, from vault to vault" (1.216–17), in the second the narrator's "eyes ran on / From stately nave to nave, from vault to vault" (2.53–4), so that "the movement of Hyperion" is repeated in the "action of the dreamer's eyes."[31] This repetition suggests that the god's action and the narrator's witnessing take shape indifferently within a movement that belongs to no agent, within an anonymous unfolding that both exemplify. Moreover, much as Hyperion's flaring from vault to vault allows him to move while finding himself still in much the same place, through an endless sequence of vaults that, like the columns in one of the early scenes of the *Fall*, lead only to mist (1.84), the narrator's spectatorship can eventuate in no act that will make a difference. Here useless mobility and empty spectatorship speak of an unproductive process that subtends them both.

How might one begin to conceive of this endless, anonymous process through which gods and poets alike are plunged into the rude wasting of old time? Here one might turn towards a feature of Lacanian theory, which suggests that the subject suffers from the endlessly persistent force of the death drive. Elucidating Lacan, Slavoj Žižek argues that his version of the death drive "does *not* lie in [the] longing to die, to find peace in death: the death drive, on the contrary, is *the very opposite of dying*, it is a name for the 'undead' eternal life itself."[32] Alluding to Søren Kierkegaard's notion of the "sickness unto death," Žižek contends that this state refers to the situation of a subject "who knows that death is not the end, that he has an immortal soul, but cannot face the exorbitant demands of this fact." Where desire "desperately strives to achieve *jouissance*, its ultimate object which forever eludes it," the drive "involves the opposite impossibility – not the impossibility of attaining *jouissance*, but the impossibility of getting *rid of it*."[33] Thus the death drive "designates the dimension of what horror fiction calls the 'undead,' a strange, immortal, indestructible life that persists beyond death," not in the "'spurious (bad) infinity' of endlessly striving to achieve the final Goal or Ideal that forever eludes our grasp, but an even *worse* infinity of *jouissance* which persists for ever, since we can never get rid of it."[34] Rather than relieving the subject of the pressure of mortality, this immortal, or rather nonmortal, drive imposes a worse fate on the finite subject, exposing it to an anguish it can never shed. Here the uncanny ceases to appear in the intrusive Real, in any apparition or visible figure that one might encounter, arising instead as the Real of a drive that infests the nonsubject itself.

This nonmortal drive is so constitutive a force in this poem that it seeps into the most pervasive elements of existence. In this regard, the poem anticipates further dimensions of recent theoretical reflection. As we have seen, Levinas suggests that in insomnia one encounters the mere *there is*, an utterly stripped-down mode of existence. Commenting on this passage in a discussion of Wordsworth's sonnets on sleep, Guyer extends it in an argument that applies almost perfectly to this poem, especially to the scene in which the narrator lingers endlessly with the fallen gods; indeed, one might well describe that scene as an instance *par excellence* of prolonged insomnia. In such a mode, Guyer remarks, a "bare, inexhaustible presence" persists for both existence and existents. "Personal insomnia unleashes the forgotten insomnia of Being," she writes, for "insomnia coincides with, but remains distinct from, the impossibility of not being." Here being has no substance, no essence: it endures as mere persistence characterized by the impossibility of not being, by the failure to get rid of being – a state unleashed by the insomniac who witnesses what was previously forgotten. To endure this condition, Guyer writes, "is not the weakness of death, but rather that of remaining incessantly in the world"; it is "an obligation that one suffers," for it requires one "to linger interminably in the excruciating interval of living on." Thus perhaps the narrator's weakness comes to the fore not in his mortality, as the passage initially suggests, but rather in the failure of his prayer for death, in his inability to die (1.396–7); like the gods, he suffers from the nameless, anonymous imperative to live on, from what one can now recognize as the death drive inherent in existence itself. This wakefulness, Guyer proposes, "happens to no one," just as, in the words of Levinas, it "is impossible to recount"; thus the narrator, if one can call him that, endures without subjectivity, without words, surviving not to bear witness at some future date but to live alongside the useless interminability of the world.[35]

What the poem evokes in this crucial passage, it explores in still further dimensions elsewhere. Indeed, *The Fall* foregrounds such questions in its very first lines. Touching on the link between the dreams of fanatics, savages, and poets, the speaker – who is also, it seems, the author – rounds out his comment with this remark: "Whether the dream now purposed to rehearse / Be poet's or fanatic's will be known / When this warm scribe my hand is in the grave"

(1.16–18). These distinctive usages of "purposed" and "rehearse" make clear that these actions take place without a subject or object, as if in the middle voice; the passage does not attribute the text to an "I," hinting instead that it arises in some other way. Moreover, insofar as these lines surmise that the value of the poem will be established only by posterity, after the author is dead, it accepts what is inevitably the case, the role that readers necessarily play in assessing a text. But the passage hints at something more than this familiar point. In writing that not he but his "warm hand" will be in the grave, the speaker hints that his voice will endure beyond his death. Acknowledging that because a text by its very nature survives its author, and that in some sense the text is posthumous from the start, Keats goes one more step, speaking *as the dead author*, suggesting that a text can survive its author precisely because there is a site within the author from which the text can emerge – a nonmortal dimension in the Real that can speak even after the body is in the grave. As the usage of the middle voice suggests, the insistence of this address is neither under the control of the conscious subject nor an object that Keats manipulates, but has a logic of its own. Furthermore, the fact that Keats can reflect on the phantom-like aspect of authorship while alive shows that it operates not only after death but also in life; it is at play in him while his scribal hand is still warm. Yet his inability to attribute it to himself suggests as well that it is present alongside ordinary subjectivity without belonging to it, without reinforcing any presumed sovereignty.

In later passages, the poem extends these reflections to still further arenas. At one point the speaker "ache[s] to see" what "high tragedy / In the dark secret chambers of [Moneta's] skull / Was acting" (1.276, 277–9), implying that this "acting" transpires on its own, that the process of memory has a logic independent of the one who remembers or witnesses. Furthermore, in an even bolder move, early in the speaker's venture into Moneta's terrain, from "white fragrant curtains" he hears "[l]anguage pronounc'd" (1.106–7). This usage, once again as if in the middle voice, hints that the pronunciation of words is an operation that takes place on its own, that in effect Moneta is only the site of a speaking, where language takes place not as the articulation of significance but the enunciation of mere sound. Here the poem synthesizes hints kept in solution in *Hyperion*, where, as Anya Taylor points out, the Titans "have difficulty bringing their words up, as if even their own bodies have ceased to obey them"; their voices "are described as voices, not as the statements of certain beings, and they rumble up as emanating sounds."[36] We have already seen how Coelus is "but a voice" that whispers to Hyperion. Oceanus speaks in "murmurs, which his first-endeavoring tongue / Caught infant-like from the far-foamed sands" (2.171–2); Clymene's voice "flow'd on, like a timorous brook" (2.300); and the "ponderous syllables" of Enceladus come "booming" like "sullen waves / In the half-glutted hollows of reef-rocks" (2.306–8). This split between wave and speech extends the pattern whereby the Titans retain an uneasy status between (presumably natural) stones and (presumably artistic) statues, in the zone of a "natural sculp-ture" (1.85) or, positioned like stones in a Druid Circle, in the mode of natural objects arranged by human artifice (2.34–5). This split seems to remain else-where in *The Fall*, especially where Moneta explains that she "humanizes" the sound of the wind in language that the speaker can understand (2.2, 4), but in fact the speaker often witnesses unmediated processes as she keeps her silence (1.388) or participates at most through explanations in voiceover. Something of the winds or tides remains in what she conveys, some anonymous process she has not yet edited into the likes of speech. Thus in its reference to this pronouncing, the poem fuses the winds and language into a material process that belongs to neither. As Mladen Dolar argues in a Lacanian vein, "What lan-guage and the body have in common is the voice, but the voice is part neither of language nor of the body."[37] The middle "voice" of the passage thus gestures towards the uncanny position of voice between the physical and the linguistic, in a region closely associated with the drive. In this moment, the poem sug-gests that Moneta's speaking is a process taking place outside any reference to sovereignty, authorship, subjectivity, or significance, making hers into a mode of nondead utterance. By implication, it also hints that the mode of memory she instantiates transpires outside its assimilation into interiority, outside the synthesis of details into a coherent tale; what transpires in her haunts her as an inexpungable, alien determination, infesting her without regard to her inten-tions or even survival. Thus the poem exposes not only the trope of modernity but also that of internalization, suggesting that when a certain externality enters the subject, it places within it a feature that is not truly in its space, displacing that interiority itself.

While it may be tempting to use the idea of a posthumous poetry or nondead speaking for an ideology of the literary, the speaker's encounter with Moneta challenges such a thought. Although Moneta declares that those who do not mount the steps "thoughtless sleep away their days," implying that those who climb into her region – those "to whom the miseries of the world / Are misery, and will not let them rest" (1.151, 148–9) – are superior in their wakefulness, she goes on to say that the speaker is "less than" they who seek "no wonder but the human face," that he is a "dreaming thing, / A fever of [himself]," and that although on earth "[e]very creature hath its home," "Only the dreamer venoms all his days, / Bearing more woe than all his sins deserve" (1.163, 168–9, 171, 175–6). The speaker, hoping that "not all" poetry is "useless," that a poet "is a sage; / A humanist, physician to all men," still feels that he is not such a heal-ing figure; Moneta, confirming his suspicion, tells him that the "poet and the dreamer" are "sheer opposite," for one "pours out a balm upon the world, / The other vexes it" (1.187, 189–90, 199, 200, 201–2). It is not obvious how these comments are consistent, for it is not clear why a poet would pour out a balm on the world if he were unaware of its miseries. Yet Moneta is not pointing the speaker towards better alternatives.[38] In their severity, her remarks help delineate the import of a posthumous poetics. Rather than allowing the narrator to claim a privileged position like that of a sage, humanist, or physician, his ascent takes him, as we have seen, into a time without time. But in that case, it also places him in a position from which he absorbs the sheer misery of the world without directly participating in it. Moneta's remarks indicate that the speaker's relation to human misery is like that to Saturn's sorrow: the dreamer endures what he witnesses without being able to intervene, suffering alongside those in time without belonging to them. He is outside of emotion, as it were, without being beyond it. Moreover, her intervention is less about her wish to share her thoughts on these questions than a translation of the nonmortal status she and he now share into explicit formulations – to allow the poem to foreground themes already embedded in its terms.

This passage further implies that in entering this domain the poet takes up a mode of discourse outside of present purposes, a writing that is outside writing while nevertheless remaining within it. Thus as Rajan argues, the poem enters the mode that Blanchot calls *désoeuvrement*, or worklessness, so that it exemplifies the "absence of the work."[39] In passages that follow, the poem encourages us to take this insight even further, to note that, as Terada points out, nothing demands of the narrator that he "produce anything in return" for witnessing the scenes transpiring within Moneta's mind; he can quite literally dispense with the activity of producing a work.[40] In effect, the poet is faced with a scene that rehearses and acts on its own, quite apart from any subject who might produce it or any audience who might receive it. Yet it does not follow that the speaker's witnessing is without import. Indeed, this aspect of the poem may well anticipate the argument of Giorgio Agamben, who suggests in a rather different context that if the survivor "speaks only on the basis of the impossibility of speaking, then his testimony cannot be denied"; his writing becomes legitimate *because* he remains silent, because a work would betray the disaster he encounters.[41] If one can apply that insight here, the speaker in this poem discovers that his task is to register the unfolding of a catastrophe in silence, to make his receptivity to that infinite event into his own workless work. Much as the gods have been dispossessed of their sovereignty, surviving under the force of a process that persists without reference to their wishes, so also poetry here endures as its own infinitely prolonged suffering of an alien process that exceeds and evacuates it. In *The Fall* one can hear the voice of a poetry that now operates in the Real, that speaks precisely where it keeps silent.

These various echoes of a time without present suggest that the poem extends its innovations with great precision across a range of registers, mobilizing the thought of Levinas, Blanchot, and Lacan *avant la lettre* perhaps even further than they do themselves. But its explorations in this regard are not accidental or naive; in fact, they are so acute that they should modify our sense of literature's position in several respects. For one thing, to take up a suggestion I made above, these prospects indicate that the concept of literature's worklessness, which at first blush seems to be opposed to historical and political engagement, actually extends the latter into a further domain, revealing literature's position not only in relation to history but to the historicity within which it takes place. In that case, the poem outlines the broader developments within which the thought of these later thinkers can arise, for in its account, literature's weakness is the feature that best enables it to register the trauma endemic to modernity, the useless negativity inscribed into the temporality of the modern world.[42]

The Fall extends its meditations in this regard in its depiction of Moneta, whose apparent criticism of the narrator for preferring to suffer the miseries of the world without limit is ironic, given the fact that she provides precisely this kind of experience to him.[43] Indeed, what she affords him slides outside of narrative per se into sheer affect. As he first takes in the situation of Saturn and Thea, he witnesses a scene that in its lack of activity or even motion scarcely belongs to what could be told in a tale; if anything, it accentuates precisely what narrative cannot encompass. Insofar as narrative relies on a series of events that lead to further events, and thus on productive action, it jettisons attention to nonevents, to scenes of waiting or inaction, and what is more, casts aside a focus on the defeated, on those whose impact on history has come to an end. In this way, the poem highlights what a progressive notion of history excludes, making visible the violence that underlies any sequential account. Various readers have suggested that the poem's treatment of the fallen Titans reveals a sympathy with the victims of historical change, even those whose suffering is caused by positive change or by a Hegelian sense of dialectical transformation.[44] Indeed, as Rajan points out, the Egyptian provenance of the Titanic statuary in both poems draws attention to a phase of Western history that in Hegel's view the historical dialectic has left behind.[45] Moneta thus makes available the counterside of narrative, what epic negates as it constitutes itself, drawing attention to the affect of what is eclipsed and forgotten. Moreover, she does so without implying that it is possible to salvage what history has discarded; as Rajan also reminds us, Moneta does not participate in any effort to cure the misery within the scenes she remembers but rather enables the speaker to affirm his "sickness not ignoble" (1.184).[46] The overall effect of this staging, then, is to confront a negativity in history for which there is no cure; despite her comments, Moneta models the possibility of suffering historical memory as an interminable sickness, of dwelling forever with the misery of the world.

This depiction of a counterside to narrative expands on the insights already present in *Hyperion*. As I mentioned above, the initial poem's emphasis on the trauma of the Titans already shifts from the narratable contents of history to its affective imprint. In *The Fall*, this perception expands to suggest that the most intimate encounter with history transpires not when one contains it within a story of events but rather when one shares in an affect that in many respects must elude discourse. Moneta is not the muse of classical epic; she is a figure who transmits what cannot be told – what cuts through any discursive genre to imprint itself traumatically on a belated witness. On this level, the poem suggests that the emphasis on a narratable history hides from view a horror intrinsic to historicity. But since this understanding of historicity is itself modern, the poem goes still further, for it makes visible a trauma embedded in the sense of modernity, suggesting that the disaster it evokes is modernity itself, that nonempirical yet sweeping event. In doing so it proposes that mere existence emerges with modernity, in that way framing the thought of Levinas and Blanchot within a modernity they do not theorize. In this respect, the poem surpasses early deconstruction, hinting that it already arrives at the historiography I outline in this book; it may thus provide the most definitive account within Romanticism of the overall trajectory in which the question of mere existence appears.

As it does so, however, the poem betrays no attempt to overcome modernity, to participate in a rebuke of it akin to what Pfau attempts in *Minding the Modern*, for as we have seen, it suggests that what modernity brings is irreversible, that no recovery from its arrival is possible. On the contrary, it embraces the task of confronting that disaster, of attending to that misery, without respite and without any hope of redemption. It does so in part by emphasizing that neither Moneta nor the speaker can exit this scene of memory; as Wolfson remarks, the narrator "discovers that he has delivered himself to the nightmare of history from which Moneta cannot awaken."[47] Although elsewhere Keats emphasizes the capacity to remain receptive to what Emily Rohrbach, following his suggestions, describes as the mist of modernity, a dark futurity that inhabits the present as what it anticipates but cannot know, here he accentuates instead the shattering effects of that modernity, its capacity to dislocate the present without providing it any temporal refuge.[48] This sense that the encounter with modernity is irreversible, that it subjects these witnesses to a horror without end, reveals even more about this poem's stance: whereas modernity conceives of itself as the result of a break that brings about a leap beyond a benighted past, and the critique of modernity imagines that one can resist or reverse this break, this poem suggests that the break unleashes a devastation – and that this event admits of no recovery.

But the poem stages modern historicity in still further terms. Just as the past scene remains perpetually available to memory, the physical remains of that past insist within and alongside the present. When the poem suggests that Saturn and Thea endure like imposing statues, waiting with seemingly endless patience under the moon, or that the assembled Titans loom together as if in a Druid stone circle (FH 1.388, H 2.34–8), it proposes that the past lives on not in the usual version of the undead, as spectres, but in another, as nondead objects of former days – objects that, even more than spectres, exemplify the inability to disappear. In doing so, it suggests that what historical narrative forgets often persists in a dimension other than memory, in the shape of objects, relics, or debris; accordingly, as Rajan suggests, the poem shifts its ground from history to archaeology, bringing renewed attention to the waste of history, the abject remainders of time.[49] Moreover, by pairing a spectralized Saturn and Thea with their statues, "like sculpture builded up upon the grave / Of their own power" (FH 1.383–4), the poem links the phantom and the ruin, memory and debris, suggesting that the insistence of the subject and the object are portions of the same process, instances of what persists after an initial context has lapsed.[50] This link hints that both exemplify the nonmortal drive, the insistence of the ruined or forgotten across time, and thereby suggests as well that this drive infests historicity itself, so that the misery produced by its refusals and violations endures perpetually within the very form that is history, hollowing it out with the force of a useless negativity. On a still further level of suggestion, the poem proposes that the task of the poet and thinker is to learn how to dwell with the debris of that history, to become receptive to the empty affect embedded in those stones, to endure what has descended into silence and darkness, and thus to bear witness to what modernity has placed out of sight and out of mind. Indeed, as Bari argues, its depiction of how Thea attends to Saturn's state suggests that the task is to "listen[] to stones," to decipher the grief encoded in that diminished state; it hints that to care for the human heart one must abide with the sorrows encrypted in apparently nonhuman forms.[51]

Embedded in Moneta's harsh comments, then, is the tacit suggestion that she and the speaker are committed to the useless labour of this limitless receptivity. Such a mode may seem surprising for a poet whose entire spiritual development seems to have led him to a poetics of soul-making, in which one attends closely to the emotions of the heart to gain a more capacious understanding of humanity.[52] But this poem does not so much depart from this project as take it further into a much more difficult endeavour.[53] To pursue the Keatsian mode, it seems, ultimately requires one to suffer the miseries of the world without respite, to accept one's fevered condition, and thus to assume the not ignoble sickness of dwelling with the world's great sorrow without rest. One could argue, with Mulrooney, that "we are most human in those moments when a coherent concept of 'subjectivity' falters"; to accept this task is to pursue soul-making by attending to a humanity always in the midst of falling, always dying.[54] But in having Moneta repudiate the speaker's reference to humanism, the poem hints that the task of soul-making necessarily takes one into a further practice, a mode of attentiveness that one finds in such thinkers as Lacan or Blanchot, that is, in those whose encounter with the "human heart" exceeds what any humanism can encompass: a receptivity to the debris of history and the useless persistence of the drive. It is thus fitting that an exemplary instantiation of this project is Moneta, who without being human does nothing but participate in this useless labour.

Thus it is all the more telling how *The Fall* depicts Moneta in the moment when the speaker gazes into her face. Her "immortal sickness" has aged her past "the lily and the snow," making her visage so harrowing, so corpselike, that for him it has become almost unthinkable: "But for her eyes I should have fled away" (1.262, 264). The "benignant light" of those eyes holds him back, despite their being "visionless entire" of "all external things," for "in blank splendour" they "beam'd like the mild moon / Who comforts those she sees not, who knows not / What eyes are upward cast" (1.65, 267–8, 269–71). The contrast between her ruined face and her mildly beaming eyes may indicate that her capacity to dwell endlessly with the misery of the world has made her, like Thea in *Hyperion*, "more beautiful than Beauty's self" (H 1.36).[55] Like Thea, "[t]hough an immortal," she too can feel "cruel pain" in her heart (H 1.44), an ability that can so deepen and expand her heart – or soul – that her eyes become most beautiful. One is almost tempted to suggest that at this moment the poem fulfils Oceanus's injunction that the new gods will be more beautiful than the old: perhaps Moneta – and by extension the narrator – will now take over for the old deities. As Brittany Pladek suggests, perhaps her immortal sickness can "infect generations of readers with the 'sickness not ignoble' necessary for developing souls."[56] But the soft light of her eyes has further, less appealing attributes. For one thing, it indicates that they cannot see anything external; they thwart any wish to enter a relationship with her or to identify with her, and what is more, make it impossible for her to know anyone, just as her incapacity to intervene into the history she remembers disables any opportunity to provide a cure.[57] Moreover, that light echoes the "silver seasons" of the moon shed upon the scene where Saturn and Thea await, hinting that those eyes, like the moon, merely shine on suffering without alleviating it.[58] Like the light of the moon, they give an impersonal comfort, addressing no one with their mild glow, healing nothing in their benign indifference. Where in "Limbo" Coleridge still maintained a distinction between the old man's blindness and the light of the moon, each incapable of gazing on the other, here Keats images a moonlight that is itself blind, eyes that, in their mild glow, cannot comfort or see. Thus the spiritual possibility that Moneta exemplifies – the power to dwell with the tribulations of finitude endlessly – is here revealed to beam forth with a *blank* splendour, giving off a light as free of consequence as that of the moon. What endlessly remembers keeps alive a vanished pain; what beams without response merely casts light on a world now well past redemption.

That the splendour of those eyes is blank speaks not only of Moneta's position beyond all response, for it also indicates that the scene she remembers is empty, devoid of fundamental logic or consequence. As Terada points out, the world at which she gazes is one without value or meaning, just as in Rajan's account the poem's worklessness "disclos[es] a negativity that is in history as much as in poetry."[59] Cut off from any origin or end, that scene transpires endlessly, indifferently. Thus this image confirms what we saw in the address of Coelus, for that light refers to two levels at once, bringing them together within a single, shared problematic: if witnessing disaster in silence allows that catastrophe to transpire without limit, it does so because it shares in the condition of the world it witnesses, having been dispossessed of its power to cure. The disaster takes place both for the world and for the witness; a certain worklessness operates in the course of things and in poetry alike. Those blank eyes bring together the uselessness of what they see with the worklessness of their seeing, revealing in a single image a process that underlies history and subjectivity alike.

The poem accentuates the nature of this process in several further details. The narrator approaches Moneta just after her ritual sacrifice is complete, just after her fire has reduced the scented wood to ash. While the smoke from that wood is fragrant – while the aroma welcomes him with its own kind of beauty – the scene overall hints that something of that fire burns within her as well, in whose eyes glow the conflagration that consumes history. Here the uselessness of history and the impotence of its witnesses come together in a new suggestion – that history itself is a perpetual consummation or endless *jouissance* that, despite one's best wishes and most intense prayers, one cannot get rid of. The flaming of this useless enjoyment leaves behind what Derrida calls the cinder, which can "recall at the delicate, charred bottom of itself only nonbeing or nonpresence," only the traceless trace of that ash.[60] In the mild glow of Moneta's eyes, a workless process shines forth with an intensity that in the end reveals nothing but itself, that refers only to its own burning passage, its flaring onward, like Hyperion, to no end (cf. FH 2.61). In the memorable words of Forest Pyle, this poem "leav[es] us with nothing but the ashes of its burning," so that in it we encounter "the gift of an all-consuming poetry that bestows us nothing at all."[61]

With these suggestions, Keats takes his spiritual project outside any hopeful scenario, even one that cherishes the act of tarrying with the heart's sorrows past any expectation of a cure. Wolfson, pointing to how Keats was aware of Hazlitt's comment that Dante "is the severest of all writers," suggests that in writing *The Fall of Hyperion* the poet sets out to adopt a "severe program" of his own.[62] Her argument is borne out in this passage, where Keats does indeed achieve a singular severity. Where the benign light of Moneta's eyes seems to hint that this tarrying can become its own reward, that looking deep into the heart can humanize and beautify, in the end even this beauty becomes a blank splendour. The comfort in those eyes can give no consolation.[63] As we have seen, at certain moments this poem suggests that the poet's primary labour is to assume the negativity at the heart of the modern West, to attend to its constitutive trauma without reserve, in this way attempting to take the measure of the cultural terrain within which it finds itself, a world haunted by all that has been destroyed. In such moments, the poem hints at something like Lacanian subjective destitution, whereby the subject assumes its nullity in a radical act of dispossession. But the poem ultimately surpasses even that act, for it proposes that tarrying with the vast scene of disaster only reveals a disaster that has befallen the witness as well. Thus the poem ultimately suggests that this labour attends to an interminable burning that, ravishing the subject and the world alike, leaves behind only the splendour of its passing, the blank illumination cast by its endless disappearance.

4 Blank Oblivion: Wasted Life in Clare's "Obscurity"

Few poets could promise more than John Clare to those interested in how Romanticism could address itself to the nonhuman. Over the course of his career, Clare composed hundreds of poems on nonhuman modes of being, ranging across the lives of birds and mammals, the vibrancy of grass and trees, and the tangled flourishings of fields, lanes, and meadows. Moreover, he forcefully registered the broader political and philosophical stakes of such a poetics; as Katey Castellano argues, he celebrated the "inhuman will to variation" in the natural world "that ranges from caprice to monstrosity," leading him to advocate for a "politicized 'neglect' that opposes the appropriation of nonhuman life."[1] Such a project committed him to exposing biopolitical attempts to subjugate human and nonhuman lives and to advocate instead for a broadly conceived politics of the commons.[2] As a result, his work can serve as a locus through which to mediate several leading concerns of those who seek to address the import of the human relation to the nonhuman, to decipher the political implications of this relation, and to think through these concerns with regard to the era that some call the Anthropocene.

Within the context of this corpus of writing, certain works explore still another challenge to a broadly humanist perspective. In several poems written in the 1820s or early 1830s, often intended for *The Midsummer Cushion*, a volume not published in his lifetime, Clare explores the possibility that time's supremely indifferent power may render humanity insignificant. On occasion he approaches this question by emphasizing how that power blasts youthful hope, and especially the young poet's ambition, in reflections that no doubt have a strong biographical resonance. In the sonnet "Nothingness of Life," for example, he writes that he never passes by a "venerable tree / Pining away to nothin[g]ness & dust" or sees "Ruins vain shades of power" but that "reflection wakes her saddest thought / & views lifes vanity in cheerless light / & sees earths bubbles youth so eager sought / Burst into emptiness of lost delight" (1–2, 3, 5–8). In another sonnet, "Ambition," Clare ponders how ambition's "ever craving wish" "Sooth[es] the rude extremities of fate" until "every hope" subsides, so that much as "grandeur" with its "fading pride doth dwell / Oer ancient walls till every stone hath fell / It falls & leaves – the song of every wind / A broken shadow of its hopes behind" (6, 9, 11–14). While both poems reflect on "lifes vanity," they place it against the background of time's power to reduce imposing structures to ruins, suggesting that any personal fate is only one event within a much vaster process, that the bursting of hope's bubble is an inevitable feature of being subject to time. Perhaps the most extensive meditation on these themes is "Triumphs of Time," a poem of over two hundred lines, which ponders how time conquers all forms of human power, so that palaces, temples, and monuments, "all all / Are swept away" to be covered in weeds (195–6).[3] Yet even these meditations contain hints at still further concerns; as we have seen, already in the first poem mentioned above Clare begins to consider how a "venerable tree" faces the prospect of disappearing into "nothin[g]ness and dust." While the poem's reference to the tree's "[p]ining" attributes a human affect to it, this passage nevertheless hints at a willingness to contemplate the subjection of nonhuman things to the operations of time. This willingness indicates that for Clare it may not be enough to fold his individual loss into the pattern whereby time defeats human ambition, for it may be necessary as well to consider how time wastes every form of life even beyond the purview of human concerns.

While Clare does not consider this suggestion directly in these poems, in three further brief poems he does so, pursuing themes that as a result are striking in their import: one complete sonnet, "Obscurity," written in the early 1830s, shortly before his move to Northborough and intended, like the two sonnets mentioned above, for the ill-fated collection, *The Midsummer Cushion*; and two nine-line poems, written in 1845, early in his stay at the Northampton Asylum, that in their shared meter and nearly identical rhyme scheme constitute a pair.[4] Scattered lines in other poems touch on these concerns, but only these three poems offer direct and concentrated treatments of the core themes; they are thus exceptional within his work, taking some of his characteristic concerns into new regions.[5] In these poems, Clare evokes a dimension further out from the human, indeed outside a reference to human existence as a whole. The formulations in these poems are conceived so radically that they raise questions beyond the purview of the approaches to Clare that critics have often used in recent years and to which I referred above. In considering how time effaces even nonhuman modes of life, erasing the significance even of aspects of the object-world, they reveal how certain moments in Romantic works anticipate that aspect of an early deconstruction that articulates a second-order negativity, an erasure even of erasure. In doing so, they hint at the argument I outlined in the introduction, at once invoking an aspect of speculative realist thought while subjecting even the object-world it invokes to further negation, as if moving through Brassier to arrive at Blanchot, thinking past the death of the sun to take up the import of an erasure that has already taken place, in this way embarking on the writing of the disaster.

Bringing these reflections to bear on this small cluster of poems enables a reader today to find within Clare's poetics a lucid, provocative rendition of subtle annihilation. The range of such resonance is broad. Insofar as this poetic cluster locates its writing of oblivion in relation to its sense of life, memory, time, and presence, as well as shelter and hospitality, inscription and its erasure, knowledge and ignorance, and sovereignty and the sublime, it allows us to conceive of a certain disaster within a surprisingly capacious range of contexts, enabling us to trace how that event unsettles a series of conceptual orientations. However brief this intervention may be, however tentative its suggestions, it opens the way towards conceiving how Clare embeds a wide range of concerns within a broader problematic that exceeds them, that of mere existence, enacting a poetics of such severe negativity that deciphering its features will require us to consider anew, and in greater depth than elsewhere, the import of several aspects of that early deconstruction with which we have been working throughout this book.

"Obscurity," the central text in this cluster, like hundreds of Clare's other poems, focuses on a certain form of nonhuman life; here again one may note the poet's well-known preoccupation with the obscure, the marginal, the forgotten, the neglected – with all those aspects of the lifeworld that ordinary attentiveness might overlook. But within that range of concern, the sonnet pushes well beyond Clare's familiar practice, for it puts something else at stake, the possibility that nonhuman life might be condemned to oblivion. Indeed, it treats this question with such rigour that it joins such poems as *The Fall of Hyperion* and *The Triumph of Life* in exploring an uncompromising negativity. Given the uniqueness of this exploration, the sonnet demands a sustained effort of close reading and resourceful speculation across related texts and theoretical traditions – an effort to which I will devote the remainder of this chapter.

Here is the sonnet itself:

Old tree oblivion doth thy life condemn
Blank & recordless as that summer wind
That fanned the first few leaves on thy young stem
When thou wert one years shoot – & who can find
Their homes of rest or paths of wandering now
So seems thy history to a thinking mind
As now I gaze upon thy sheltering bough
Thou grew unnoticed up to flourish now
& leave thy past as nothing all behind
Where many years & doubtless centurys lie
That ewe beneath thy shadow – nay that flie

> Just settled on a leaf – can know with time
> Almost as much of thy blank past as I
> Thus blank oblivion reigns as earths sublime[6]

Here again Clare attends to the fate of an old tree, considering its fate under the impress of time, delving more deeply into the theme that arises in the sonnet mentioned earlier. On a first impression, this poem's reference to the tree's condemned life may imply a strong contrast between Clare's failure to notice this tree and his more typical practice of attending to the lifeforms surrounding him in the landscapes he knew intimately over the first several decades of his life. On this score, the poem might seem to point back to the establishing framework of human witnessing. Yet the poem is not merely attempting to acknowledge the prior absence of such attention; it attempts to apprehend what transpires without reference to him. It sets out to register not his own affect but what happens, has happened, and will happen apart from him – except for his encounter with this happening.

By recording Clare's response to a process that transpires without reference to him, the sonnet enters that apparently paradoxical terrain familiar in our moment. Here too, as in speculative realism, one asks how one can begin to apprehend things or events that take place without our apprehension. As the sonnet suggests, the "history" it outlines is as it "seems" to a "thinking mind" (7). By drawing attention to this seeming, the poem joins a questioning that is taking place today as well. We can thus register the force of this sonnet's intervention best if we sense in that implicit reference to human consciousness in its opening lines not a privileging of that consciousness but a deliberate turn away from it, a turn that foregrounds and privileges a sharply different mode of relation. That turn also takes Clare beyond the poetics of living things, which always bear an implicit reference to human existence, and into a new problematic, for it shifts focus from the attributes of the tree's life to its oblivion, from its place within the interrelation of living things to its thoroughly evacuated condition. Here Clare dwells on how a form of life, buffeted by a force as blank as itself, does not register, comes to seem as nothing; without witnesses, its life is "condemn[ed]" to nullity.

As it formulates this initial sense of the tree's blank state, the poem relies on a complex figural construction. On one level, it states that the tree's life is blank and recordless *as* the wind, thereby linking the tree's life and the wind through a simile and suggesting that the empty and invisible movement of an oblivious wind serves as an apt comparison to an oblivion already characteristic of the tree's life. Yet in this figural register, the poem also hints at a causal relation, suggesting that because of the wind's disappearance, none could possibly recover the impress of the life of that tree. As a result, the poem suggests that the blank status of the tree's life is simultaneously figurally prior to the wind and brought about by the latter. The sonnet resolves this apparent paradox, however, by suggesting that the significance of a life depends on its place within the field of recording, reception, or inscription; in a logic familiar from intersubjective relations, the intrinsic here is knowable only through the extrinsic, through being acknowledged by other objects, lives, processes. The blank movement of the latter, then, speaks of – and brings about – the blank oblivion of the former.[7] Here again, as in certain moments in Blanchot, the blank condition arises from a loss or incapacity embedded in relationship, from the subtle devastations inherent in alterity.[8] The nonrelation between the tree and the wind, then, produces that oblivion, that erasure of its life.

Through this emphasis on the import of the wind's passage, the sonnet proleptically engages with, and surpasses, the stance of speculative realism. In foregrounding the figure of the wind, the sonnet evokes not phenomena from the pre-human past or posthuman future – Quentin Meillassoux's archefossil or Brassier's death of the sun – but a perpetual, nameless process that, extending across all temporal sites, incorporates them into an indifferent, devastating flow that bears upon the apparent present as well.[9] On first impression, the poem's rendition of the wind's movement over the tree's young shoots might seem to echo "Mont Blanc," a poem crucial to how we think about Romanticism's anticipations of speculative realism. When in that poem the "chainless winds still come and ever came / To drink" the odours of the "giant brood of pines" and "their mighty swinging / To hear – an old and solemn harmony," in effect the winds, listening to the sound that they cause, serve as a remarkably efficient metaphor for Shelley's theory of perception, according to which "[a]ll things exist as they are perceived: at least to the percipient."[10] But in Clare's sonnet, the wind registers nothing, evacuating any apparent import of what it moves. The sonnet thus evokes the opposite prospect, that of a nonreceptive, thoroughly indifferent movement over the world's lifeforms. By implying that the wind could register what it moves yet emphasizing that it does not, the sonnet starkly effaces the process Shelley's lines encapsulate, hinting that if perception is essential to existence, then where it has been rendered blank, the tree ceases to exist altogether.[11]

But both Shelley and the sonnet go further. Since the sonnet nowhere proposes that the narrator's encounter salvages the tree from its ruined state, it implies one further step: when one witnesses the life of a tree, one does not give that tree existence; on the contrary, one discerns the incapacity of perception to do so. The sonnet might thus seem to explore a stance unlike Shelley's. Yet insofar as Shelley writes that all things exist as they are perceived "at least to the percipient," he hints that things may exist outside the domain of perception, anticipating one of the cardinal themes of speculative realism. What Shelley only implies, however, the sonnet makes palpable; it transforms the wind into a "recordless," unperceiving force and thereby displaces the centrality of human perception, depicting an agency to which that mode of perception and its effects are subordinate. Human perception, it seems, cannot overcome the effects of a process that transpires without regard to human concerns.

Yet in the next lines the sonnet displaces these provisional inferences. This process of recordless passage gives way to another erasure, the utter disappearance of those winds. The process of effacement itself disappears, for "who can find / Their homes of rest or paths of wandering now"? The wind that figurally effaced the life of the tree has no proper place, no stable position that one might decipher to understand its work; what subjects the tree to oblivion has itself entered a similar state. The work of the erasure redoubles itself, cancels even cancellation. It thus exemplifies not an intrusive, marked instance of the Real but rather a version that, surpassing that mode, hollows out the phenomenal realm as such, obliterating the traces even of this obliteration, producing as a result a condition beyond the very possibility of inscription, significance, or memory, a mode of existence outside existence – the condition of mere existence. Under the force of this doubled erasure, the tree is condemned to oblivion, to wasted life.

If we are unsure as to whether Clare would wish to carry out such a philosophically radical step, we need only turn to the paired lyrics, mentioned above, that he composed over a decade later, for they amply confirm his capacities in this regard. In contrast to the sonnet, these lyrics vividly testify, through their affect and tone, to what Eugene Thacker describes as horror, the "non-philosophical attempt to think about the world-without-us philosophically."[12] The first poem, to which I will refer as "Old times forgetfull," makes more explicit a logic already present in the sonnet:

> Old times forgetfull memories of the past
> Are cold & drear as snow upon our graves
> In books less then a shadows doom will last
> But Fragments there each stranded volume saves
> Like some rich gems washed up from ocean waves
> But now no summer dwells upon the spot
> Nor flower to blossom – the eternal blast
> Oblivion leaves the earth in which they rot
> Darkness in which the very lights forgot[13]

Here the fragments thrown up from a disastrous inundation are effaced once again by an "eternal blast / Oblivion [that] leaves the earth" only a "[d]arkness in which the very lights forgot" (7–9). Such a double negation appears as well when snow and flowers, winter and summer, as well as the earthly life that revolves through the seasons, are all subjected to an eternal blast, as if absolute "[d]arkness" can condemn the life of the earth itself. Furthermore, the forgetting with which this poem begins is itself erased by a darkness that forgets the light, that forgets even what memory – or indeed forgetfulness – might be.[14]

A similar logic is at work in the second poem, which I will call "Where are the citys," which at once confirms and varies the logic of the first:

> Where are the citys Sodom & Gomorrah
> The marble pallaces upon the plain
> Citys to day & a dead sea tomorrow
> & what they was they ne'er will be again
> That earth is lost & all its city slain
> By the oerwhelming waves entombed & gone
> Search for its ruins now is void & vain
> & but one witness saw that ruin done –
> The ever burning bright eternal Sun

The devastating process wipes out not only the "citys" but the earth, carrying out in an initial blow the full sequence at play in "Old times forgetfull." This is not a story of mere slaying or death, nor of ruins or entombment, but of the erasure even of the ruins. This second negation, in turn, takes place before the witness of an "ever burning bright eternal Sun," an apparent counterpart to "the eternal blast / Oblivion," though taking the form of an eternally scorching brightness. This pair of poems thus cultivates a sharp indifference on the question of whether absolute darkness or absolute light is a better figure for this second erasure. As if responding to the figural patterns of Romanticism and beyond, which as we will see in chapter five tend to accentuate either an expired or a supremely bright sun, this pair suggests that either is a suitable figure for a scorching, blasting process that destroys all and erases any memory or residue of that devastation as well.

The sweeping annihilation of the second negation makes clear that pure process bears not only on the life of a tree but on all life and all objects, indeed on the matrix that can sustain any particularity, for it rots the earth and annihilates even the memory of light. These short poems thus foreground what is already present in the sonnet, the realization that oblivion condemns the life of human beings as well. But it would be a mistake to claim that these second-order negations bear primarily on human self-regard, for they cut against any such implication. Insofar as that first erasure is a blow to human narcissism, it retains a tacit nostalgia for human significance. The further negation, however, insists that the logic of pure process erases any memory of human centrality, any resentment regarding its loss. These poems thus do not merely decentre the human from its apparent pride of place; they speak instead of a voiding of the human, an erasure so absolute that it would be vain ever to seek it.

It is thus quite tempting to see in these poems anticipations of Derrida's suggestion that the trace is "constituted" not only by the "disappearance" of "selfhood," but by the "disappearance of its disappearance."[15] In this moment, Derrida proposes that the movement of the trace not only evacuates whatever it traverses but also eradicates any mark of that evacuation. But as we have seen, the sonnet goes even further. By describing the wind as "blank and recordless," it depicts even its initial passage as without inscription, and thus outside *écriture*, beyond the operation of *différance*. While one might immediately suspect that this stance provides refuge from the severe negations of deconstruction, calling upon a cryptic version of presence, in fact it evokes a process even more severe, one that operates without reference to writing or the trace – a movement of what one could call, with apologies to Derrida, *indifférance*. It takes place on a level even less attuned to the human than language, in a mode that never relies on the signifier, in a manner that never even promises the mirage of meaning. The sonnet thus carries out a negation even of Derridean erasure, as if to apply to that version of deconstruction the procedures characteristic of an earlier, less linguistic deconstruction; as it turns out, perhaps that earlier version, already evident in the sonnet, is even more adventurous than the Derridean form, expunging the positivity that lurks even in the trace as it evokes the traceless, the movement of what can never be inscribed.

One might begin to explore this arena by noting that the sonnet participates in the task of writing the disaster, conceived here not as anything one could witness in empirical reality or historical time but that, in its hyperbolic force, erases any trace of such an event. This erasure of history or the event might thus seem to take these poems far beyond political terms; after all, the leap beyond empirical experience into an absolute darkness threatens to become a suspect leap outside the political as well. But the references to Sodom and Gomorrah and certain "marble pallaces" in "Where are the citys" allude to themes Clare broaches in one of his more political lyrics, "The Flitting," written in 1832, shortly after the sonnet (and after his move to Northborough). This poem proposes that the familiar molehills, weeds, and blossoms of his former landscape are "[a]ll tennants of an ancient place," "Coeval … with adams race," as if they remain perpetually at the origins and keep alive the primordial freshness of the world.[16] This emphasis culminates in the final stanza, where the opposition between marble cities and enduring grasses captures Clare's disdain for all pomp and grandeur, all claims to human privilege:

Time looks on pomp with careless moods
Or killing apathys disdain
– So where old marble citys stood
Poor persecuted weeds remain
She feels a love for little things

That very few can feel beside
And still the grass eternal springs
Where castles stood and grandeur died (209–16)

According to this poem, time carelessly accepts the shattering, levelling effects of history, cultivating instead a unique affection for those "persecuted weeds" that history neglects and protecting them from its own ruinous effects. Here a certain endless temporal process protects and sustains the earth, exempting it from the historical process that lays waste to all human constructions. In this conception of nonhuman process, the apathy of time does not condemn life but makes it "coeval" with "adams race," affirming any form of life, human or nonhuman, that finds its place with "little things," with what is marginal to history.[17] Here the politics of the commons becomes one of what the human and nonhuman commons share, a politics of the persecuted. These final stanzas of "The Flitting" elucidate well what is at stake in recent thinking that contests human privilege and emphasizes instead a shared vibrant life or a democracy of objects.[18]

But "Where are the citys," invoking the stance of "The Flitting," at once sustains and exceeds it. It carries out a second-order negation, pushing beyond a politics of the marginal, erasing that erasure of a certain human privilege, and yet, through the very logic, remaining continuous with the first. The "eternal blast / Oblivion," it seems, erases the eternal grass; its pure process began before and will continue after any reference to "adams race." In that case, through this gesture the poem undermines the claim that "little things" are given a perpetual flourishing outside history, in this respect anticipating the ubiquitous recent critiques which expose the costs of an idealizing notion of Nature. Thus "Where are the citys" undercuts a poetics of the earth through which even an apparently humble humanity may anchor its claims to a more-than-historical origin. In consequence, a more capaciously conceived political stance becomes clear: this cluster of poems outlines a politics of severe fragility – a fragility not of Dasein (which experiences its thrownness within a distinctly human temporality) nor of "little things" (which despite their vulnerability are guaranteed endurance) but rather of entities whose lives have been condemned, erased, forgotten – and thus endure a condition of mere existence. It conceives of a politics well outside the reach of any biopolitical regime or indeed of any human sovereignty – one that arises in a nullity held in common, a shared oblivion.[19]

The tenderness for such fragile entities is not explicit in these short poems but is evident at once in the sonnet, which begins with an apostrophe to the tree that seems to express a certain nonanthropocentric solidarity with its condition: "Old tree oblivion doth thy life condemn."[20] It might seem odd for the sonnet to develop this tone of tenderness in a context so devastating, for the oblivion bestowed by pure process could be understood to erase any basis for concern.

Yet the sonnet makes clear that despite the process that has condemned the life of the tree, it continues to flourish; the nullity that has befallen it does not bring its thriving to an end. Somehow, its life continues in the void of that life's undoing; it belongs to an earth that is long forgotten yet somehow persists.

What might this strange conjunction of oblivion and persistence suggest? Here it may be best to note the strong resonances between the sonnet's stance and Blanchot's theory of disaster, which lingers with a similarly elusive theme. The tree, no trace of whose earlier life can be found, has grown up "to flourish now" (8); it follows that oblivion, in Blanchot's words, "ruins everything, all the while leaving everything intact."[21] The tree's life is condemned to nullity, yet the tree thrives; to borrow from Brassier, one might say that like everything else, the tree is dead – yet it lives on.[22] The event, then, is obscure, beyond any ordinary concept of condemnation or destruction. "When the disaster comes upon us, it does not come," writes Blanchot; "it does not happen."[23] Its advent is so elusive we cannot arrive at any knowledge of it, for it is "related to forgetfulness – forgetfulness without memory," or the disappearance of a wind that never registered the significance of the "young stem" in the first place.[24] The sonnet thus seems to anticipate Blanchot's disaster precisely, except that by discerning a disaster that has befallen a tree, rather than a human being, it expands his rendition of disaster to include *all* entities over which a wind might flow.

How might Blanchot's articulation of this quiet disaster bear on the treatments of such an event in speculative realism? For Brassier, as for Clare and Blanchot, the condemnation comes not in a distant future but has already taken place. Brassier makes clear that the empirical death of the sun is ultimately a figure for a contingency that underlies all physical realities, one that is intimate to any living thing. The arche-fossil does similar work for Meillassoux; as he argues, the category of the ancestral that it captures "designates an event *anterior* to terrestrial life and *hence anterior to givenness itself.*"[25] One could thus surmise that the chronological distance of any ancestral thing or terminal event figures the elusiveness of this perpetual process, its taking place below the threshold of ordinary perception. Whatever produced the arche-fossil or will kill the sun is already rotting the earth and condemning the life of a tree; that process operates already in every conceivable time or place.

But even this formulation falls short; as both Clare and Blanchot suggest, one can never locate that event in time, for as an event that cancels even forgetfulness and wipes out the attributes of any temporality – that "does not happen" – it befalls every entity through a constitutively self-erasing dimension of temporality itself. The sonnet captures this complex structure through its figure of a wind that flows over the tree in a movement that can take place only in time while erasing the significance of any difference between past and present. The disaster "does not happen" because it evacuates a happening that nevertheless continues to flow.[26]

This reading of temporality in "Obscurity" might seem to cut against its formulations, for in lines seven and eight it twice invokes the term "now," as if for a moment it proposes counting the past as nothing in relation to a present in which the tree flourishes and the speaker gazes upon it. But the poem's insistence both on blank oblivion and its equally blank reception highlights instead the utter erasure of that now, its incapacity to escape or evade the obliterating flow of the indifferent wind. Within that context, the sonnet makes explicit how the reiteration of this blank now produces what Blanchot describes as a "time without present," a time without a now that could count itself as such – a time that is not time, a time that erases itself.[27]

Such an insight, however, bears on the notion of eternity as well – and especially on the notion, appearing in "Old times forgetfull," of an "eternal blast / Oblivion." If oblivion wipes out every temporal location, even the present, does life subsist under the impress of an eternal now, an endless present that is sovereign over all moments? On the contrary, this sonnet works out the temporal consequences of living under oblivion, ultimately suggesting that one can never be present in, for, or with the eternal blast of that oblivion, that it is precisely the effacement of any present – even an eternal present – and thus constitutes instead a perpetual capacity to void time.

Here again this small cluster of poems bears on a question of central, vexing concern within speculative realist thought: how and whether to think time outside or beyond human reference.[28] This gesture, along with several others, undermines nearly every category crucial to Heideggerian phenomenology, carrying the sonnet not only into *post*phenomenology, to which, as Rajan argues, many "poststructuralist" theorists belong, but beyond such theorists into a mode of *non*phenomenological writing, sharing and extending this feature of speculative realism.[29] In this broad terrain, one might provisionally argue that the obliteration of the tree's life puts it in a zone that, in Blanchot's words, "escapes the possibility of experience," for without a present, the self-evidence of experience – or the priority of experience as an explanatory framework – is subtly condemned.[30] One might say as well that the sonnet evokes what Blanchot describes as a condition "outside being" – a state not of anti-being, which still invokes the possibility of being, but one in which the very possibility of being is effaced.[31] These poems thus evoke a state very like the night of Levinas, where one confronts the mere *there is*, except that here something more devastating than night is taking place – a darkness in which light is forgotten, where the metaphor of night itself must fall away.

Such a severe anticipatory reworking of phenomenology operates not only in the poem's subtle erasures of temporality and being but also of another key category in Heideggerian speculation: the notion of dwelling. In this regard, the poem extends an emphasis that pervades Clare's work; indeed, within the English literary tradition, there may be no better utterance of the poetics of the local than can be found in his poetry. Thus in this sonnet, as in hundreds of other poems and biographical episodes associated with Clare, one senses that for him, as for Heidegger, space is not given *a priori* but arises from the power of a specific location. Here, as in the later philosophical text, there inheres in the conditions of life, along with the relation to place, things, and space, a certain dwelling. "To say that mortals *are* is to say that *in dwelling* they persist through spaces by virtue of their stay among things and locations," Heidegger writes; one might say as much of the tree, except that, in "leav[ing its] past as nothing all behind," it hardly claims to persist where it is found, even over centuries, and thus abandons its claim to be.[32] Furthermore, in the sonnet, as in Heidegger's essay, dwelling implies a mode of protection, a capacity for sheltering the fly in its branches or the ewe in its shade; something is made possible under the tree, some sustaining provision of life, except that neither the fly nor ewe nor even the speaker can claim anything about it, suggesting that no mode of being has any privilege in its domain. In this sonnet, at least, these apparently local forms of life have been subsumed under a process that moves without reference to any ground or moment that could anchor it or make it legible: here even place is displaced, location unlocatable, the ground groundless.

This evacuation of a place's claim to be has important implications for the ewe, fly, and speaker who thrive under the tree's "sheltering bough" (7). When the poem places the human alongside nonhuman animals outside being in this space of utter erasure, it may seem to articulate the stance of one who, according to Giorgio Agamben, in an argument that responds in part to the work of Heidegger, has learned not merely to let the animal be, but also "to let it be *outside of being*," in a zone "beyond both knowing and not knowing … beyond both being and the nothing."[33] This gesture, Agamben tentatively proposes, might enable as well the arrival of a certain ignorance which suspends the hiatus between human and animal and lets both be, outside of being.[34] Clare's sonnet seems to anticipate these threads of Agamben's argument, but it does so not because it finds a place of suspension between the human and nonhuman, as Agamben ponders, but rather subjects both to a non-Heideggerian process, a nontemporality indifferent to the human and nonhuman alike. The sonnet marks neither a moment of messianic suspension nor of the condition of bare life one might overcome through it, but of subtle disaster, of wasted life, which flourishes in a state none can overcome.[35]

This resistance bears on other possibilities that Agamben explores. A key question arises when the sonnet refers to *that* ewe and *that* "flie," when it enacts an explicit gesture of deixis, treating certain living things as particular, as unique. It suggests that the ewe and fly persist alongside the speaker in their unique *thatness*. Perhaps they are instances of what Agamben in *The Coming Community* describes as singularity, characterized not by belonging to any category or having any property but rather by the very fact of their "taking-place," their "being-*such*." If so, they share a "common and absolutely exposed singularity" and thus "enter into a community without presuppositions and without subjects."[36] In that case, the sonnet would convey a perspective on things that Clare explores in hundreds of poems across his career, texts that perpetually evoke singular places, things, and encounters. But while Clare often suggests that "little things" endure in proximity to an edenic state, as we have seen, much as Agamben theorizes that singularities are themselves a form of revelation, in this sonnet they appear in a state of wholesale erasure, evacuated by oblivion. The poem thus explores an alternative to an Adamic poetics, offering us singularities defined by their "taking-place" in a groundless place and in a time outside of time so that, to borrow on Blanchot, they happen in a way that does not happen. The utter obliteration of being allows them to occur through this non-occurrence. Yet for Clare, each remains irreducible, singular, so that each transpires as *that* nullity, *that* nonevent.

But is this rendition of the sonnet's exploration of a redoubled negativity too hasty? What about the sonnet's speaker, who apparently does notice what the tree does not and surveys the past years, "doubtless centurys," that lie behind? What difference does the intrusion of this "thinking mind" make as it sees that none can find those stray winds that once fanned the tree in its youth? No difference at all: while the human subject might register the wind's recordless movement, that act does not undo the fact that time's nonpassage, like that of the wind, is blank, that the tree endures under a regime other than the poet's gaze. Furthermore, by suggesting that the ewe and fly can know almost as much about the tree's blank past as the speaker, the poem meditates on the uselessness of human witnessing. The poet beholds a process that transpires identically with or without his observation.

One might object that such a reading runs aground on the poem's final line – "Thus blank oblivion reigns as earths sublime" – which seems to evoke the aesthetic payoff of the sublime. But what, after all, is *earth's* sublime? Perhaps it is not a sublimity for the speaker, not a payoff for human consciousness, but rather a sublimity afforded *to the earth*, one that "condemns" earthly life while leaving it intact – giving it, through that intervention, access to something other than its immediate condition. A sublime proper to the earth, of course, would not be filled with a plenitude provided by the human mind's imaginings; on the contrary, it would remain utterly vacant in a mode best described as "blank oblivion." Thus the poem maps out a contrary analytic of the earthly sublime, whereby natural forms, passing through a violence that interrupts merely biological life, would ultimately gain access to a more effaced condition. Such a sequence would rehearse within the aesthetic register the unusable negativity of a counter-Hegelian descent towards the more severe nullity sketched above.

What significance does this earthly sublime then bear for the poet who inscribes it? As I have suggested, for the most part the poem thematizes its concerns by attending to the consequences of a stunningly nonhuman pure process; nevertheless, it acknowledges that its addressee must be human, separating the speaker from the ewe and the fly with that minimal word "almost" (13) and thereby hinting at the human relevance of what it captures. But rather than subsuming its themes under the sovereignty of human response, the poem subjects the speaker to oblivion's reign, locating him not so far from the ewe and fly under the shelter of the tree. In doing so, it suggests that the domain of human time, whose pages – including those of the poem itself – are apparently not blank, relies on the protection of natural oblivion. Evidently the tree offers not a hospitality to disaster, of which Scott J. Juengel unforgettably writes in another context, but a hospitality *of* disaster, so that the human and the poetic find shelter under what is rendered blank, as if to receive a pointless care from the process of obliteration itself.[37]

Here the sonnet proleptically intervenes into the speculations of the late Derrida, suggesting that the notions of pure gift and absolute hospitality apply not to human beings, for whom even in his account they are impossible, but rather to a temporality that operates without regard for us.[38] To any human gift, after all, one may respond with gratitude, an affect that in his view at least in small measure cancels out the absoluteness of the initial gesture and thus disqualifies it from being considered an instance of pure generosity. No human act can entirely overleap its place within the field of mutual relations; none can qualify as a pure gift. In contrast, temporality may well be capable of bestowing an absolute hospitality to the life of a tree, ewe, fly, or poet, for it remains absolutely indifferent to any gratitude that might return. It may therefore enable and condemn any life *in the same gesture*, in which case disaster and flourishing are two faces of the same flowing – a possibility that goes far towards unpacking Blanchot's account of disaster.

This reversal of sovereignty, whereby the poet takes shelter under the sign of disaster, applies to the poem as well. While the sonnet does leave a record, it registers a disaster to which it is subject, proposing that it too is buffeted by a condemnation that effaces its frail form. Thus even a poetic reception of that oblivion is only marginally distinct from the response of a ewe or fly, knowing very little more than they about the nontemporality to which all of them are subject.[39]

How does the poem offer itself to our reading in the wake of such a recognition? The sonnet implicitly addresses this question when it depicts how the tree receives its condition: "Thou grew unnoticed up to flourish now / & leave thy past as nothing all behind" (8–9). That past, the poem suggests, is indeed nothing, as blank as a disappeared wind; but in treating that past *as* nothing, the tree abandons that blank past, fails to record the fact of that recordless fate. Because of its blank receptivity, the tree endures these obliterations without reference to what it seems to have lost. To follow Blanchot once again, it endures in a mode of a radical passivity so severe it no longer sustains any link to the possibility of action.[40] This erasure of the very possibility of action should remind us of the second negation in which darkness erases the very memory of light; the wind's indifference to the lifeforms over which it flows is replicated in the tree's indifference *to* that indifference. The tree does not notice that it grew up unnoticed. If the wind utterly effaces the tree's history, the tree in turn utterly effaces that effacing.

By bringing forward this aspect of the tree's life, the sonnet goes far towards deprivileging the potentially disabling weight of oblivion. It gives us a moment of horror, pointing to how a blank movement condemns the tree's life to sheer inconsequence, but unlike the paired poems, it just as quickly turns its back on its own insight, as if to register that horror precisely in the gesture of turning away. In doing so, it spurns one possible response to condemned life, the cultivation of anguish over such a condition, and explores a nonanthropocentric alternative. It exemplifies instead what Anne-Lise François theorizes as recessive action, whereby one might encounter such a revelation and not take it up, not accept it as a determining gift. Invoking Wordsworth's line, "Stop here, or gently pass," François suggests that it "scandalously grants permission to pass, implying an indistinct continuity between the act of stopping to listen and that of letting lapse or fall behind."[41] Wordsworth's "or" may hint at a choice between two options, but as François proposes, it may also highlight the fact that each option may stand in for the other. Clare's sonnet addresses a similar question in another vein: suggesting that the tree is capable of responding blankly to the blank wind, it points to another continuity, this time between oblivion and its reception.

In identifying how the logic of negation is replicated yet again, the sonnet may remind us of a Hegelian dialectic whereby the negation of the negation sublates spirit into a higher level. But in this sonnet, no such sublation takes place; on the contrary, each further cancellation makes more severe the initial erasure, making more apparent a radical nullity. The renewed negation happens, as it were, not through Hegel but through Blanchot, where the opposition between light and dark leads not to a synthesis but a renewed cancellation through which the very possibility of the first term disappears. The poem underlines this logic in its reiterations of the term "blank," which it first introduces in the key phrase "Blank & recordless," then replicates twice in the final two lines as it refers to the tree's "blank past" and the "blank oblivion" that condemns it (2, 13, 14). In this way, the poem's figurations respond, as it were, to the productive capacities of Hegelian negativity through a workless counterpart, what Rajan calls in another context "unusable negativity," which evacuates the temporal sequence of self-consciousness towards absolute knowledge through what is here a nontemporal sequence towards a nonknowledge, an anonymous receptivity without consciousness.[42]

Through this repetition of effacement, then, the sonnet opens up a seldom considered response to the possibility that all life transpires in a state of severe abandonment: it leaves that state "as nothing all behind." The contrast between this sonnet and the stance of Brassier, who elaborates such insights into a version of nihilism, suggests that even speculative realism at times still clings too closely to the search for an ultimately rewarding framework for existence. The turn away from such expectations, in contrast, exposes their premises by abandoning them. The sonnet ceases to remember a prior claim and makes possible instead a radical passivity in the face of an unredeemable condition.

Thus in this sonnet, Clare at once invokes the poetics that obtains virtually across the rest of his writing and surpasses it. This slender sonnet bears a substantial burden: it outlines the contours of his most frequent practice but also indicates that it is possible to move beyond it into an even more adventurous and rigorous position. While this statement remains rare in his work, it demonstrates that a blank poetics does not have to await the work of Blanchot to receive articulation; moreover, it shows that such a stance could emerge not only within capacious genres (such as the epic or the triumph, as in Keats and Shelley) but also in briefer responses to aspects of place. In its daring formulations, the poem retains the power to intervene even into the stances of our own moment, to challenge us with an austerity more severe than virtually anything in more recent arguments. In reading it, we may reach the limit-experience of an encounter with erasure, at least of the modes of encounter that texts within the tradition make available to us. But for that reason, this poem has the power to anticipate a stance that may become necessary to us today, when we must take into account the possibility that humanity could become extinct in the relatively near future – an event that offers to us the urgent prospect that thought itself may soon fall into eclipse. We may find ourselves today in Clare's sonnet, condemned to wasted life under the movement of an oblivion that will itself disappear.

Yet the sonnet's turn away from the seductions of annihilating affect or searing insight, its abandonment even of a thought of thought's imminent extinction, leads the sonnet in the direction of a rather surprising minimalism – one that contrasts sharply with the lavish attention that other texts give to these concerns. The poet does not give the insights of these poems too great a weight; on the contrary, he enacts what one might call, following François, a recessive mode of writing, taking it so far that on these matters he cultivates near-silence. The fact that Clare included the sonnet within scores of poems on other themes for *The Midsummer Cushion*, returned to these concerns in two short poems, and touched on similar themes only briefly elsewhere suggests that he knew how he might "gently pass." Like the tree, he could treat his sense of oblivion as nothing. If Coleridge explores a mode of "blank attachment" in his Dejection Ode, as Noel Jackson proposes – a state of receptivity without prospect – here

Clare attributes to the wind, the tree, and himself a state of blank *non*attachment, a receptivity that abandons what it apparently receives.[43] In doing so, he authorizes us as well to extend this gesture in our turn, to recognize that we may best acknowledge our place under the shelter of oblivion by turning away – by evoking that sheltering briefly, implicitly, or in silence.

5 Blank Light: Annihilating Radiance
   in Turner

The fact that the light of the sun is not an object like any other has had far-reaching consequences within the metaphysics of the West. As Hans Blumenberg demonstrates, in the allegory of the cave in Plato's *Republic*, that light, as "the origin of knowability, Being, and essence," "stands out ... above beings." It does so because "that which gives everything else visibility and 'objecthood' cannot, in the same way, itself have the character of an object. Light is only seen in what it lets become visible."[1] In his discussion of this work, Derrida deciphers the metaphysical import of this stance, showing how Socrates regards the sun as a "hidden illuminating, blinding source of *logos*"; because it is what "enables one to speak," one cannot speak of it. Thus Socrates has "recourse to logos as that which *protects us from the sun*, protects us under it and from it ... in the *analogous* order of the sensible or the visible."[2] The domain of speech and the visible, which the sun illuminates, protects us from regarding the source of illumination itself, which by enabling speech and sight lies beyond them in the realm of the Good.

What happens, then, when one begins to look at the sun? Such an action would jeopardize its privilege; rather than regarding it as the unseen source of light, something that stands above and apart from the visible, and thus an instantiation of the metaphysical basis of phenomena, one would consider it as a source that at the same time appears within the visible – a source of light that one can see. By abandoning the modes of protection against it, one would also perforce regard it as an entity for whose appearance one cannot account, insofar as it would belong neither to the category of invisible, unquestioned origin nor in any straightforward way to the world it makes visible. No longer grounding the world of appearances as a transcendental principle, it would become an exceptional object, at once visible and too bright to look at for more than an instant. In many ways, then, it would serve as an exemplary instance of what survives after the cancellation of transcendence: a factor that perpetually disrupts the world that it once presumably guaranteed. If we follow Derrida's suggestion that the classical figure of the sun as origin grounds the realm of speech and the sensible alike, we can infer that the newfound status of the sun would constitute a problem for the arts that work with either words or images, unsettling the premises that had long obtained in both arenas.

Through what resources might one capture the import of such an uncanny brightness? There may be no better instance of the challenge in attempting to do so in a literary work than the moment in Percy Bysshe Shelley's late, unfinished masterwork, *The Triumph of Life*, in which the narrator recounts how, amid the dancing throng, he saw the light of the figure that later receives the name of Life: "And a cold glare, intenser than the noon / But icy cold, obscured with [ ] light / The Sun as he the stars" (77–9).[3] What one faces in this passage is not the adjective "blank," as we see in every other textual instance I discuss in this book, but a missing word where one would expect to find an adjective. (In the manuscript, the poet had initially written "fascinating light," but struck out "fascinating" without replacing the word, leaving a line without the requisite number of feet.)[4] When she edited the poem for publication, Mary Shelley filled in this gap with the word "blinding," a word whose meter is suitable for the line and whose import is seemingly appropriate for the context. Yet it is clear that Percy could have used that word here and did not do so; instead, he left that gap in the manuscript open, a gap that the poem's most recent and authoritative editors have indicated with a blank space between brackets (as cited above). The fact that a word is missing in the initial manuscript becomes evident in the modern edition, where it represents in visual form a verbal, metrical, and conceptual absence in the poem's articulation.

The absence of a word in that position is quite revealing. Perhaps the poet left that gap unfilled because he hoped he would find a better word later in the process of composing the poem. But it is equally plausible that he could find no word that could fit this context; the absence of a word may be at least partially intentional, in which case the incompleteness of this passage may stand in for what the poet regards as the incapacities of language. This moment may thus designate an impasse constitutive to speech as such – an impasse that befalls it once language, ceasing to be authorized by an origin, becomes infected by a gap or void that reveals its structural incapacity. But as this passage suggests, such an impasse falls on light as well – a light it attributes to Life as well as the sun – revealing a similar incapacity that operates in the visual domain. That "[ ] light" might appear precisely as such in an artistic reflection on the affordances of that domain. This moment, then, indicates that language may share a constitutive fault with visuality, in which case poetry and art may be able to capture, each in its own way, the import of that fault, the strange implications of that gap.[5]

While the poem makes these suggestions in a brief gesture, a student of Romanticism can pursue their implications much further, for such a student fortunately has access to a set of brilliant and original examinations of visuality's impasse in this period in the painting of J.M.W. Turner. The brief suggestion in Shelley's poem points to a problematic that operates far more broadly in Turner's painting, and accordingly I will consider the poem precisely in these terms below – as an opening that ushers us into the explorations Turner pursues in his work. In contrast to Shelley, Turner lived long enough to explore this devastating brightness at length, pursuing a range of strategies for evoking its force through the affordances of his visual medium. In certain ambitious works, Turner shows how the light of the sun, which makes visibility possible, can also eradicate eyesight and thus destroy that visibility; the light that seems to call the world into being can ultimately cause it to disappear. What was once a foundational principle becomes in his work a force that erases the world. Since this shift to a new understanding of the sun's light dismantles the classical and theological regime of representation, it leads to changes across a further series of registers, including nationalist ideologies, understandings of perception, the premises of visual representation, and the subject's sense of embodiment.

For much of the painter's career, then, the sun becomes a catastrophic presence in the world and in the visual field; it is an equivalent of a spectacular version of the Real, a singular intervention, the event of ruination. But Turner does not remain content with evoking that version of the Real. In two of his last paintings, *Norham Castle: Sunrise* and *Sunrise with Sea Monsters*, he takes a further step, moving from the spectacular, intrusive Real to the blank Real beneath it, to a condition where light itself has been dispossessed, depicting a condition that, outside visuality, is still visible in the strange light that illuminates nothing for no one. The catastrophic sun, these images suggest, eventually gives way to the bliss of a state before life or after death, outside the subject – the eerie, blank splendour of mere existence.

I

One might best sketch aspects of this problematic in a preliminary fashion by considering certain details of the missing word in Shelley's manuscript. At first, one might assume that the gap in *The Triumph of Life* remains empty because of the unfortunate circumstance of the poet's death. As Paul de Man remarks, this poem was reduced "to the status of a fragment brought about by the actual death and subsequent disfigurement of Shelley's body.... This defaced body is present in the margin of the last manuscript page and has become an inseparable part of the poem."[6] While this remark is quite fanciful, since no such body actually appears on that page, it is nevertheless true in nearly a literal sense: sketches of sails and sailboats are scattered throughout the manuscript, including arguably on its final page, signs of the fascination that soon led to the poet's death by drowning. Thus a reminder of the poet's death is indeed visible in the manuscript, as if to confirm de Man's suggestion.[7] One could take this fact quite far; in an initial account, one could say that "figuration and cognition are actually interrupted by an event which shapes the text but which is not present in its represented or articulated meaning." Yet this response to the poem must give way to another; as de Man continues, "the reading of *The Triumph of Life* establishes that this mutilated textual model exposes the wound of a fracture that lies hidden in all texts. If anything, this text is more rather than less typical than texts that have not been thus truncated." This condition is the case, he argues, because of a pattern in the poem that his reading has already traced: "The rhythmical interruptions that mark off the successive episodes of the narrative are not new moments of cognition but literal events textually reinscribed by a delusive act of figuration or of forgetting."[8] For de Man, the contingent interruption of the poem is already reflected in the poem's practice of interrupting itself; the poem explicitly affirms its incomplete state in advance.

Here de Man expands on themes we encountered in Blanchot, replicating the temporal transposition so central in the latter's work – the transformation of a final, catastrophic event into a ruination that has already taken place and that dislocates experience from itself – in a shift from the interruption of the manuscript at Shelley's death to the intrinsically fractured status of textuality as such. Moreover, he brings these two levels together, suggesting that the fissures in *The Triumph* speak of death and textuality at once, that a certain feature mutilates life and work alike. Following this logic, one may equally well argue that the gap in the manuscript, while seemingly accidental, speaks of its ruined state, its already unworked condition. As Mazur remarks in relation to a blank space in another Romantic work – Friedrich Schelling's *Clara* – such a space suggests that the "(un)published is the presence of nothing, or, better yet, the presence of non-being."[9]

The passage brings into view several further instances of this overall logic as well. As Amanda Goldstein demonstrates, the poem displays Life as a figure of a material, temporal process, a catastrophe that operates endlessly in the domain of what Monique Allewaert calls "materialist figuration."[10] Life can obscure the sun because its movement captures a temporality in which our familiar sun, like any other, was once formed and will be dissolved. In this poem, as in "Mont Blanc," Shelley invokes developments in natural history, which had begun to argue that the stars and earth formed over the course of deep time through a dynamic that exemplifies the influence of vast, inhuman forces, which are themselves further instances of the imposition that applies throughout the poem. But *The Triumph* pushes beyond the suggestions of natural history, for it interprets them not in relation to a Deist theology, which many researchers in these fields invoked, but rather what it inherits from Lucretius, to whose *De Rerum Natura* it alludes in many passages.[11] Yet the poem cuts through even these invocations, for it suggests that it is not enough to trace how a material process initially emerged and will eventually disappear; the Lucretian account of origins out of a random *clinamen* or swerve proposes the more radical insight that this dynamic is constituted by a turbulence without a core, an effervescence without essence.

These echoes of Lucretius indicate why it may be difficult to provide an adjective for the light of this figure. Is there a strategy for naming a light beyond light, a light that obscures light itself? In *Paradise Lost*, Milton faces a similar dilemma when, addressing God, he attempts to describe the divine brightness as at once invisible and as the source of light: "Fountain of Light, thyself invisible / Amidst the glorious brightness where thou sit'st / Thron'd inaccessible" (3.375–7). Soon thereafter, the passage outlines another paradox, suggesting that God's light is so bright it is dark while still dazzling: "Dark with excess of light thy skirts appear / Yet dazzle heaven, that brightest Seraphim / Approach not, but with both wings veil thir eyes" (3.380–2).[12] Inheriting this passage, Shelley resists writing similarly oxymoronic formulations, for doing so would imply that his figure shares the status of Milton's deity. Yet even under this constraint, he wishes to suggest that Life's brightness exceeds that of brightness itself in the form of the sun, that its light obscures mere light. As a result, the manuscript he leaves behind does so not through dissonance between positive terms, as Milton's poem does, but rather between a positive term and an absent one. Through its turn against those paradoxes, the passage resists evoking a biblical or Platonic origin for the world of appearances, an essence for which the sun has often served as a metaphor, but rather exposes a light without any such attribute. It does so as well by attributing the absent feature of this light not merely to the poet's gesture but to a structural incapacity in the formation of phenomena themselves; the evacuation of transcendence leaves behind not an immanent fountain, an instance of origin embedded in a natural theology, but a void that evacuates any substantial ground.

By evoking that void through a poetics of excessive brightness the poem pursues an approach quite distinct in its own moment and ours. Several poems in the Romantic era rely on a nearly opposite prospect, the absence or extinction of the sun: Coleridge's "Limbo"; Byron's "Darkness" (1816); and John Clare's short lyric, "Old times forgetfull," which we saw in the previous chapter. Such a pattern extends into our own era: as noted earlier, Brassier, pursuing a suggestion by Lyotard, argues that the eventual death of the sun is a catastrophe for the horizon of thought, undoing the very conditions for philosophical questioning itself.[13] As these examples demonstrate, the death of the sun is a recurring trope for how the preconditions of our embodied condition lack substance; it replicates on a cosmic scale the Levinasian night in which one encounters the bare *there is*. Ironically, however, this trope leaves in place the potential inference that because the sun is not yet extinct, neither is the metaphysics for which it can serve as a metaphor. Thus it may be a more telling gesture for Shelley to invoke not darkness but excessive light (as Clare does in another short lyric,

"Where are the citys"); in this way he assaults the metaphysical privilege of the sun more directly than otherwise, avoiding even the thematics of night familiar in Levinas and Blanchot to suggest instead that light may subvert itself, that the field of the visible is already a world without world.[14]

II

These indications derived from a brief moment in *The Triumph of Life* may prepare us for the expansive treatment of the problematic in the work of Turner. Pursuing these links, at least initially, is feasible because the premises that underlie that poetic line and the latter work share a great deal. Much like Shelley, Turner sought to make his art consistent with new findings in the history of the earth; as Gerald Finley demonstrates, he incorporated aspects of geological knowledge into his painting over many decades.[15] He cultivated friendships with geologists and brought aspects of their findings into his lectures at the Royal Academy, giving this field such sustained attention that James Hamilton remarks that "through his unique means of expression Turner was also a geologist."[16] The assumptions of geology fit well within Turner's overarching sense that all earthly phenomena emerged within the dynamic interplay between the elements; accordingly, he incorporates Hutton's theory of the earth as a collision of elements into many of his paintings, creating a sequence of cataclysmic events in *Snow Storm, Avalanche and Inundation* (1837), in which, as Barry Venning points out, "the snowstorm sets off the avalanche, which in turn causes the flood.[17] Elsewhere I have discussed how the reception of a geological sense of earthly history over the course of deep time undercut belief in the rainbow covenant, in which God promised never again to unleash a Deluge on the earth, leading Wordsworth to explore a post-covenantal poetics in his account of encountering the geological majesty of the Alpine landscape in Book 6 of *The Prelude*. For his part, Shelley deploys a geological interpretation of the Alps in "Mont Blanc," even as he suspends it in favour of insisting on humanity's inability to grasp the Power that transcends phenomena, a Power he associates with the peak of that mountain.[18]

In all these instances, the breach in a covenantal framework opens the way for an encounter with an unfettered and ultimately disastrous interplay of elements, one that comports well with an aesthetics of the sublime, to be sure, but also with a new sense of humanity's vulnerability.[19] As Inés Richter-Musso argues, Turner's images often emphasize the "transitory nature of the natural world" in a painting style that "suggests unfinished business and rejects objectivism."[20] In effect, Turner takes what Koselleck regards as the temporalization of history another step, insisting that materiality itself is undefined and open, its contours always in process. In this way he moves, as does Shelley, from substantial forms to their movement and collision, but also cuts through the reliance on any enduring framework for interpretation, any cultural system that would claim to understand or ground reality itself. Such a stance inevitably leads Turner to destabilize even the viewer's perspective, as he does most famously in *Snow Storm – Steam-boat off a Harbour's Mouth making Signals in shallow Water, and going by the Lead. The Author was in this Storm on the night the Ariel left Harwich* (1842). This title draws attention to how the image is presented from a viewpoint in motion, suspending the longstanding privilege of a secure station from which one can survey what the painting depicts, to emphasize an ungrounded, rather dizzying spatial and temporal position in the midst of what it perceives.[21] In these and other paintings, Turner subjects objects and subjects alike to unfinished, undefined movements, a world always in flow, a clash of forces whose ultimate import nothing can secure.

This transition from objects to flows includes a further, similarly transformative shift from painting what is perceived to the dynamics of perception. In a note to an essay included in *The Round Table* (1817), William Hazlitt, remarking that Turner is the "ablest landscape painter now living," complains that his paintings are "representations not so properly of the objects of nature as of the medium through which they are seen."[22] This aspect of his art finds a passionate advocate in John Ruskin, whose *Modern Painters* (1843–60) sets out a host of arguments insisting on how brilliantly Turner captures what actually appears in the visible world, including the way in which the images of objects reach the eye through the medium of the atmosphere.[23] Turner's work, however, was not unique in this regard; it emerged within a period that saw a range of new inquiries into visual phenomena. For one thing, scientists first captured images of the sun's surface, thereby demonstrating that investigators could treat it as a natural object, if a uniquely challenging one. It is likely that this development was well known to Turner; in 1801, the astronomer Sir William Herschel gave a series of papers on the nature and appearance of the sun to fellows of the Royal Academy in rooms of Somerset House directly adjacent to the space in which Turner was exhibiting one of his paintings. As Hamilton points out, Herschel "looked *at* the sun" and considered it "as an object, with physical features, naming its parts, giving it a new reality, against the old view of the sun as an unknowable, unseeable object."[24] In his *Theory of Colour* (1810), Goethe recounts the results of his looking directly at the sun, capturing the retinal phenomena that follow, and some decades later, researchers examined similar retinal images, both describing new aspects of the process of perception.[25] Jonathan Crary points out that many of the scientists who researched these afterimages damaged or lost their eyesight as a result, but in doing so discovered how the body was "the site and producer of chromatic events," coming to "a piercing realization of the corporeality of vision."[26] Evidently, Turner himself participated in aspects of these new developments, for at least on one occasion late in his life a fellow artist noticed him gazing directly at the sun.[27] Thus Turner's own work contributed to the shift whereby, as Crary argues, "the process of perception itself had become, in various ways, a primary object of vision." This shift to the experience of vision, however, led to "the irrevocable loss of a fixed source of light, the dissolution of a cone of light rays, and the collapse of the distance separating an observer from the site of optical experience."[28] The move towards the observer largely displaced the privilege of the sun as the external source of light.

This last suggestion, however, ultimately indicates that the move towards an emphasis on perception brings about an even more profound transformation. Insofar as these changes in representations of the sun and of optical experience dissolve the idea of an unseen source of light that illuminates the world, they exemplify the abandonment not only of the mode of visual representation modelled on the camera obscura, which in Crary's account dominated throughout the early modern period, or of an Enlightenment conception of light, which had a major influence in the decades before Turner's work, but also of the classical understanding of light inherited from Plato, whereby the sun makes the world of objects visible and thereby establishes the domain of what can be known.[29] The move towards mediation, in short, suspends the assumptions that had dominated since Plato in favour of the ungrounded domain of a temporalized perception. Thus Turner's originality consists not only in his observing how phenomena of the visual world appear to the eye but also in dislodging the framework that had for millennia established the validity of the visual world itself.

That transformation, however, inevitably bears on the medium of art as well. If reality is to be found less in the domain of visible objects than in the experience of perceiving it, and if painting's task is to highlight what results from the dynamics of perception, it follows that the painter must also become aware of the effects of mediating that process through the resources of his art. Thus it is not surprising that, for Turner, an attention to how light appears to the eye became a rigorous examination of how the capacities of paint might capture the most telling features of such appearances. Indeed, for Lawrence Gowring, he went so far as to subordinate his interest in nature to the exploration of his medium.[30] This tendency is especially pronounced in watercolour, which "allowed Turner to meditate on some unexplored property of his vast technical resources, some possibility inherent in colour and in paint itself." The drawings he made on a visit to Italy in 1819 "leave a magical impression that the specific details of a real place grew out of colour instead of the reverse."[31] The watercolours of Venice in the 1830s have a similar quality; as Lindsay Stainton argues, within them "solid forms blend into the surrounding water and sky, [and] objects are hardly more substantial than their reflections" – even as the choice of colour "[does] not reproduce a familiar reality but create[s] a new one."[32]

One consequence of these changes is that Turner is less invested in representing the objects of the visible world than his predecessors. While the painter invokes the traditions and genres characteristic of European high art, and especially of certain Old Masters such as Claude, he does so while departing from them, suspending the effort to provide a detailed representation of his ostensible subjects. At times, his contemporaries scoffed at the results. Hazlitt writes that these images "give pleasure only by the excess of power triumphing over the barrenness of the subject.… The utter want of a capacity to draw a distinct outline with the force, the depth, the fulness, and precision of this artist's eye for colour, is truly astonishing."[33] But what Hazlitt criticized is precisely the intervention that Turner wished to achieve; as Gowring points out, "He was intent on the scheme and the effect of a picture, and intent on outdoing whichever master it had come from."[34] By invoking those traditions, however, Turner kept them in play as a necessary context for understanding his art; in effect, he wished to make visible the dissonance between prior assumptions and those in his own work.

Turner's practice in this respect suggests that it is not enough to note that he participated in the transition into a visual practice focused on the process of perception. His wish to draw attention to the break required to inaugurate this practice shows that he wished to accentuate as well how it entailed the destruction of prior theological and political assurances. In his choice of subject, Turner often sought to make the larger implications of this shift explicit, not least in visible signs of humanity's vulnerability to the indifferent courses of nature or of history. For him, the transition towards a mediated sense of perception could not exhaust itself in an art of pure mediation, for it also had to indicate what follows from the lapse of those prior guarantees. Thus Turner's is not a reassured practice of immanence; it is instead an art that perpetually depicts the groundlessness of experience, the erosion of reassurance – what he calls, in a poem he claims to be writing throughout his career and from which he draws quotations that accompany many of his paintings, *The Fallacies of Hope*. (Because no manuscript of this poem was ever found after his death, it enjoys the status not of an actual poem but of a governing intention he could invoke at any time, a touchstone of his overall project as a painter.)[35]

Turner makes the implications of this stance evident across his career. In various paintings on subjects that offer him the opportunity to contain the representation of horrific violence through comforting religious or political explanations, he chooses instead to place an abundance of corpses in a central position and thereby to repudiate the speciousness of such ideological appeals. A timely and courageous instance in this regard is *The Field of Waterloo* (1818; Figure 1), which shows grieving widows moving through a field of bodies in search of their dead husbands. Philip Martin argues that the painting's "composition and content make no deferential gestures to the conventional aesthetics governing history painting," for in depicting "this startling and traumatic scene … it produces a remarkable recasting of Waterloo as an anthem to doomed

Figure 1   J.M.W. Turner, *The Field of Waterloo* (1818). Photo: Tate Gallery, CC-BYNC-ND (3.0 Unported).

youth, the antipathy of glorious victory," for it emphasizes instead "the extent of the casualties, the grief, and the pathos."[36] Moreover, as Philip Shaw points out, by undoing the separation of the military and the domestic, the painting displays "the vulnerable body that can be maimed and killed." In that way, it "disturbs the ideology that perpetuates war," the notion that it will prevent violence from invading the home.[37] Taking this approach further, Leo Costello suggests that "the picture itself, with its twisting, intricately complex forms strewn across the center of the canvas, looks not unlike an open wound, or viscera spilled out onto the ground."[38] Rather than assembling images into a "central, climactic narrative moment," Turner does the opposite, for by featuring this open wound on which the widows cast their searching light, he pursues "the decomposition of the body and a loss of its singularity and individual integrity."[39] One might say of this image, as a reviewer did of the roughly contemporaneous painting by Theodor Géricault, *The Raft of the Medusa* (1819), that this "picture is a heap of corpses from which one turns away."[40] Turner's sharp response to Waterloo does not fade with time; as Martin points out, while in a watercolour of 1833 he shows "rows of rude stones marking the interred bodies," he also "plac[es] a skeleton in the left foreground as a potent reminder" of that heap of corpses and "the impossibility of their permanent interment."[41] Something in this scene exceeds the practice of burial, refusing to be absorbed either into the earth or into the myths of history. Overleaping the psychology of humanitarian regret or retrospective sympathy, this image makes visible what had been a feature of the scene all along, its resistance to any justification, and thus exposes what Slavoj Žižek, following Lacan, calls the lack in the Other, the gap in the ideological framework that structures social reality.[42]

This painting exemplifies how Turner, already sensitive to the ungrounded dynamics of earthly history and of embodied perception, discerns the temporalization of history as well. As Costello argues, over the course of his career he was "increasingly aware that both history and painting were characterized by the dynamics of formation, disintegration, and reformation."[43] Crucial in this regard is the fact that "Turner consolidated his career in the first decade of the century as a painter of destruction *par excellence*," as well as that "a number of paintings from the period immediately following Waterloo into the 1830s consistently depict empire by referring to its demise."[44] His paintings of the burning of the Houses of Parliament, the decline of the Carthaginian Empire, and the slow decay of Venice all exemplify this concern.[45] As we have just seen, he conveys this concern in part by challenging the conventions of historical painting, opening up the viscera of the image, as it were, and thus challenging the integrity of the viewing subject. His treatment of these themes extends and complicates his evocation of the elements; the clash between Rome and Carthage, for example, which stands in for the war between empires in his own moment, echoes the collision of fundamental forces in earth's history, as the juxtaposition of these two arenas in *Snow Storm: Hannibal and his Army crossing the Alps* (1812) suggests. Extending this theme in *Rain, Steam, and Speed – The Great Western Railway* (1844), he treats the train as wielding a force akin to those of the elements, a power capable of cutting through earth and air alike, already pointing towards humanity's capacity to disturb the relation between elements and thus signalling the arrival of what some have recently begun to call the Anthropocene.[46] In his career overall, then, he consistently elaborates on the temporalization of history, nature, perception, and representation, challenging the ideologies that had obtained in each of these domains.

Thus it is no surprise that a respondent such as Hazlitt, still attached to an earlier regime of representation, brings out the implications of Turner's practice in a way seldom attempted by any other critic. As we have seen, Hazlitt contests the painter's move away from the object world towards mediation, but his concern applies as well to the painter's refusal of metaphysical guarantees on every level. This turn, Hazlitt writes, suggests that Turner ultimately "delights to go back to the first chaos of the world, or to that state of things when the waters were separated from the dry land, and light from darkness, but as yet no living thing nor tree bearing fruit was seen upon the face of the earth." Since in the biblical account the creation consists in part of the differentiation of elements,

Turner's practice reverses the creation and returns us to a phase much closer to the primordial state. In those paintings, Hazlitt continues, "All is 'without form and void.' Some one said of his landscapes that they were *pictures of nothing, and very like*."[47] For Hazlitt, insofar as these paintings dissolve all the elements into a primaeval flow, they depict a world without substance and without ground – a world that is at its core nothing at all. Precisely by resisting this mode of art, Hazlitt provides a striking insight into its implications, showing that for Turner the emphasis on process ultimately discloses something beyond it, the absence of any feature that governs it, the sway of what one might call the void.

If all this is the case, how might one best interpret the Turner paintings which feature the violently blazing light of the sun? The emphasis on atmospheric mediation, which disperses sunlight, ironically draws attention to what is now the highly exceptional status of a direct sight of the sun's disk itself, just as the attention to perception makes all the more evident how gazing at the sun has an exceptional impact on the retina. Thus the source of light that in its neutral sovereignty once established the integrity of the visual world now becomes a figure for visual and optical violence, transforming from the agent of a guarantee into the site of cataclysm. While this newly violent sun in some respects seems to fit within a Burkean account of the sublime, it does so while threatening the survival of the medium of representation itself – the eye and thus the visual field *tout court* – thereby potentially destroying the means for treating it as a sublime image in the first place.[48] An exception even for an aesthetics of the sublime, it becomes a problem for the entire regime of visual representation. Accordingly, if one seeks an image of what Hazlitt describes as the void that defines Turner's practice, one could scarcely do better than consider his sun.

As one might expect, Turner engages with the question of the sun's light in a range of key paintings. Here I will discuss only a small number of distinctive but telling instances in this regard. In *Regulus* (initially exhibited in Rome in 1828 but reworked considerably and exhibited in London in 1837; Figure 2), one of the first paintings in which he delves into this distinctive problematic, Turner alludes to a story Oliver Goldsmith tells in *Roman History* regarding Regulus, a Roman general who was captured by the Carthaginians and in due course tortured by them, having his eyelids cut off and placed in a position facing the sun, before being put into a barrel pierced by nails pointing at his body, where he remained until he died. Turner sets this painting at the port of a city, perhaps Rome or Carthage, but presents us neither with an image of a heroic figure nor with the sight of Regulus under torture. Instead, the primary feature of this painting is a sun that has become a vast swath of extreme luminescence that nearly engulfs the entire scene. As Matthew Beaumont remarks, it "metastasises across the sky and threatens to contaminate or corrode the cityscape that … lies unprotected beneath it."[49] But where is Regulus in this extraordinary scene? One must conclude that he is in the position of the viewer, that as

Figure 2 J.M.W. Turner, *Regulus* (1828, 1837). Photo: Tate Gallery, CC-BY-NC-ND (3.0 Unported).

Beaumont suggests, the painting "situates painter and viewer in the position of Regulus as he is being tortured."[50] One is caught in the situation of gazing at the sun without reprieve, unable to protect one's eyesight from its brightness and thus on the verge of going blind. One could argue, then, that when the painting associates viewers with Regulus, it subjects them to another instance of torture. Thus it is somehow fitting that in 1863, Walter Stephenson, a visitor to the National Gallery, was so dismayed by the painting that he slashed it with a penknife. Beaumont comments, "Perhaps the violence of the painting itself, a violence that shapes its composition and its pictorial content alike, provoked these responses."[51]

Such a response to the painting accurately registers the fact that in *Regulus* Turner departs from his practice of attending to the dynamics of perceiving the landscape. But this departure reveals a further concern. The painting demonstrates that he wishes to indicate that the light of the sun is not simply an object among others, for it can potentially undermine the perceivability of the world;

in this painting the sun nearly blanks out every other object, creating a mist of brightness that obscures all other things. In forcing his viewers to confront these attributes of the sun's light, the painter insists with singular urgency on this new question. Invoking the conventions of historical painting in order to breach them, he foregrounds a question regarding the medium of painting, and more radically, of perception as such. The sun is necessary if one is to see the visible world, as the classical regime of representation maintained, but it is also the source of a light that can annihilate the visibility to which it provides access. Thus Turner suggests that perception rests upon a precondition that can potentially contradict itself and that must remain as a result undecidable.

This painting thus depicts what is at stake when a "[ ] light" appears in Shelley's poem. Here we see a visual counterpart of what Shelley suggests in his key lines: this cold glare, dimming all other objects through the violence of its own brightness, does indeed obscure the world. But does that sun constitute a blank light? That central, blazing portion of *Regulus* is bereft of colour, feature, or form. But rather than arising from something missing – as is the case in the poem – it emerges instead from the artist's intense, public activity in laying an abundance of white paint across the image.[52] Although the presence of this glaring paint might inspire one to argue that it is not blank in the sense of entirely lacking any feature, in his time and ours viewers frequently describe its effect as dazzling or violent, a fact already made evident in the response of Stephenson, which indicates that he saw it as akin to a light that exceeds what the eye can absorb. In this respect, then, *Regulus* explicitly transgresses the practices visible elsewhere in Turner's work. Precisely because Turner elsewhere remains focused on the mediation of light, this assault on perception and colour alike is especially striking. The painting demonstrates that he is acutely aware that an excessive brightness must intrude into what otherwise might seem to be the seamless interweavings of mediation. Here one can say, with Gilles Deleuze and Felix Guattari, that a Turner canvas "is pierced by a hole, a lake, a flame, a tornado, an explosion," that it is "truly broken, sundered by what penetrates it."[53] Cancelling the metaphysical privilege of the sun produces this conflagration in the fabric of the world, this explosion in the field of vision.

The painting's violation of the visible bears on further aspects of its reception as well. Beaumont argues that the painting organizes the legend of Regulus "not as a historical tableau but as a landscape," for it depicts his departures from both Rome and Carthage in a single image. Moreover, as he notes, the tiny figure in a toga descending the stairs of the palace on the right is Regulus, while the cask that four men roll on the left is most likely that into which Regulus was placed for the purposes of torture. Thus the painting juxtaposes several distinct moments "synchronically," capturing a "subjective topography" in the "nightmarish gaze of the general," recombining various moments from his experience into a single, dreamlike image.[54] If we can follow Beaumont in this reading, the painting aligns an assault on the embodied process of perception with one on the temporal coordinates of subjectivity, taking the subject to the verge not only of blindness but also of delirium, to the edge of a dismemberment at once physical and psychoanalytic. For Turner, it seems, visuality is more than a purely visual space; it establishes the framework within which the subject figures itself. To eclipse the visible is to undo the coordinates of subjectivity itself.

In these various ways, then, *Regulus* deciphers the import of the blank sun with singular rigour. As a result, this image may delineate better than any other the significance of what Turner is reputed to have said in his final weeks, "The sun is God": for him, this figure does not have the properties of the Christian God, who creates and sustains, nor of a pagan god, one of many figures in a pantheon of deities, but rather of a force whose violence is more supreme than any other.[55] It is well worth pausing over the import of this declaration. Responding to his depiction of light across his career, Jeremy Robinson places Turner in the tradition of Christian mysticism, invoking predecessors such as Pseudo-Dionysus and St John of the Cross to argue that he was a devotee of the eternal light.[56] This stance takes further the classical metaphysics of light; as Blumenberg points out, the brightness of Plato's sun becomes absolutely bright in Neoplatonism, in which "the coincidence of seeing and not-seeing found in the dazzling effect of pure light is the fundamental confirming experience of all mysticism, in which the presence of the absolute attests itself, in which all thinking and speaking is surpassed, and which represents the uniquely adequate way of encountering transcendency."[57] But as we have seen, Turner's exploration of the reception of the sun's light ultimately leads him to see in this "coincidence of seeing and not-seeing" not the pure essence of being but rather a process that ungrounds all things, not a divine light but an annihilating force. Thus it may be better to argue that his work anticipates the atheological mysticism of Georges Bataille, especially his ecstatic apprehension of a pure, useless expenditure: *Regulus* may well be an act of homage to this extravagance without reserve.[58] In a similar vein, Deleuze and Guattari declare that Turner is not merely "far ahead of his time," for in such paintings something "comes to us from an eternal future, or flees toward it," an eternal future that rests not with God but with the void that unworks all temporality, that decimates embodied experience *tout court*.

The intervention of *Regulus* is so immense in its implications that Turner clearly had ample room to explore them further in many paintings in the ensuing years. Of the many images one could explore in this regard, one of the most telling is *Light and Colour (Goethe's Theory) – the Morning after the Deluge – Moses writing the Book of Genesis* (1843, Figure 3), which as its title suggests brings together the artist's preoccupation with aspects of his medium, including colour, the problem of the Deluge along with its geological associations, and the

Figure 3   J.M.W. Turner, *Light and Colour (Goethe's Theory) – the Morning after the Deluge – Moses writing the Book of Genesis* (1843). Photo: Tate Gallery, CC-BY-NC-ND (3.0 Unported).

status of biblical revelation.[59] It does so while also retaining aspects of the compositional structure and imagistic details present in a series of closely related paintings. The strange tangle of dark figures in the central foreground, for example, replicates, albeit in a less representational mode, the heap of corpses on the field of Waterloo. Moreover, through the bodies of those floating in much of the painting's lower half, the image alludes to many paintings that display those destroyed by Deluge, shipwreck, or the deliberate tossing of bodies overboard at sea, as in one of his most pivotal images, *Slavers throwing overboard the*

Dead and Dying, Typhon [*sic*] *coming on* (1840), hinting that the painter here ascribes a similarly tyrannical brutality to the God of the Deluge. The painting undercuts biblical narrative, for it treats the mass death caused by the Deluge as a dark area on what is otherwise an excessively bright luminescence – an open wound, as it were, on the field of divinity. If on this level one can take the light of the sun as a figure for divine revelation, then that dark tangle intrudes as a blot on that brightness, a sign that within transcendence there lurks a lethal hostility to human beings that even revelation cannot expunge, or worse, that is intrinsic to revelation itself.

The implications of this suggestion go far. As the title of this painting indicates, it offers a sustained interrogation of Goethe's theory of colours, responding to its explorations of the polarity of light and darkness, the relations between primary colours, and the affective import of different hues. Finley demonstrates that Turner's response in this painting is complex, for he sustains aspects of Newtonian colour theory while adapting elements of Goethe's analysis as well, arriving at an approach that is his own.[60] Goethe argues that colours derive from the interplay of light and dark, for example, while Turner insists that only light can confer colour or shade.[61] But while Turner's engagement with these and many other questions is visible in *Light and Colour* and its companion piece, *Shade and Darkness – The Evening of the Deluge* (1843), his concerns go further than this discussion implies, for as he demonstrates in *Regulus*, the power to call forth the visible is *at the same time* the power to erase it. As we have seen, in *Light and Colour* he builds on that intuition, suggesting that revelation itself contains the power to destroy. In doing so, he takes seriously his rethinking of the sun as the origin of light. Insofar as the concept of revelation relies on the privilege of light, as Blumenberg points out, a reconception of light must bear on the status of revelatory light as well.[62] Thus at least in one of its dimensions, this painting dissolves the opposition between light and darkness, undoing the terms on which previous reflections, including those of Goethe, relied.

The painting's concern with the process of perception, central to Goethe's theory of colour, is evident as well in its awareness that the circular image of the sun is echoed in the afterimage retained by the retina. The collapse of the difference between the sun's light and its devastating effect on sight, already evident in *Regulus*, here advances to an identification between one circular image and another. But since this image hardly renders an actual landscape, it refers instead to a reception of transcendence per se; it thus treats visual perception as a metaphor for a mode of apprehension that applies on another level, the perspective that a vulnerable, temporalized subject must take on ultimate concerns. In effect, the painting treats the retinal afterimage of the sun as a metaphor for the reception of a disastrous transcendence within the contours of finitude.

Given the scope of these concerns, the painting intervenes on a scale even larger than Crary suggests. It undoes not only what had once been the spectatorial privilege of the viewer, but also the stability of a viewer's existence, expanding upon a practice that, as we have seen, applies in many earlier paintings. The skeletal remains of Waterloo which remind the viewer of an unexpungable death, the assault on the viewer's eyesight in *Regulus*, and the unstable position of painter and viewer alike in *Snow Storm* (1842) demonstrate that Turner finds an array of strategies to undermine the classical privilege of the viewer.[63] He deploys a similar strategy here as well, for the dark area of the drowning in the central foreground – surrounded by other bodies bobbing in the field of light nearby – extends downward to the spot where the viewer presumably stands.

In this feature of the painting, Turner interweaves suggestions he makes in a series of related works and takes them further. The composition of this painting shares much with that in the *Snow Storm*, which places the image of a steamboat in the centre surrounded by the swirls and heaves of the storm and water, as well as *Shade and Darkness*, which features the swirling motion of the tempest above darker images of those who survived the flood. In *Light and Colour*, however, the tempest circles around what one could call a sunscape similar to that in the later painting *The Angel standing in the Sun* (1846), in which an angel as well as characters from biblical tales appear inside the sun's fiery world.[64] In *Light and Colour*, Turner directly juxtaposes stormscape and sunscape, painting the swirling tempest in such a way that it also outlines the circle of the sun. One could argue that here the sun gives rise to the Deluge and is partially shrouded in its effects. But because the vortex of the tempest directly outlines the shape of the sun, in this painting the Deluge and the sun are part of a single phenomenon, a destructive process that encompasses them both. Furthermore, because Turner deemphasizes the rectilinear frame on which he relies in virtually all of his other works and accentuates instead the circular outline of the image, forcing the viewer to peer into this image from a site amid the maelstrom, he suggests that this disastrous swirling expands limitlessly beyond the canvas. Rather than establishing the privilege of the viewer, he implies that the catastrophe it depicts engulfs all human beings, indeed all forms of life subject to that destructive process. Here we encounter that feature of Turner that, according to Deleuze, does not merely represent catastrophe but creates paintings that are "catastrophes in themselves and for those who view them."[65]

Through these various suggestions, this painting offers a stunningly precise counterpart of what Shelley's poem evokes through the figure of Life, for both depict a force that exceeds even the sun as it produces a devastating temporal and material process. Like the poem, this painting incorporates this overall view into its local details as well. If one looks closely, one can see that the painting makes it difficult to distinguish between the heads of the drowning and bubbles; it thus hints that human beings are little more than froth upon these turbulent seas. In this regard, the painting is significantly bolder than the caption Turner appended to it from *The Fallacies of Hope*:

> The ark stood firm on Ararat: th' returning Sun
> Exhaled earth's humid bubbles, and emulous of light,
> Reflected her lost forms, each in prismatic guise
> Hope's harbinger, ephemeral as the summer fly
> Which rises, flits, expands and dies.[66]

These lines suggest that the sun, on coming out after the Deluge, draws forth from the earth its "humid bubbles," which rise up, in nearly Burkean parlance, as summer flies to flit about and then expire. This imagery recalls a moment near the end of Canto 4 of *Childe Harold*, a poem Turner knew well, in which Lord Byron refers to the bubbles rising to the surface of the sea from those drowning after shipwrecks; they may also allude, as Gage proposes, to a passage in *Prometheus Unbound*, which Turner seems to have encountered by this time, in which the sun sucks bubbles from watery depths.[67] But the painting goes much further than such allusions suggest. By associating the bubbles with floating human beings, the painting depicts the latter as ephemeral as the flies of a summer day; it is not merely the human exhalations that become bubbles, but those human beings themselves.

Further aspects of the painting's bubbles point to still other implications. By painting the bubbles not only in the darker encircling zone but also in the field of light, Turner suggests that they are engulfed in a sea of bright fire, inundated by the storm that is the sun. Indeed, the poetic lines hint at this possibility, for if we take them literally, the sun itself exhales those bubbles. Thus it is appropriate that John Gage suggests that these prismatic bubbles are "emblems of fallacious hope," for while they visually substitute for the biblical rainbow, their emphemeral status undermines the notion of a covenant.[68] Despite the title and caption, the sun is not returning after the Deluge but is an intrinsic part of it, a fiery inundation in which these bubbles are suspended; rather than surviving the Deluge, as the reference to Ararat implies, humanity becomes froth on the surface of these seas, denizens of the materiality of a post-covenantal world. Here the painting draws close to *The Triumph of Life*, which describes those caught up in the tempest as "like bubbles on an eddying flood" (458) – a flood, one must remember, that swirls around Life's cold glare, much as Turner's vortex surrounds this glaring sunscape. But both poet and painter dare to go a further step: Shelley associates the figure of Life with the "bubble" on which "[f]igures ever new" arise and fade away (248–9), hinting that this blank orb is also a mere bubble, another shape surrounding a void. In much the same way, Turner paints these bubbles as little versions of the sun itself, small echoes or reflections of the larger red circle surrounding a yellow centre; as a result, the sun begins to appear as a bubble in its own right, a bright but empty radiance. Indeed, as Costello argues, the viewer sees the sun *through* a bubble, as the movement of colour across the painting's central, round surface suggests, a possibility that accentuates once again the process of perception.[69] But this possibility hints in turn that, as Pressly remarks, this "entire composition is one giant bubble that, emulous of light, will soon burst asunder."[70] The bubble of the subject is also the sun, its perception, and its representation, for the nullity on each level ramifies across the rest. The blank light speaks of a logic that operates across all these domains, hollowing out every dimension of visuality.

III

By the early 1840s, then, Turner had taken his exploration of the sun's obliterating light quite far, making explicit several of the most telling implications of the shift to a new regime of representation. The close affinities between Turner's paintings and a moment in *The Triumph* point to a wholesale cultural transformation that took place in the arenas of poetry and painting alike and that produced a series of related changes across a host of interlinked registers. In pursuing these concerns, moreover, Turner clarified how the void that now operates through a post-covenantal materiality can appear precisely as a blank light, a force that, while eliciting phenomena, can cancel them as well.

But his achievement in this respect does not bring his consideration of these themes to an end; in some of his final paintings, he ponders key questions anew, sketching alternative ways to consider still further implications of these concerns, depicting what transpires after the sun and world have both disappeared, when both give way to a light that is nothing more than light, to the visibility of the mere *there is*. While one must be cautious in interpreting these late images, many of which were left incomplete, several are nevertheless in a sufficiently finished state to indicate new approaches that interested him in his final phase.[71]

As we have seen, Turner had long verged on effacing details of landscape in favour of accentuating colour, whether in certain watercolours or in the oil paintings on which Hazlitt comments. In one of his final paintings, *Norham Castle, Sunrise* (c. 1845, Figure 4), he pursues this exploration further. Speaking for virtually the entire critical tradition, Andrew Wilton remarks that in this painting, "the whole scene seems to dissolve in light."[72] This image ostensibly depicts the soft light of dawn, a quiet brilliance that radiates from the undramatic, tender moment of the sun's emergence. A muted light blanks out the details of the world, forcing one to guess at its features without actually discerning them clearly. But this ravishing light is not innocent: by taking us further away from objects into pure colour, by effacing the difference between entire categories of earthly forms, the painting takes us further into what Hazlitt

Figure 4 J.M.W. Turner, *Norham Castle, Sunrise* (c. 1845). Photo copyright Tate Gallery, Creative Commons, CC-BY-NC-ND (3.0 Unported).

called the void, into a domain almost completely released from the visibility of the world.

Thus *Norham Castle: Sunrise* verges on becoming an image of an absolute light. D.H. Lawrence, responding to this aspect of the painting, asserts that it is "the last word that can be uttered, before the blazing and timeless silence." With only one more step, the painter would have entered wholly into that silence: "If Turner had ever painted his last picture, it would have been a white, incandescent surface."[73] But in that case, blank incandescence is already at work here through the painting's power to convey this suggestion. What Turner elsewhere depicts as the sun's power to erase the world appears here through an implied event that has evacuated the landscape's objects and forms – one that, as Blanchot would propose, has already taken place, displacing the visible field from itself. An annihilating power lies beneath the colours of this painting, so that the white light of which Lawrence speaks makes possible the emergence of the supremely fragile loveliness of these colours. In effect, the painting depicts what transpires in the space of an erasure that has already taken place, a blanking out that has left this worldless world behind: this light evokes enough of the world that one can sense the force of that prior annihilation. Here the atheological mysticism I mentioned above appears in a new mode, not in the frenzy of a Bataillean expenditure but in the serenity of disappearance, not of an absolute light but of an absolutely muted visual domain. The result is an image that blends a blank light and what can still be seen, the invisible and the visible, nonbeing and being, nothing and something, in a stunning luminescence on the verge of disappearing.

By taking us into this liminal domain, Turner moves past Shelley and draws closer to those aspects of Wordsworth's poetry we explored in chapter one. As we have seen, Wordsworth suggests that by discovering the power of sound, one can "breathe an elevated mood by form / Or image unprofaned," survive one's thoroughly ungrounded state, and enter into an absolutely minimal existence. In much the same way, *Norham Castle: Sunrise* proposes that by responding to the power of light that obscures both form and image, one may apprehend that state. In both cases, the appeal of a severely denuded affect – one without content, without the attributes of any specific mood – arises in response to what Lyotard calls a "timbre, tone, nuance in one or other of the dispositions of sensibility" – including, as we can now see, colour – and can thus apprehend the *there is*, the sheer facticity of a world. But where Wordsworth depicts this state as arising before the entry into a fully conscious, affective life, Turner paints a state after the subject has dissolved into what colour can convey. In erasing the forms of the world, he evokes the mood of those who, having lived on through a certain annihilation, enter into another version of the "sentiment of being," the empty bliss of mere existence.

But one should not suggest that this painting captures the whole of the late Turner. Other perspectives on these themes appear at virtually the same moment. In *Sunrise with Sea Monsters* (c. 1845, Figure 5), a pale white and yellow light sweeps across most of the upper two-thirds of the image, referring neither to sunrise, nor any phase of the day, nor any feature of an actual landscape. Here Turner blanks out the world without hinting at what has vanished, leaving only a light without origin and without a world to make visible. This image displays the full consequences of dismantling the classical regime of representation: without a source in the sun, without making the world of objects appear, light now insists as nothing more than light itself, making only itself visible, shining with a blank radiance without justification or alibi.

Yet the painting does not allow the viewer to melt away into a scene of pure disappearance. On the lower third of the image or so it presents us not so much with monsters as portions of fish or sea life that it assembles in such a way that two separated eyes, above something that almost suggests a mouth, seem to respond cryptically, obliquely, to the viewer, as if providing a hideous distortion

Figure 5   J.M.W. Turner, *Sunrise with Sea Monsters* (c. 1845). Photo: Tate Gallery, CC-BY-NC-ND (3.0 Unported).

of human gaze or speech. This image does not attempt to represent a mytho-logical, historical, or empirical reality, for it evokes instead the dissolution of human embodiment not simply into the nonhuman but also into a disorga-nized, incoherent, unrecognizable version of the nonhuman. It thus reminds us of the Rousseau who appears to be an old tree root with discoloured grass in *The Triumph of Life* or of the unbearably aged face of Moneta who speaks in *The Fall of Hyperion*. In a similar fashion, Turner tries out a proto-surrealist composite image, assembling various features of what are no longer coherent sea creatures into what does not quite come together as a face, hinting in his own way at what Keats evokes with Titans whose words bubble and lash in the rumbles of the waves. It is as if in this scene the void addresses us, garbling up a ragged sound to announce the world's dissolution.

In providing an image of such horror, *Sunrise with Sea Monsters* transforms a range of suggestions that appear in Turner's earlier works. Here again, as in *Regulus*, one enters into a kind of dream or hallucination that, empirically impossible, nevertheless captures the subject's incoherence in visual form. In this image, one sees the very thing of which the Lacanian mirror stage is meant to relieve the subject: the lack of the unity of the body and its dispositions.[74] Here one encounters a shattering of the visuality on which the initial version of the ego founds itself. Thus one cannot explain these images by tracing them back to Turner's late, quasi-scientific interest in painting sea creatures, nor further back to his longstanding use of reptilian creatures as signs of earth's geological and paleontological history or of what witnesses and survives the Deluge, for they do not possess the form of those emblems, lacking the integrity even of chthonic embodiment.[75] These formless forms may evoke instead the possibility Turner explores in the unfinished canvas *Disaster at Sea* (c. 1833–5), which contains fragments of human bodies, the images of which, according to Costello, indicate that "Turner, in his search for more and more extreme moments of decomposition, has come to the very limit of representability."[76] In *Sunrise with Sea Monsters*, Turner moves past that limit, capturing an element of dismemberment not through human but creaturely fragments, not in a scene of drowning but of what persists after the Deluge has mutilated creaturely existence.

By juxtaposing these upper and lower portions, the painting suggests that what blanks out the world may also radically deform embodiment, cancelling the versions of gaze, voice, and personhood embedded in the viewing subject. This image coheres only on the level of speculative thought, for Turner proposes that the unworking of phenomenology is simultaneously that of psychoanalysis. It is impossible not to conclude that this painting operates on as sophisticated a level as the philosophical or poetic works of the period; indeed it makes clear, if it were not already clear enough, that a profoundly speculative ethos shaped Turner's work throughout his career. This painting captures what it takes to be the unworking of the world on both levels at once: it moves beyond the narratives implied in the histories of the earth or of life, but also beyond a subject who can orient itself in the world through its identification with a coherent body. It plunges us into a condition after being, appearance, subjectivity, and embodiment have all been dissolved.

One might be tempted to say that in this painting, Turner confronts the fact of his own mortality, knowing that after this phase of his work he had little time left in which to live. Might this image arise from his attempt to practise a being-towards-death, to cultivate an authentic response to his demise? But this scene includes no human figure, not even the minimal, almost abstract surrogate visible in a roughly analogous painting, Caspar David Friedrich's *Monk by the Sea*; on the contrary, here no one sees, no subject endures to register this sight. Should one then suggest that the painting captures what appears when the world is gone, when humanity is extinct, when the dynamics of natural history have erased the species? Is this the world without us? But in this image the sun (and any sunrise or sunset) is gone as well: this is not a substantial world from which human beings have disappeared but the void from which the world arose and into which it will dissolve, from which the sun itself emerged and into which it too will die, the void that has always been present within and as the world itself.

Yet the light that flows across this canvas is beautiful – not with the beauty one can recognize from any empirical object but rather a beauty on another level, one that inheres in what Lyotard would call the timbre of the *there is*, in the useless persistence of existence, the implacable flow of nonmortality. Who knew that the void was beautiful? Yet Turner juxtaposes this beauty with the horror of that mutilated nonbody, the persistence of an assemblage after its destruction, or the radical incoherence that has always persisted but that the mirror image masks. One might see in this single image, then, *both* bliss and horror. One might as a result conclude that these two affects arise when emotion, having been emptied out, registers the event of that erasure. But since, as Wordsworth would suggest, the bliss of being is also the bliss inherent in being itself, one might better surmise that this juxtaposition, rather than pointing back to any affective response, speaks instead of a bliss or horror that, arising where subject and world have both disappeared, exceeds any such terms, eludes even these scenarios. Thus the painting hints at this beauty and this horror but evacuates them as well under the serene light of what dissolves affect into the scene itself.

This is no sunrise with sea monsters; this is a blank light flowing over the nonsubject – not over the sea of time and space, but over the sheer *there is* of the void. Here subject and object, viewer and viewed, evaporate into a sensibility that uselessly insists without purpose and without end. Here shines a light without light, the moodless mood of a time without present, the blank splendour of mere existence.

Notes

Introduction

1 See Part Two of the 1798–9 *Prelude*, lines 354–6, 357–8. Here I rely on the edition of the poem presented in Wordsworth, *The Prelude, 1798–1799*, ed. Stephen Parrish (Ithaca, NY: Cornell University Press, 1977), 43–67.

2 I thank Tilottama Rajan for pointing out the relevance of this passage in a response to a presentation of an early version of chapter one below. That comment contributed greatly towards my eventually discerning the themes of this book.

3 Emmanuel Levinas, *Existence & Existents*, trans. Alphonso Lingis (Pittsburgh, PA: Duquesne University Press, 1978), 52–3.

4 Levinas, 56.

5 Here I borrow the term "nonsubject" from Rei Terada, *Feeling in Theory: Emotion after the "Death of the Subject"* (Cambridge, MA: Harvard University Press, 2001), 154.

6 Levinas, 55, 58.

7 Maurice Blanchot, *The Step Not Beyond*, trans. Lycette Nelson (Albany: State University of New York Press, 1992), 1. On the complexity of the terms in the book's title, see Nelson's introduction, xvi-xvii.

8 See Rodolphe Gasché, *The Idea of Form: Rethinking Kant's Aesthetics* (Redwood City, CA: Stanford University Press, 2003), 18–26, 97. The phrase "bare existence" might seem to allude to a range of passages in Romantic literature that rely on the adjective "bare" with a specific resonance of their own; it might also call to mind Giorgio Agamben's concept of "bare life," which has a precise significance quite removed from the themes of this book. See Agamben, *Homo Sacer: Sovereign Power and Bare Life*, trans. Daniel Heller-Roazen (Redwood City, CA: Stanford University Press, 1998).

9 Denis Hollier, "The Dualist Materialism of Georges Bataille," *Yale French Studies* 78 (1990): 133.

10 Jacques Derrida, *Margins of Philosophy*, trans. Alan Bass (Chicago: University of Chicago Press, 1982), 7.

11 Tilottama Rajan, *Deconstruction and the Remainders of Phenomenology: Sartre, Derrida, Foucault, Baudrillard* (Redwood City, CA: Stanford University Press, 2002).

12 Rajan, 72.

13 Rajan, 80.

14 See Blanchot, "Literature and the Right to Death," where literature is "the presence of things before the *world* exists, their perseverance after the world has disappeared, the stubbornness of what remains when everything vanishes and the dumbfoundedness of what appears when nothing exists." *The Gaze of Orpheus and Other Literary Essays*, ed. P. Adams Sitney, trans. Lydia Davis (Barrytown, NY: Station Hill Press, 1981), 47. For Blanchot in this essay, literature is itself the *there is*, as he signals in a note directly referring to Levinas on the *there is* and reinforces when he depicts the literary work as the "horror of existence deprived of the world" (51n, 52). On Blanchot's deployment of the *there is* in his initial theory of literature, see Rajan, 82, and Leslie Hill, *Blanchot: Extreme Contemporary* (New York: Routledge, 1997), 62–3, 110–16; cf. Gerald L. Bruns, *Maurice Blanchot and the Refusal of Philosophy* (Baltimore: Johns Hopkins University Press, 1997), 56–77.

15 Rajan, 80.

16 Blanchot, *The Space of Literature*, trans. Ann Smock (Lincoln: University of Nebraska Press, 1982), 112, 113, 116.

17 Blanchot, *Space*, 117.

18 Blanchot, *Space*, 155. On being-towards-death, see Martin Heidegger, *Being and Time*, trans. John Macquarrie & Edward Robinson (London: SCM Press, 1962), 307; for the various elaborations of his critique of Heidegger, see Blanchot, *Space*, 87–119, 147–55; *The Step Not Beyond*, 93–100, 106–10, 123–5; and *The Writing of the Disaster*, trans. Ann Smock (Lincoln: University of Nebraska Press, 1986), 3, 13–33, 39–40, 65–72, 117–18, 121. On the response to Heidegger in *Space*, see Hill, 114–27.

19 *The Step Not Beyond*, 123; John D. Caputo, *The Prayers and Tears of Jacques Derrida: Religion without Religion* (Bloomington: Indiana University Press, 1997), 84.

20 Blanchot, *The Writing of the Disaster*, 1, 5, 8, 9, 15.

21 See *Pas*, translated as "Pace Not(s)," in Derrida, *Parages*, ed. John P. Leavey, trans. Tom Conley et al. (Redwood City, CA: Stanford University Press, 2011), 78.

22 See Blanchot, *Space*, 103: "Whoever dwells with negation cannot use it." In this regard, of course, Blanchot shares much with one of his chief interlocutors, Georges Bataille, whose perpetual theme was precisely an expenditure without return, a heterology that can never be incorporated into any economy. For a key statement in this regard, see Bataille, "The Notion of Expenditure," in *Visions of Excess: Selected Writings, 1927–1939*, ed. and trans. Allan Stoekl (Minneapolis:

University of Minnesota Press, 1985), 116–29; for a classic discussion of this theme in Bataille, see Derrida, "From Restricted to General Economy: A Hegelianism without Reserve," in *Writing and Difference*, trans. Alan Bass (Chicago: University of Chicago Press, 1978), 251–77.

23 See Quentin Meillassoux, *After Finitude: An Essay on the Necessity of Contingency*, trans. Ray Brassier (New York: Continuum, 2008), especially 8–27.

24 Ray Brassier, *Nihil Unbound: Enlightenment and Extinction* (New York: Palgrave Macmillan, 2007), 223. See Lyotard, *The Inhuman: Reflections on Time*, trans. Geoffrey Bennington and Rachel Bowlby (Redwood City, CA: Stanford University Press, 1991), 9.

25 Brassier, 232.

26 For the foremost treatments of process in the speculative realist canon, see Iain Hamilton Grant, *Philosophies of Nature after Schelling* (New York: Continuum, 2008) and "Mining Conditions: A Response to Harman," in *The Speculative Turn: Continental Materialism and Realism*, ed. Levi Bryant, Nick Srnicek, and Graham Harman (Melbourne: re.press, 2011), 41–6. For a recent analysis of the place of a Lucretian understanding of process within Romanticism, see Amanda Jo Goldstein, *Sweet Science: Romantic Materialism and the New Logics of Life* (Chicago: University of Chicago Press, 2017).

27 David Collings, *Disastrous Subjectivities: Romanticism, Modernity, and the Real* (Toronto: University of Toronto Press, 2019), 3–21.

28 Reinhart Koselleck, *Futures Past: On the Semantics of Historical Time*, trans. Keith Tribe (New York: Columbia University Press, 2004), 22.

29 Joan Copjec, *Imagine There's No Woman: Ethics and Sublimation* (Cambridge, MA: MIT Press, 2002), 95–6, 94.

30 I borrow the term "state-thought" from Stefano Harney and Fred Moten, *The Undercommons: Fugitive Planning & Black Study* (Brooklyn: Minor Compositions, distributed by Autonomedia, 2013), 54.

31 Slavoj Žižek, *The Parallax View* (Cambridge, MA: MIT Press, 2006), 4.

32 Blanchot, *Space*, 163.

33 On this aspect of *The Monk*, see Collings, *Monstrous Society: Reciprocity, Discipline, and the Political Uncanny, c. 1780–1848* (Bucknell, PA: Bucknell University Press, 2009), 149–54.

34 For the reading of the Wordsworth passage on which I rely here, see *Disastrous Subjectivities*, 84–108.

35 Hill, 195.

36 Donald H. Reiman, *The Study of Modern Manuscripts: Public, Confidential, and Private* (Baltimore: Johns Hopkins University Press, 1993), 1–37.

37 Marc D. Mazur, *Unread: The (Un)published Texts of Romanticism* (The Electronic Thesis and Dissertation Depository, 2018), number 5784, 12. https://ir.lib.uwo.ca/etd/5784/. See Blanchot, "The Essential Solitude," in *Space*, 19–34.

38 Mazur, 29, 30–1.

39 See Jean-Luc Nancy, *The Inoperative Community*, ed. Peter Connor, trans. Connor et al. (Minneapolis: University of Minnesota Press, 1991), and the response by Blanchot, *The Unavowable Community*, trans. Pierre Joris (Barrytown, NY: Station Hill Press, 1988). The French title of Nancy's text, *La communauté désoeuvrée*, invokes the term *désoeuvrément*, or worklessness, central to Blanchot's thought; on this question see Joris, "Translator's Preface" to *The Unavowable Community*, xxii–xxv.

40 Novalis [Friedrich von Hardenburg], *Fichte Studies*, ed. Jane Kneller (Cambridge: Cambridge University Press, 2003), 3.

41 Novalis, 15. The original act does not take place in infancy, prior to language, but rather in a state prior to reflection. On the question of language, see Giorgio Agamben, *Infancy & History: Essays on the Destruction of Experience*, trans. Liz Heron (New York: Verso, 1993), 47–8.

42 Jane Kneller, "Introduction" to Novalis, *Fichte Studies*, xiv. As Alexander M. Schlutz argues, this situation leads to the rather tricky relation between feeling and reflection: "[S]ince feeling is not a conscious form of knowledge, it remains dependent on reflection to determine its content, which would otherwise never be known. Feeling thus needs reflection, just as reflection depends on feeling, and the hierarchy between the two modes of thought constantly subverts itself." See Schlutz, *Mind's World: Imagination and Subjectivity from Descartes to Romanticism* (Seattle: University of Washington Press, 2009), 169.

43 Novalis, 31.

44 Novalis, 6.

45 Thomas Pfau, *Romantic Moods: Paranoia, Trauma, and Melancholy, 1790–1840* (Baltimore: Johns Hopkins University Press, 2005), 61.

46 Martin Heidegger, *The Fundamental Problems of Metaphysics: World, Finitude, Solitude*, trans. William McNeill and Nicholas Walker (Bloomington: Indiana University Press, 1995), 65, as modified and quoted in Pfau, 10.

47 Pfau, 10.

48 Levinas, 68, 71.

49 Kate Singer, *Romantic Vacancy: The Poetics of Gender, Affect, and Radical Speculation* (Albany: State University of New York Press, 2019).

50 Forest Pyle, *Art's Undoing: In the Wake of a Radical Aestheticism* (New York: Fordham University Press, 2014), 4–5.

51 Certain moments in meditative prose works in the period, especially those regarding the troubled affective state of solitary men wandering in the natural landscape, establish their tone by hovering perpetually at one remove from the condition of mere existence, recording its imprint, as it were, without entering more closely into it. They thus highlight, by contrast, the unique status of those works that dare to become more intimate with radical erasure. For relevant instances in this regard, see the meditation on "the corrosive power that lies concealed in the natural universe" in Johann Wolfgang von Goethe, *The Sorrows*

of Young Werther, trans. Michael Hulse (New York: Penguin, 1989), 66; the protagonist's "hopeless thought that all was but a dream" in Georg Büchner, "Lenz," *The Major Works*, ed. Matthew Wilson Smith, trans. Henry J. Schmidt (New York: Norton, 2012), 87; and the remark on the incertitude, uselessness, and emptiness of all things in Étienne Pivert de Senancourt, *Obermann* (London: William Rider & Son, 1907), 17.

52 Georg Wilhelm Friedrich Hegel, *Hegel's Science of Logic*, trans. A.V. Miller (Atlantic Highlands, NJ: Humanities Press International, 1969), 82–105.

53 Heidegger, *Being and Time*, 32, 34.

54 Rebecca Comay and Frank Ruda, *The Dash – The Other Side of Absolute Knowing* (Cambridge, MA: MIT Press, 2018), 91.

55 On this contrast between Derrida's work with *écriture* and Blanchot's with *écrire*, see Rajan, 83.

56 Craig Dworkin, *No Medium* (Cambridge, MA: MIT Press, 2013), 31.

57 Slavoj Žižek, *Interrogating the Real*, ed. Rex Butler and Scott Stephens (New York: Continuum, 2005), 313.

58 Jean-François Lyotard, *The Inhuman: Reflections on Time*, 99, 112.

59 Lyotard, 140. I thank Rasmus Simonsen for drawing my attention to these passages in Lyotard in response to a presentation of an early version of chapter one below, passages that have helped me shape my argument here and elsewhere in this book.

60 Lyotard, 90.

61 See Rajan, "Mary Shelley's 'Mathilda': Melancholy and the Political Economy of Romanticism," *Studies in the Novel* 26 (1994): 46; and "Keats, Poetry, and 'The Absence of the Work,'" *Modern Philology* 95 (1998), 350.

62 Sara Guyer, *Romanticism after Auschwitz* (Redwood City, CA: Stanford University Press, 2007), 154–9.

63 Anne-Lise François, *Open Secrets: The Literature of Uncounted Experience* (Redwood City, CA: Stanford University Press, 2008).

64 Jacques Khalip, *Anonymous Life: Romanticism and Dispossession* (Redwood City, CA: Stanford University Press, 2009).

65 David L. Clark, "Schelling's Wartime: Philosophy and Violence in the Age of Napoleon," *European Romantic Review* 19 (2008): 139–48; "Goya's Scarcity," *Constellations of a Contemporary Romanticism*, ed. Jacques Khalip and Forest Pyle (New York: Fordham University Press, 2016), 88–121; and "Insult to Injury: Romantic Wartime and the Desecrated Corpse," *European Romantic Review* 30 (2019): 275–85.

66 Khalip, *Last Things: Disastrous Form from Kant to Hujar* (New York: Fordham University Press, 2018), 9, 13.

67 Khalip, *Last Things*, 22.

68 Khalip, *Last Things*, 68.

69 David Collings, *The Rubble of Culture: Debris of an Extinct Thought* (London: Open Humanities Press, 2023), 13–15; Jan Zalasiewicz et al., "Stratigraphy

of the Anthropocene," *Philosophical Transactions of the Royal Society A*, 369 (13 March 2011): 1038.

70 On thinking the death of thinking, see Brassier, 223; on how the extinction of humanity includes "those who would think this idea and bear witness to its reality," see Eugene Thacker, "Notes on Extinction and Existence," *Configurations* 20 (2012): 137.

71 Cf. Brassier's concluding sentence (239), in which he suggests that one must recognize that "philosophy is neither a medium of affirmation nor a source of justification, but rather the organon of extinction."

Chapter 1

1 I use the designation "quasi-cognitive" not to indicate any reservation about interpreting mood as cognitive but rather to be precise about what region of cognition it occupies – that is, a zone prior to and underlying conscious articulation. In doing so, I rely on the approach outlined by Pfau in *Romantic Moods*, 12–13.

2 Pfau, *Romantic Moods*, 10.

3 Pfau, *Romantic Moods*, 12.

4 Pfau, *Romantic Moods*, 11, 25.

5 I discuss this shift in slightly different terms in *Wordsworthian Errancies: The Poetics of Cultural Dismemberment* (Baltimore: Johns Hopkins University Press, 1994), 18–49. Because I wish to focus on the shift between moods, my argument here leaves out of view the place of melancholy in the tropological relations between moods. In principle, however, it must be possible to decipher melancholy's position within those relations.

6 Martin Heidegger, *Being and Time*; Pfau, *Romantic Moods*, 2; 4–7.

7 On post-Kantian engagements with mood, especially in Novalis, Hegel, and Hölderlin, see Pfau, 27–74.

8 For an exemplary discussion of the troping of figural evocations of mood, see Terada's account of de Man's arguments regarding the rhetoric of mood; see Terada, *Feeling in Theory*, 48–89.

9 In my discussion of these poems, I draw on aspects of the argument in my *Wordsworthian Errancies*, 100–17. The poet revises the contents and title of the poem "Old Man Travelling" in later editions; here I discuss the 1798 version. Although "The Old Cumberland Beggar" was not published until the 1800 edition of *Lyrical Ballads*, Wordsworth composed it in January to March 1798, in the midst of the process of composing many poems for the first edition of 1798. See *William Wordsworth*, ed. Stephen Gill, 687.

10 In discussing these poems, I draw on aspects of the argument in *Wordsworthian Errancies*, 69–99. See MS. D of *The Ruined Cottage* in Wordsworth, *The Ruined*

Cottage and *The Pedlar*, ed. James Butler (Ithaca, NY: Cornell University Press, 1979), 43–75.

11 Collings, *Wordsworthian Errancies*, 69–99.

12 Compare Joel Faflak, *Romantic Psychoanalysis: The Burden of the Mystery* (Albany: State University of New York Press, 2008), 79–91.

13 Maurice Merleau-Ponty, *Phenomenology of Perception*, trans. Colin Smith (New York: Routledge, 2002).

14 Wordsworth, *The Prelude, 1798–1799*, 43–67.

15 Here I pursue the possibility, broached by Nancy Yousef, that one cannot read these lines as referring simply to the death of the mother; see *Isolated Cases: The Anxieties of Autonomy in Enlightenment Philosophy and Romantic Literature* (Ithaca, NY: Cornell University Press, 2004), 124.

16 Levinas, 45–60.

17 Blanchot, *The Step Not Beyond*, 123.

18 Geoffrey H. Hartman, *The Unremarkable Wordsworth* (Minneapolis: University of Minnesota Press, 1987), 22.

19 Yousef, *Isolated Cases*.

20 Samuel Taylor Coleridge, *Opus Maximum*, ed. Thomas McFarland and Nicholas Halmi (Princeton, NJ: Princeton University Press, 2002), 119–33. On Coleridge's theory of the person in that work, see Pfau, *Minding the Modern: Human Agency, Intellectual Traditions, and Responsible Knowledge* (Notre Dame, IN: University of Notre Dame Press, 2013), 565–6, 574–5; for a contrast between Coleridge's position here and related passages in *The Prelude*, see the same work, 576–8.

21 For relevant discussions of the ethical dimension of this level of phenomenological experience, see Levinas, *Totality and Infinity: An Essay on Exteriority*, trans. Alphonso Lingis (Pittsburgh, PA: Duquesne University Press, 1969), and *Otherwise than Being: Or Beyond Essence*, trans. Alphonso Lingis (Pittsburgh, PA: Duquesne University Press, 1998).

22 The passage may not be fully integrated into the rhetoric of its context because Wordsworth wrote it originally as a separate manuscript draft emerging out of work for the Pedlar. Never incorporating it into a draft of *The Ruined Cottage*, he eventually revised it and brought it into *The Prelude* in the present context: see *The Ruined Cottage* and *The Pedlar*, 371.

23 Lyotard, 140–1.

24 Lyotard, 142.

25 Adam Potkay, "Wordsworth and the Ethics of Things," *PMLA* 123.2 (2008): 400.

26 Lyotard, 141.

27 In *Looking Away: Phenomenality and Dissatisfaction, Kant to Adorno* (Cambridge, MA: Harvard University Press, 2009), 3–4, Rei Terada suggests that "[a]fter Kant, one needs *particularly ephemeral phenomenal experiences*, perceptions that seem below or marginal to normal appearance, to figure the possibility of fleeting relief

from the pressure to endorse what Kant calls the world 'as is.'" This passage thus opens up the possibility that the poet may seek that relief or attempt to curb it; on this question, see the discussion of the Ode below.

28 Novalis, 15, 6.

29 On the grammatical complexity of "sentiment of being," compare Potkay, "Wordsworth," 397.

30 Potkay, "Wordsworth," 397.

31 Heidegger, *What Is Philosophy?* (London: Vision, 1963), 51–3, 79–85.

32 William Wordsworth, *William Wordsworth*, ed. Stephen Gill (Oxford: Oxford University Press, 1984), 147.

33 *Wordsworth*, ed. Gill, 255; 269–70.

34 On the happiness of the dead and on the poem's questioning of why one should fear death, see Mary Jacobus, *Romantic Things: A Tree, a Rock, a Cloud* (Chicago: University of Chicago Press, 2012), 117.

35 In my discussion of the Ode I rely on *Wordsworth*, ed. Gill, 297–302.

36 For a treatment of the figurative structure of the Ode that establishes that these lines in stanza nine are unusual for not being affiliated with other moments in the poem, see Helen Vendler, "Lionel Trilling and the Immortality Ode," *Salmagundi* 41 (1978): 82.

37 It would not be difficult to bear out this point by following the practice of several generations of critics and citing Wordsworth's discussions late in his life of his childhood experience. But I prefer to rely on the evidence of the poems themselves, keeping the focus on a philosophically weighted poetics rather than on the poet's biography.

38 Levinas, *Existence*, 51–60.

39 Simon Jarvis, *Wordsworth's Philosophic Song* (Cambridge: Cambridge University Press, 2007), 198.

40 See the discussion of the mathematical sublime in Immanuel Kant, *Critique of the Power of Judgment*, ed. Paul Guyer, trans. Paul Guyer and Eric Matthews (Cambridge: Cambridge University Press, 2000), 141–3.

41 Vendler, 70, 84. For a critical discussion of Vendler's argument, see Jeffrey C. Robinson, "The Immortality Ode: Lionel Trilling and Helen Vendler," *The Wordsworth Circle* 12 (1981): 64–70.

42 Terada, *Looking Away*.

43 For two key arguments that the Ode marks the poet's political retreat, see Marjorie Levinson, *Wordsworth's Great Period Poems: Four Essays* (Cambridge: Cambridge University Press, 1986), 80–100, and Jamison Kantor, "Immortality, Romanticism, and the Limit of the Liberal Imagination," *PMLA* 133 (2018): 508–25.

44 Khalip, *Last Things*, 9.

45 Here I allude to the subtitle of Rei Terada, *Feeling in Theory: Emotion after the "Death of the Subject."*

Chapter 2

1 Tilottama Rajan, "Coleridge, Wordsworth, and the Textual Abject," *The Wordsworth Circle* 24 (1993): 61–8.

2 On the relation to Wordsworth, see Rajan, 62.

3 Rajan, "Coleridge," 68.

4 For a classic study of Coleridge's shift from a pantheist to a Trinitarian theology, see Thomas McFarland, *Coleridge and the Pantheist Tradition* (Oxford: Clarendon Press, 1969).

5 Pfau, *Minding the Modern*.

6 Immanuel Kant, *Critique of the Power of Judgment*, ed. Paul Guyer, trans. Paul Guyer and Eric Matthews (Cambridge: Cambridge University Press, 2000), 231–346.

7 Howard Caygill, *Art of Judgment* (Oxford: Basil Blackwell, 1989), 2–3; Jean-François Lyotard, *Lessons on the Analytic of the Sublime*, trans. Elizabeth Rottenberg (Redwood City, CA: Stanford University Press, 1994).

8 All quotations from Coleridge's poetry are taken from Samuel Taylor Coleridge, *The Complete Poems*, ed. William Keach (New York: Penguin, 1997) and will be cited by title and line number. This phrase is taken from "Human Life: On the Denial of Immortality," line 14, which appears on page 362.

9 On the speaker's mode of distancing in this passage, see Jean-Pierre Mileur, *Vision and Revision: Coleridge's Art of Immanence* (Berkeley: University of California Press, 1982), 41.

10 Cf. Mileur, 51.

11 Rajan, "Coleridge," 62–3, 66–7.

12 Cf. Rajan, "Coleridge," 64.

13 Mileur, vii–ix, 1–24.

14 Rajan, "Coleridge," 64.

15 Ben Brice, *Coleridge and Scepticism* (New York: Oxford University Press, 2007), 3.

16 Brice, 172.

17 Brice, 178–9.

18 Brice, 188. For similar points, see Eric Wilson, *Coleridge's Melancholia: An Anatomy of Limbo* (Gainesville: University Press of Florida, 2004), 27, 86. For an earlier, foundational analysis of the instabilities in Coleridge's conception of the relation between God and nature, an analysis pivotal to the discussion in Brice and in this chapter, see Raimonda Modiano, *Coleridge and the Concept of Nature* (Tallahassee: Florida State University Press, 1985).

19 Edward Kessler, *Coleridge's Metaphors of Being* (Princeton, NJ: Princeton University Press, 1979), 8.

20 Kessler, 137–8.

21 *The Notebooks of Samuel Taylor Coleridge*, ed. Kathleen Coburn, vol. 3: 1808–1819 (Princeton, NJ: Princeton University Press, 1973), entry 3911; as Wilson

comments, in such passages Coleridge is "pining for a completeness realized only through its absence": Wilson, 31.

22 On the contrast between "Constancy" and "Limbo," see Stephen Prickett, *Coleridge and Wordsworth: The Poetry of Growth* (Cambridge: Cambridge University Press, 1970), 200–4.

23 Murray Evans, *Sublime Coleridge: The* Opus Maximum (New York: Palgrave Macmillan, 2012), xiii, 17, 27, 29. For an extended discussion of one such demonstration, see 105–17.

24 The fact that this poem responds to that of John Donne, whom Coleridge conceived as a metaphysical poet, confirms this reading. For the relevant notebook lines from which "Limbo" and other poems are drawn, see *Notebooks*, entry 4073–4. On the response to Donne in these lines, see *Notebooks*, vol. 3: 1808–1819, *Notes*, ed. Coburn (Princeton, NJ: Princeton University Press, 1973), notes for entry 4073, and Morton Paley, *Coleridge's Later Poetry* (Oxford: Clarendon, 1996), 42–6. For more on Coleridge's response to Donne, see the discussion of this poem's final lines below.

25 I first encountered this passage in a quotation in Kessler, 83. For the correct language (Kessler writes "contemplatable" for "contemplable"), see Coleridge, *Literary Remains*, vol. 3, ed. Henry Nelson Coleridge (1838; Project Gutenberg, 2003), note to *Unum Necessarium; or the Doctrine and Practice of Repentance*, s. 1. p. 166. https://www.gutenberg.org/files/8956/8956-h/8956-h.htm. Coleridge makes a similar point in a Notebook entry of September to October 1810: "Space & Time not in God – But except under the forms of Space and Time we can predicate nothing, can bring no one even of the most abstract intellections to consciousness – What follows? – That concerning God we can neither talk sense or nonsense – except as far we talk piously or impiously.... Alas! why do we all seek by instinct for a God – a supersensual – but because we feel the insufficiency, the unsubstantiality, of all *forms*, and formal Being of itself ... and then make the <very> weakness the substratum of the Strength." See *Notebooks* 3, entry 3973.

26 See *Notebooks* 3, entry 4078; see also Frederick Burwick, "Coleridge's 'Limbo' and 'Ne Plus Ultra': The Multeity of Intertextuality," *Nineteenth Century Contexts* 9 (1985): 42–3.

27 Kessler argues that the old man awaits a response from God, "but the skies remain black and silent"; thus he is "Coleridge's most striking embodiment of the Christian paradox" (Kessler, 161).

28 Paley, 54.

29 *Marginalia*, vol. 2: *Camden to Hutton*, ed. George Whalley (Princeton, NJ: Princeton University Press, 1984), 559.

30 One should note that here the poem also alludes to Jakob Böhme's argument that the damned souls are, in Eric Wilson's words, "divorced from time and thus from meaningful action, from reality." See the thirty-fourth question (What is the miserable and horrible Estate of the Damned?) in Böhme, *Forty Questions*

Concerning the Soul, trans. John Sparrow (London: Simmons, 1647), Early English Books Online, 133–4, https://www.proquest.com/books/xl-questions-concerning -soule-propounded-dr/docview/2264190163/se-2?accountid=9681; Wilson, 12; cf. Paley, 43.

31 Kessler, 103; Wilson, xvii.

32 Kessler 69–80; Onita Vaz-Hooper, "'If Dead We Cease to Be': The Logic of Immortality in Coleridge's 'Human Life,'" *European Romantic Review* 20 (2009): 529–44. Insofar as the poem pursues this approach, it deploys a strategy characteristic of the late theological writings. A key passage of the *Opus Maximum*, for example, maintains that "[w]e affirm" that work's central postulate "<not> because we ... comprehend the affirmation, but because we clearly comprehend the absurdity of the denial" (221). On this form of negative demonstration, see Evans, 139.

33 Cf. Wilson, 169.

34 As Coleridge writes in a notebook entry, "[T]he presumption of [immortality] is at the bottom of every hope, fear, and action. Suppose for a moment an intuitive certainty that we should cease to be at a given time – the *Whole* feeling of futurity would be extinguished at the first feeling of such a certainty – and the mind would have no motive for not dying at the same moment." See *Notebooks*, entry 4356. On this passage see Kessler, 72–3.

35 My thanks to Brian McGrath for the suggestion that "gust" resonates with the theme of the ghost and phantom throughout the poem.

36 *Poetical Works, Volume II (Variorum Text)*, Part 2, ed. J.C.C. Mays (Princeton, NJ: Princeton University Press, 2001), 1101. For a contrasting reading of the revision of this line consistent with her overall account, see Vaz-Hooper, 538–9.

37 Blanchot, *Space*, 117.

38 On a flat ontology, see Levi Bryant, *The Democracy of Objects* (Ann Arbor, MI: Open Humanities Press, 2010); on the undoing of ontology through a hauntology, see Jacques Derrida, *Spectres of Marx: The State of the Debt, the Work of Mourning, & the New International*, trans. Peggy Kamuf (New York: Routledge, 1994).

39 For a key intertext here, see the passage in which Sara Guyer follows Barbara Johnson's discussion of lyric animation, apostrophe, prososopeia, and abortion; Guyer, *Reading with John Clare: Biopoetics, Sovereignty, Romanticism* (New York: Fordham, 2015), 11–20. "Human Life" for a moment deploys similar tropes to figure what one might call an animated instance of nonlife (or abortive creation), but it eventually resorts to a slightly different set of tropes as discussed below.

40 Cf. Mileur, 63–6. The prospect of interpreting nature as a nullity with restless hands would, of course, ordinarily vex Coleridge, but such a rendition of nature is not entirely outside the realm of his thought; on his difficulty in establishing a firm interpretation of nature within the context of natural religion, see Brice.

41 Kessler, 78–9; Wilson, 170–1; Vaz-Hooper, 536–7.

Chapter 3

1 On the trope of modernity, see Fredric Jameson, *A Singular Modernity: Essay on the Ontology of the Present* (New York: Verso, 2002), 34.

2 Joshua Wilner, *Feeding on Infinity: Readings in the Romantic Rhetoric of Internalization* (Baltimore: Johns Hopkins University Press, 2000), 20.

3 As Christoph Bode remarks, "If Apollo were to embody the new kind of poetry … then since the change would have occurred before the narration began, the whole epic would have to be written in this new diction." Thus the poem "collapses in self-contradiction or *aporia*." See Bode, "Hyperion, 'The Fall of Hyperion,' and Keats's Poetics," *The Wordsworth Circle* 31 (1999): 34.

4 All quotations from the poems of Keats are taken from *The Poems of John Keats*, ed. Jack Stillinger (Cambridge, MA: Harvard University Press, 1978). Passages from these poems will be cited in the text by canto and line number. For *Hyperion*, see 329–56; for *The Fall of Hyperion*, see 478–91. For "blank splendor," see *The Fall*, 1.269.

5 Reinhart Koselleck, *Futures Past*, 22. On how the poem embeds Christianity within its concerns, especially in Oceanus's declaration that "From Chaos and parental Darkness came / Light" (2.191–920), see Ronald A. Sharp, *Keats, Skepticism, and the Religion of Beauty* (Athena: University of Georgia Press, 1979), 135.

6 On how the poem is unusual for focusing exclusively on the gods, see Geoffrey Hartman, *The Fate of Reading and Other Essays* (Chicago: University of Chicago Press, 1975), 60.

7 For discussions that outline this historical allegory while complicating it, see Paul Sherwin, "Keats's Struggle with Milton in *Hyperion*," *PMLA* 93 (1978): 383–95; Alan Bewell, "The Political Implication of Keats's Classicist Aesthetics," *Studies in Romanticism* 25 (1986): 220–9; Daniel P. Watkins, *Keats's Poetry and the Politics of the Imagination* (Rutherford, NJ: Fairleigh Dickinson University Press, 1989), 91–103; Michael O'Neill, "'*When this warm scribe my hand*': Writing and History in *Hyperion* and *The Fall of Hyperion*," in *Keats and History*, ed. Nicholas Roe (Cambridge: Cambridge University Press, 1995), 143–64; Greg Kucich, "Keats's Literary Tradition and the Politics of Histriographical Invention," in *Keats and History*, 238–61; and Nicola Trott, "Keats and the Prison House of History," in *Keats and History*, 262–79.

8 Rei Terada, "Looking at the Stars Forever," *Studies in Romanticism* 50 (2011): 279–80, 289–90, 305.

9 Marjorie Levinson, *Keats's Life of Allegory: The Origins of a Style* (Oxford: Basil Blackwell, 1988), 210.

10 Carol L. Bernstein, "Subjectivity as Critique and the Critique of Subjectivity in Keats's *Hyperion*," in *After the Future: Postmodern Times and Places*, ed. Gary Shapiro (Albany: SUNY Press, 1990), 44.

11 Joel Faflak, "Romantic Psychoanalysis: Keats, Identity, and '(The Fall of) Hyperion,'" in *Lessons of Romanticism: A Critical Companion*, ed. Thomas Pfau and Robert F. Gleckner (Durham, NC: Duke University Press, 1998), 311.

12 Pfau, *Romantic Moods*, 11. While Pfau analyses Keats in relation to melancholy (see 309–78), the *Hyperion* poems depart from that pattern, for they explicitly situate themselves as evocations of trauma.

13 Jonathan Mulrooney, "How Keats Falls," *Studies in Romanticism* 50 (2011): 260. For a searching discussion of the trauma endured by Saturn and Thea, see Shahidha K. Bari, *Keats and Philosophy: The Life of Sensations* (New York: Routledge, 2012), 118–49.

14 Friedrich Nietzsche, *The Gay Science with a Prelude in Rhymes and an Appendix of Songs*, trans. Walter Kaufmann (New York: Vintage, 1974), 283.

15 Hartman, *The Fate of Reading*, 59.

16 Jacques Lacan, *The Seminar of Jacques Lacan*, ed. Jacques-Alain Miller. *Book VII: The Ethics of Psychoanalysis*, trans. Dennis Porter (New York: Norton, 1992), 184.

17 On this moment, see also Sharp, 138, and Nancy Moore Goslee, *Uriel's Eye: Miltonic Stationing and Statuary in Blake, Keats, and Shelley* (Tuscaloosa: University of Alabama Press, 1985), 83.

18 Thus as Eric Lindstrom comments, Hyperion's failure represents a "paradigm shift" in the status of the gods so that "Hyperion glosses the sunrise, but cannot control it." But this moment "presents the antitype" of the fiat that obtains far more often in Romantic poetry, the "'command to nature' to do what it always does." See Lindstrom, *Romantic Fiat: Demystification and Enchantment in Lyric Poetry* (New York: Palgrave Macmillan, 2011), 51.

19 On the poetics of watchfulness and attention in the *Hyperion* poems, see Lily Gurton-Wachter, *Watchwords: Romanticism and the Poetics of Attention* (Redwood City, CA: Stanford University Press, 2016), 141–77. On the exchange between Coelus and Hyperion and its echoes, see 144–9.

20 Terada's essay, "Looking at the Stars Forever," constitutes a *tour de force* reading of *Hyperion* through the lens of this passage, suggesting that here and elsewhere Keats resists the naturalization of political stasis in the wake of the Restoration, as noted above. Here I focus instead on what one might call the naturalization of nature, on the formation of an understanding that departs from traditional understandings of divine sovereignty over the natural world, a change with its own profound implications.

21 Marie-Hélène Huet, *The Culture of Disaster* (Chicago: University of Chicago Press, 2012), 3–4.

22 On Saturn's absolute "seclusion" even from time and space, see Bari, 120.

23 Collings, *Disastrous Subjectivities*, 84–7.

24 Collings, *Disastrous Subjectivities*, 85–6, 91–2, 96–108.

25 Bari, 132.

26 On the contrast between the first and second scenes of transformation, see Stuart M. Sperry, Jr., "Keats, Milton, and the Fall of Hyperion," *PMLA* 77 (1962): 80.

27 Blanchot, *The Step Not Beyond*, 1.

28 Blanchot, *Space*, 112; cf. *The Writing of the Disaster*, 15.

29 Blanchot, *The Writing of the Disaster*, 15. On the speaker's similarity to Moneta, see Levinson, 218; O'Neill, 163.

30 Bari, 139.

31 Susan Wolfson, *The Questioning Presence: Wordsworth, Keats, and the Interrogative Mode in Romantic Poetry* (Ithaca, NY: Cornell University Press, 1986), 358.

32 Slavoj Žižek, *The Ticklish Subject: The Absent Centre of Political Ontology* (New York: Verso, 1999), 292; italics in the original.

33 Žižek, 293.

34 Žižek, 294.

35 Sara Guyer, *Romanticism after Auschwitz* (Redwood City, CA: Stanford University Press, 2007), 155, 158; Levinas, *Existence*, 67. On the failure not to be, compare Aaron Schuster, who while meditating on a passage of *Oedipus at Colonus* in a Lacanian vein writes, "The human being is the sick animal that does not live its life but lives its failure not to be born." (This sentence is italicized in the original). See Schuster, *The Trouble with Pleasure: Deleuze and Psychoanalysis* (Cambridge, MA: MIT Press, 2016), 15.

36 Anya Taylor, "Superhuman Silence: Language in Hyperion," *Studies in English Literature, 1500–1900* 19 (1979): 676.

37 Mladen Dolar, *A Voice and Nothing More* (Cambridge, MA: MIT Press, 2006), 73; this sentence is italicized in the original.

38 Balachandra Rajan remarks that "Moneta's function … is to provoke as much as to expound, to sting her pupil into acts of definition." See Rajan, "The Two *Hyperions*: Compositions and Decompositions," in *Romanticism: A Critical Reader*, ed. Duncan Wu (Oxford: Basil Blackwell, 1995), 283.

39 See Tilottama Rajan, "Keats, Poetry, and 'The Absence of the Work,'" *Modern Philology* 95 (1998): 335. On *désoeuvrement*, Rajan cites Blanchot, *The Space of Literature*, 46. The latter passage is highly relevant to a reading of this moment in *The Fall*, for here Blanchot refers to an art that has "taken leave of the ordinary world" and thus becomes "the silence of the world, the silence of what is usual and immediate in the world": see *Space*, 47. For a related discussion, see Blanchot, "The Absence of the Book," in *The Infinite Conversation*, trans. Susan Hanson (Minneapolis: University of Minnesota Press, 1993), 422–34. Arkady Plotnitsky quotes another relevant passage from Blanchot on the "absence of the book" at the culmination of his argument on this poem and *The Triumph of Life*: see Plotnitsky, "Beyond the Inconsumable: The Catastrophic Sublime and the Destruction of Literature in Keats's *The Fall of Hyperion* and Shelley's *The Triumph of Life*," in *Cultures of Taste / Theories of Appetite: Eating Romanticism*, ed. Timothy

Morton (New York: Palgrave Macmillan, 2004), 178, quoting Blanchot, *Infinite Conversation*, 350.

40 Terada, "Looking," 298.

41 Giorgio Agamben, *Remnants of Auschwitz: The Witness and the Archive*, trans. Daniel Heller-Roazen (New York: Zone Books, 2002), 164. In turning to Agamben here, I follow the lead of Guyer, who cites this passage as she works through the question of poetry as testimony; see Guyer, 32.

42 Here I engage with Tilottama Rajan, who in a response to Marjorie Levinson argues that Keats's *Hyperion* poems are caught between the notion of literature as cultural work and a conception of its worklessness, placing these two traditions of thinking within British and German conceptions of the literary respectively. See Rajan, "Keats, Poetry," 334–51 and Levinson.

43 Compare Tilottama Rajan, *Dark Interpreter*, 191.

44 See Bewell 229; Balachandra Rajan, 278.

45 Tilottama Rajan, "Keats, Poetry," 349–50.

46 Tilottama Rajan, "Keats, Poetry," 347. On how these poems refuse a "therapeutic cure to explore identity's interminable pathology," see Faflak, *Romantic Psychoanalysis*, 230. For a discussion of how the *Hyperion* poems ultimately value a sickness without cure, see Brittany Pladek, "'In Sickness Not Ignoble': Soul-Making and the Pains of Identity in the *Hyperion* Poems," *Studies in Romanticism* 54 (2015): 401–27. This sickness may appear as well in the nausea that in the draft of *The Fall* the narrator experiences when in the poem's opening scene he first attempts to enjoy the scent of incense; see Denise Gigante, 'The Endgame of Taste: Keats, Sartre, Beckett," in *Cultures of Taste*, ed. Morton, 185.

47 Wolfson, 354; compare Plotnitsky, 167.

48 Emily Rohrbach, *Modernity's Mist: British Romanticism and the Poetics of Anticipation* (New York: Fordham University Press, 2015). See especially 2–3 on Keats and the mist of futurity; 11–12 on Jameson's treatment of the trope of modernity; and 22–3 on her decision to emphasize futurity rather than trauma. For her discussion of Keats's Odes in the context of this argument, see 77–105.

49 Tilottama Rajan, "Keats, Poetry," 348.

50 Cf. Goslee, 127.

51 Bari, 125. Mary Jacobus, drawing on the work of Jean-Luc Nancy, considers the weight of bodies and of stones in relation to the weight of meaning, but in these Keats passages, such weight may gesture towards the weight of a meaningless persistence, or rather of a meaning that persists outside meaning. See Jacobus, 121–2.

52 For the classic study of how Keats works through various positions to arrive at a religion of soul-making, see Robert Ryan, *Keats: The Religious Sense* (Princeton, NJ: Princeton University Press, 1976).

53 Cf. Hartman, *The Fate of Reading*, 66; Wolfson, 353; and Vincent Newey, "*Hyperion, The Fall of Hyperion*, and Keats's epic ambitions," in *The Cambridge*

Companion to Keats, ed. Susan J. Wolfson (New York: Cambridge University Press, 2001), 81.

54 Mulrooney, 268, 269–70.

55 Cf. Pladek, 420.

56 Pladek, 422.

57 On how Moneta's eyes thwart relationship, see O'Neill, 163; on how her visage refuses the speaker's identification with her, see Faflak, 316; see also Jacques Khalip, *Anonymous Life*, 176–7.

58 On the link between the moon's light and the light of Moneta's eyes, see Goslee, 128.

59 Terada, "Looking," 299; Tilottama Rajan, "Keats, Poetry," 335.

60 Jacques Derrida, *Cinders*, trans. Ned Lukacher (Minneapolis: University of Minnesota Press, 2014), 21.

61 Forest Pyle, *Art's Undoing*, 101–2.

62 Wolfson, 356.

63 Here I follow Mulrooney, who argues that "Keats's poetry remains relentlessly committed to the life that exists, and only exists, beyond consolation" (255).

Chapter 4

1 Katey Castellano, *The Ecology of British Romantic Conservatism, 1790–1837* (New York: Palgrave Macmillan, 2013), 159.

2 For recent, compelling accounts of Clare's opposition to his moment's biopolitical imperative, see Chris Washington, "John Clare and Biopolitics," *European Romantic Review* 25 (2014): 665–82 and Sara Guyer, *Reading with John Clare: Biopoetics, Sovereignty, Romanticism* (New York: Fordham University Press, 2015).

3 John Clare, *Poems of the Middle Period: 1822–1837*, general ed. Eric Robinson, vol. IV, ed. Robinson, David Powell, and P.M.S. Dawson (Oxford: Clarendon Press, 1998), 278, 268, 494. I am grateful to Katey Castellano for pointing out the relevance of "Nothingness of Life" and "Triumphs of Time" to the concerns of this chapter.

4 In one of the very few discussions of "Obscurity," Adam Phillips cites its exploration of obscurity to specify what he considers Clare's resistance to exposing himself as a poet to the public, reading it as "one of his finest poems, or anti-poems" that uniquely dares to celebrate oblivion; see Adam Phillips, "The Exposure of John Clare," in *John Clare in Context*, ed. Hugh Haughton, Phillips, and Geoffrey Summerfield (Cambridge: Cambridge University Press, 1994), 187. But this reading understates how Clare, rather than seeking obscurity, long attempted to cultivate an audience on whatever terms were available to him; for a lucid treatment of these concerns, see Alan Vardy, *John Clare: Politics and Poetry* (New York: Palgrave Macmillan, 2003). Indeed, the two sonnets mentioned earlier indicate that for Clare, oblivion burst the bubble of his youthful hope for distinction and perhaps fame; they speak of the dashing of his poetic hopes. Yet

as I argue here, "Obscurity" goes well beyond biographical contexts to consider broader themes.

5 For short poems that touch on related concerns, see the poems beginning with "There is a chasm in the heart of man," "The present is the funeral of the past," and "Is nothing less than naught" in *The Later Poems of John Clare, 1837–1864*, general ed. Eric Robinson, vol. I, ed. Robinson and David Powell, associate ed. Margaret Grainger (Oxford: Clarendon, 1984), 165, 173, 250.

6 Clare, *Poems of the Middle Period*, vol. IV, 256. Further references to this poem will be cited by line number in the text.

7 The sonnet thus touches on a problematic broached in the late lyric "I Am," where the absence of an other effaces the speaker's identity; Clare, *Major Works*, ed. Eric Robinson and David Powell (New York: Oxford University Press, 1984), 361. On Clare's attempt to craft a notion of identity that could subsist apart from another, see Guyer, 57–77.

8 Here I refer once again to the key passage in *The Step Not Beyond*, 123, which I discussed in the introduction.

9 On the archefossil, see Meillassoux, 8–27; on the death of the sun, see Brassier, 223.

10 Percy Bysshe Shelley, "Mont Blanc," in *Shelley's Poetry and Prose*, 20, 22–4; "A Defence of Poetry," 533. For a discussion of these lines on which I build here, see also Earl R. Wasserman, *Shelley: A Critical Reading* (Baltimore: Johns Hopkins University Press, 1971), 225. On "Mont Blanc" and speculative realism more generally, see among others Greg Ellerman, "Speculative Romanticism," *SubStance* 44 (2015): 166–70; Anne C. McCarthy, "The Aesthetics of Contingency in the Shelleyan 'Universe of Things,' or 'Mont Blanc' without Mont Blanc," *Studies in Romanticism* 54 (2015): 355–75; and Evan Gottlieb, *Romantic Realities: Speculative Realism and British Romanticism* (Edinburgh: Edinburgh University Press, 2016), 161–81.

11 In this regard the sonnet anticipates Emily Dickinson's "Four Trees," which as Lily Gurton-Wachter suggests "presents a landscape with no one watching it," except for one who might pass by; it thus complicates the thematics of attention she finds throughout important strands of Romantic poetics. See Gurton-Wacher, *Watchwords*, 188.

12 Eugene Thacker, *In the Dust of the Planet*, vol. 1 of *Horror of Philosophy* (Washington, DC: Zero Books, 2011), 9.

13 For this fragment as well as the one cited shortly below, see *The Later Poems of John Clare, 1837–1864*, vol. I, 211.

14 The loose syntax of the passage gestures towards still further implications, for it suggests that the *lights* "forgot" – perhaps that they forgot to shine, or forgot that they were lights at all, and thus participating, even where they shine, in what doubly negates them. The passage inscribes a double negation within the apparently positive regime itself, hinting that disaster might befall in a way that may remain seemingly invisible – in a logic to be explored below.

15 Derrida, *Writing and Difference*, 230. I thank Alexander Schlutz for his suggestion that the sonnet's stance anticipates this discussion of a traceless trace.

16 Clare, "The Flitting," in *Major Works*, 250–6, lines 129, 131. In "Songs Eternity," nonhuman song is depicted as similarly coeval, with Adam and Eve and surviving far longer than cities or books; see *Major Works*, 122–4.

17 The emphasis on "little things" here is borne out in other Clare poems, indeed across virtually the entire corpus of his writing. For an example in this respect, see "Sudden Shower," a poem of the Helpston period, in which the "little things like you and I / Are hurrying through the grass to shun the shower." The speaker finds shelter under an ash tree, where "[t]hat little Wren knows well his sheltering bower / Nor leaves his dry house tho we come so near[.]" See *Major Works*, 102. I thank Alan Vardy for drawing my attention to the resonances of this poem in the present context. For the implications of Clare's reference to *that* wren, see the discussion of singularity below.

18 See Jane Bennet, *Vibrant Matter: A Political Ecology of Things* (Durham, NC: Duke University Press, 2010) and Bryant, *The Democracy of Objects*.

19 On this shared condition, see Jean-Luc Nancy, *The Inoperative Community* and the response in Blanchot, *The Unavowable Community*.

20 This instance raises key questions about the figure of apostrophe, for analyses of that figure rely on the assumption that nonhuman lives share a condition clearly distinguishable from that of human subjects. For an extended treatment of apostrophe and related figures in Clare, see Guyer, 11–24.

21 Blanchot, *The Writing of the Disaster*, 1.

22 For considerations of the Blanchotian resonances of the phrase "living on" relevant in the present context, see Derrida, "Living On," trans. James Hulbert, in *Parages*, 103–91.

23 Blanchot, *The Writing of the Disaster*, 1, 5.

24 Blanchot, *The Writing of the Disaster*, 3.

25 Meillassoux, 20.

26 Such a rendition of temporality suggests that this sonnet's stance shares much with Derridean deconstruction's account of the radical destructibility intrinsic to temporality; for an exemplary account of the latter, see Martin Hägglund, *Radical Atheism: Derrida and the Time of Life* (Redwood City, CA: Stanford University Press, 2008) and "Radical Atheist Materialism: A Critique of Meillassoux," in *The Speculative Turn*, 114–29. However, as noted above, by depicting the wind as moving without inscription, the sonnet proposes that it operates beyond what deconstruction elucidates, for it does so not only in the movement of what I have called *indifférance*, but also in what I will shortly describe as a time without time, a temporality that cancels temporality itself.

27 Blanchot, *The Writing of the Disaster*, 15. Tim Chilcott makes a related point, writing that in "Obscurity," "even time itself seems subject to the greater force of oblivion." Chilcott, '*A Real World & Doubting Mind': A Critical Study of the Poetry*

of John Clare (Hull, UK: Hull University Press, 1985), 126. I thank Billy Galperin for a comment that inspired this line of argument.

28 On this theme, see Meillassoux, *Time without Becoming* (Milan: Mimesis International, 2014) and Peter Gratton, *Speculative Realism: Problems and Prospects* (New York: Bloomsbury, 2014), especially 210–16. For an approach that explores the "temporal undulations" of quantum time and the nonpresent of the relations of interobjectivity, see Timothy Morton, *Hyperobjects: Philosophy and Ecology after the End of the World* (Minneapolis: University of Minnesota Press, 2013), 55–68, 81–95.

29 Tilottama Rajan, *Deconstruction and the Remainders of Phenomenology*. For a discussion of how speculative realism challenges core aspects of the phenomenological tradition, see Tom Sparrow, *The End of Phenomenology: Metaphysics and the New Realism* (Edinburgh: Edinburgh University Press, 2014).

30 Blanchot, *The Writing of the Disaster*, 7.

31 Blanchot, *The Writing of the Disaster*, 5.

32 Martin Heidegger, "Building Dwelling Thinking," in *Basic Writings*, ed. David Farrell Krell (New York: Harper & Row, 1977), 335.

33 Giorgio Agamben, *The Open: Man and Animal*, trans. Kevin Attell (Redwood City, CA: Stanford University Press, 2004), 91.

34 Agamben, 92.

35 For Agamben's reflections on bare life in the context of the human and animal, see *The Open*, especially 33–8, 75–7. I am grateful to David Clark for pointing out the relevance of these passages to this argument.

36 Agamben, *The Coming Community*, trans. Michael Hardt (Minneapolis: University of Minnesota Press, 1993), 15, 2, 65. I thank Anne McCarthy for pointing out the particularity of the ewe and fly and Alexander Schlutz for drawing my attention to the sonnet's telling use of deixis; their comments illuminate Clare's practice across most of his poetry and have inspired this line of argument.

37 Scott J. Juengel, "Mary Wollstonecraft's Perpetual Disaster," in *Romanticism and Disaster*, ed. Jacques Khalip and David Collings, *Romantic Circles Praxis* 2012, http://www.rc.umd.edu/praxis/disaster/HTML/praxis.2012.juengel.html paragraph 31.

38 For representative statements along these lines, see Derrida, *Given Time: I. Counterfeit Money*, trans. Peggy Kamuf (Chicago: University of Chicago Press, 1992), 34–70; *Of Hospitality: Anne Dufourmantelle Invites Jacques Derrida to Respond*, trans. Rachel Bowlby (Redwood City, CA: Stanford University Press, 2000); and *The Gift of Death*, second edition, with *Literature in Secret*, trans. David Wills (Chicago: University of Chicago Press, 2008).

39 The poem emphasizes the absence of knowledge through a fine irony, suggesting that a fly might know almost as much as the speaker about a blank past "with time" – that is, with the lifespan of a fly – and thereby reinforces in another way the theme of a self-cancelling temporality.

40 Blanchot, *The Writing of the Disaster*, 13.

41 Anne-Lise François, *Open Secrets*, 10.

42 Rajan, "Mary Shelley's 'Mathilda,'" 46. Over the course of its reiterations of this blank condition, the sonnet thus figures with unusual rigour the theme of anonymous life; for an exemplary treatment of the latter, see Khalip, *Anonymous Life*. I thank Libby Fay for her astute reflections on the sonnet's doubled usage of "blank," thoughts that led me to the argument outlined here.

43 Noel Jackson, "Coleridge's Criticism of Life," *Coleridge Bulletin* n.s. 37 (2011): 21–34.

Chapter 5

1 Hans Blumenberg, "Light as a Metaphor for Truth: At the Preliminary Stage of Philosophical Concept Formation," in *Modernity and the Hegemony of Vision*, ed. David Michael Levin (Berkeley: University of California Press, 1993), 33.

2 Jacques Derrida, *Dissemination*, trans. Barbara Johnson (Chicago: University of Chicago Press, 1981), 82–3; italics in the original.

3 All quotations from *The Triumph of Life* are taken from Percy Bysshe Shelley, *Shelley's Poetry and Prose*, second edition, 483–500, and will be cited by line number in the text.

4 See Percy Bysshe Shelley, *The Bodleian Shelley Manuscripts*, ed. Donald H. Reiman, vol. 1: *Peter Bell the Third* and *The Triumph of Life* (New York: Garland, 1986), 148.

5 While the authoritative edition provides bracketed, blank spaces later in the poem – in the line on Aristotle and Alexander the Great as well as that on Francis Bacon (260, 269) – in those instances the difficulty may be in characterizing specific historical figures in words that fit the poem's meter. The missing adjective before Life's light, however, is much less metrically daunting, even as it has a much more sweeping import. Moreover, that absent word modifies "light" in a telling way, adding an uncanny element to the poem precisely through that absence.

6 Paul de Man, "Shelley Disfigured," in *The Rhetoric of Romanticism* (New York: Columbia University Press, 1984), 120.

7 See Shelley, *The Bodleian Shelley Manuscripts*, 146, 166, 176, 196, 198, 232, 240, 252. On the reverse of the draft of the poem's final lines appears what could be a rudimentary sketch of a sail with a slight indication of a boat beneath; see 272. The image is so bare it becomes almost abstract, but because of the context established by the many prior sketches, it is not amiss to interpret it as the last image in that series. If that reading is plausible, then this final, barren image is no bad counterpart to what de Man figuratively locates on the manuscript's last page.

8 De Man, 120–1.

9 Mazur, 42. Mazur goes on to cite Reiman's contention that one cannot deconstruct *The Triumph of Life* because the poem had been left in an incomplete state;

see Reiman, 63. In effect, the transposition of death into life, of disaster into phenomena, and of incompletion into the work are already instances of a certain deconstruction.

10 Amanda Goldstein, "Growing Old Together: Lucretian Materialism in Shelley's 'Poetry of Life,'" *Representations* 128 (2014): 60–92; Monique Allewaert, "Toward a Materialist Figuration: A Slight Manifesto," *English Language Notes* 51 (2013): 61–77.

11 For useful accounts of the poem's evocations of Lucretian themes, see Hugh Roberts, *Shelley and the Chaos of History: A New Politics of Poetry* (University Park: Pennsylvania State University Press, 1997); Michael A. Vicario, *Shelley's Intellectual System and Its Epicurean Background* (New York: Routledge, 2007); and Goldstein. For my discussion of these themes see Collings, *Disastrous Subjectivities*, 140–6.

12 John Milton, *Complete Poems and Major Prose*, ed. Merritt Y. Hughes (Indianapolis: Odyssey Press, 1957), 267. These lines are quoted from *Paradise Lost*, Book III, lines 375–7, 380–2.

13 Brassier, *Nihil Unbound*, 223; Lyotard, *The Inhuman*, 8–23.

14 The question of how the poem treats the metaphor and image of light is, of course, immensely complex, not least because of the interplay between Life and the shape all light. For my earlier, extended discussion of light in the poem, see *Disastrous Subjectivities*, 156–62.

15 Gerald Finley, *Angel in the Sun: Turner's Vision of History* (Montreal: McGill-Queen's University Press, 1999), 148–73. Turner's emphasis on natural process leads him at times to emphasize the shift from mythic figures to those processes, the same transformation that takes place at key moments in Keats's *Hyperion* poems. As James A.W. Heffernan argues, in *Ulysses Deriding Polyphemus* (1829), the "prime mover" is not Ulysses but the sun, much as the sea displaces "Poseidon's vengeful rage." See Heffernan, *The Re-Creation of Landscape: A Study of Wordsworth, Coleridge, Constable, and Turner* (Hanover, NH: University Press of New England, 1984), 89.

16 James Hamilton, *Turner and the Scientists* (London: Tate Gallery, 1998), 119. See also Hamilton's discussion of Turner's overall engagement with geology and magnetism, including Mary Somerville's work on the latter: Hamilton, 115–28.

17 Barry Venning, "'Water, the Image of the Mind': Turner's Artistic Metaphors," in *Turner and the Elements*, catalogue by Inés Richter-Musso and Ortrud Wetheider (Munich: Hirmer Verlag, 2011), 85.

18 Collings, *Disastrous Subjectivities*, 84–108, 140–3.

19 Thus it is telling that Turner displaces the sublime through his unique emphasis on how it dwarfs humanity; as Ronald Paulson comments, Turner's version of the sublime "makes part of the terror the unimportance in every sense of the human survivors." See Paulson, *Literary Landscape: Turner and Constable* (New Haven, CT: Yale University Press, 1982), 77.

20 Inés Richter-Musso, "Fire, Water, Air and Earth: Turner as a Painter of the Elements," in *Turner and the Elements*, 49–50.

21 Thomas Sorger, "In the Eye of the Storm: Images of Spacetime in Turner and Poe." *Interdisciplinary Humanities* 28 (2011): 66.

22 William Hazlitt, *The Complete Works of William Hazlitt*, ed. P.P. Howe (Toronto: J.M. Dent, 1930–4), 4:76n.

23 John Ruskin, *Modern Painters*, in *The Works of Ruskin*, ed. E.T. Cook and Alexander Wedderburn, vols. 1–5 (London: George Allen, 1909).

24 James Hamilton, "'Earth's Humid Bubbles': Turner and the New Understanding of Nature 1800–1850," in *Turner and the Elements*, 53.

25 Johann Wolfgang von Goethe, *Scientific Studies*, ed. and trans. Douglas Miller (New York: Suhrkamp Publishers, 1988), 174–5. On Goethe's place in the shift to an emphasis on the process of perception, see Jonathan Crary, *Techniques of the Observer: On Vision and Modernity in the Nineteenth Century* (Cambridge, MA: MIT Press, 1992), 67–74; on Goethe's discussion of the retinal afterimage, 97–9.

26 Crary, 141. Leo Costello makes a similar point on how Turner's interest in the "physical, sensual relationship of the artist to the external world … brought about a very different kind of pictorial subject than the model of history painting that Turner inherited": see Costello, *J.M.W. Turner and the Subject of History* (Burlington, VT: Ashgate, 2012), 11.

27 When the fellow artist "expressed his wonder" at Turner's doing so, he is said to have replied, "It hurts my eyes no more than it would hurt yours to look at a candle." See Anthony Bailey, *Standing in the Sun: A Life of J.M.W. Turner* (New York: Harper Collins, 1997), 386.

28 Crary, 138.

29 For two discussions of Turner's response to an Enlightenment notion of light, see Paulson, 84–6 and Matthew Beaumont, "Reason Dazzled: The All-Seeing and the Unseeing in Turner's *Regulus*," *British Art Studies* 15 (2020), https://britishartstudies.ac.uk/issues/issue-index/issue-15/turners-regulus.

30 Lawrence Gowring, *Turner: Imagination and Reality* (New York: Musem of Modern Art, 1966), 13.

31 Gowring, 19.

32 Lindsay Stainton, *Turner's Venice* (New York: Braziller, 1985), 25, 27.

33 Hazlitt, 18:14.

34 Gowring, 10.

35 On the absence of any such manuscript and the uses to which Turner put this title, see Sam Smiles, *The Late Works of J.M.W. Turner: The Artist and his Critics* (New Haven, CT: Yale University Press, 2020), 172–4.

36 Philip Martin, "The Plains of War: Byron, Turner, and the Bodies of Waterloo," in *Literature as History: Essays in Honour of Peter Widdowson*, ed. Simon Barker and Jo Gill (New York: Continuum, 2011), 89.

37 Philip Shaw, *Waterloo and the Romantic Imagination* (New York: Palgrave Macmillan, 2002), 22.

38 Costello, 87.

39 Costello, 90.

40 This comment is quoted in Pyle, *Art's Undoing*, 22.

41 Martin, 92.

42 See Slavoj Žižek, *The Sublime Object of Ideology* (New York: Verso, 1989), 118–28.

43 For an earlier argument along similar lines, see Karl Kroeber, "Romantic Historicism: The Temporal Sublime," in *Images of Romanticism: Verbal and Visual Affinities*, ed. Kroeber and William Walling (New Haven, CT: Yale University Press, 1978), 149–65.

44 Costello, 5, 150–3.

45 See Costello, 97, 144, 166–7.

46 Ronald Paulson comments that the train in this painting constitutes "a substitute" for the sun, "an alternative, a black sun": see Paulson, 93.

47 Hazlitt, 4:76n; emphasis in the original.

48 In his chapter on light, Burke briefly addresses the sublimity of the sun's light, but soon moves to the greater sublimity of darkness. He then cites Milton's line on the darkness of God's light to refer to how a glance at the sun leaves black spots on the eyes, a fact that indicates how these apparent opposites come together in producing the sublime. His comments in this respect anticipate reflections on the process of perception of interest to Turner; it thus seems likely that Burke's theory of the sublime already participates in the shift of focus towards an aesthetics based on perception. His work, however, does not pursue the implications of the sun's light as far as Turner's. See Edmund Burke, *A Philosophical Enquiry into the Origin of our Ideas of the Sublime and Beautiful* (Oxford: Oxford University Press, 1990), 73–4.

49 Beaumont, 17–18.

50 Beaumont, 22. Here Beaumont builds on a brief remark by John Gage, *Color in Turner: Poetry and Truth* (New York: Praeger, 1969), 143.

51 Beaumont, 15.

52 Joyce Townshend explains that this canvas, sustaining "a large, curved tear in the sky" after its return from Italy, required extensive repair work, and that after applying an "extraordinarily thick" layer of paint to cover this tear in his studio, Turner added further paint during the varnishing days. See Joyce H. Townsend, *How Turner Painted: Materials & Techniques* (New York: Thames & Hudson, 2019), 84–7. According to John Gilbert, who witnessed Turner in action, the painter drove white paint "into all the hollows, and every part of the surface," gradually creating the sense "of brilliant sunshine absorbing everything, and throwing a misty haze over every object." Gilbert's account is quoted in Andrew Wilton, *Turner in His Time* (London: Thames & Hudson, 2006), 164 and Beaumont, 23–4. For images

that capture the damage to *Regulus* from this tear, as well as from the knife attack in the 1860s, see Townsend, 85.

53 Gilles Deleuze and Félix Guattari, *Anti-Oedipus: Capitalism and Schizophrenia*, trans. Robert Hurley, Mark Seem, and Helen R. Lane (Minneapolis: University of Minnesota Press, 1983), 132.

54 Beaumont, 21–2. Cf. Crary, "Nineteenth-Century Visual Incapacities," in *Visual Literacy*, ed. James Elkins (New York: Routledge, 2008), 69–70.

55 On references to Turner's saying "The sun is God," see Ruskin, *Works*, 28:147 and 36:543.

56 Jeremy Robinson, *The Light Eternal: A Study of J.M.W. Turner* (London: Crescent Moon, 1989). See especially chapter nine, "The Light Eternal," 92–106.

57 Blumenberg, 45. B.R. Nelson points out that while Turner was familiar with aspects of Neoplatonism from teachings to which he was exposed at the Royal Academy, he ultimately pursued a "subtle exploration of the psychology of sensory perception" instead; see Nelson, *Forms of Enlightenment in Art* (Cambridge: Open Angle Books, 2010), 142. But as I suggest in this chapter, Turner goes further still, for he also raised the question of how to conceive of absolute light from within the mode of that perception.

58 For his central discussion of cosmic abundance in the context of general economy, see Georges Bataille, *The Accursed Share: An Essay on General Economy*, vol. I, *Consumption*, trans. Robert Hurley (New York: Zone, 1988), 19–41; on the place of solar expenditure within this general economy, see 28–9.

59 On the geological references of the portrayal of the Deluge in this painting, see Finley, 167–9.

60 See Finley, 200–8.

61 Finley, 202–3.

62 Blumenberg, 34.

63 In his discussion of *Slavers* within the context of the *Zong* massacre, Ian Baucum argues that the devastating scene it portrays stops short at the painting's frame, exempting viewers and thereby allowing them "to stand sympathetically outside this historical scene" and thus indulge from a safe distance in the sentiments of a romantic liberalism. See Baucom, *Specters of the Atlantic: Finance Capital, Slavery, and the Philosophy of History* (Durham, NC: Duke University Press, 2005), 292. But as the paintings I have just mentioned demonstrate, the fact that viewers stand outside the frame of a Turner painting is not sufficient to guarantee that they enjoy a stable, external vantage point; on the contrary, Turner pursues a variety of strategies to undermine their privilege. For discussions of how Turner allows the processes he depicts in his paintings to bear on the mode of representation and on the position of viewers, see Costello, 73, 76, 102–3; for an extended discussion of how *Slavers* implicates its viewers, see Costello, 203–32.

64 On references to biblical figures within this painting, see Morton D. Paley, *The Apocalyptic Sublime* (New Haven, CT: Yale University Press, 1986), 117–18; Finley, 179–81; and Smiles, 216.

65 Here I quote a depiction of Deleuze's reading of Turner in James Williams, "Deleuze on J.M.W. Turner: Catastrophism in Philosophy?," in *Deleuze and Philosophy: The Difference Engineer*, ed. Keith Ansell Pearson (New York: Routledge, 1997), 234.

66 J.M.W. Turner, *The Sunset Ship: The Poems of J.M.W. Turner*, ed. Jack Lindsay (Lowestoft, Suffolk: Scorpion Press, 1966), 88. For discussions of Turner's poetry see Lindsay, "Turner and Poetry," in *Sunset Ship*, 11–75, and Andrew Wilton, *Painting and Poetry: Turner's* Verse Book *and His Work of 1804–1812* (London: Tate Gallery, 1990).

67 Gage 186, citing *Prometheus Unbound* II.ii.71–73. See Lord Byron, *Childe Harold's Pilgrimate*, Canto 4, 1603–11; see also 1648–56, where Byron writes that "my joy / Of youthful sports was on thy breast to be / Borne, like they bubbles, onward" and that "I was as it were a child of thee, / And trusted to thy billows far and near, / And laid my hand upon thy mane – as I do here." The simile thus associates the narrator with bubbles, nearly anticipating the suggestions that appear in Shelley's *Triumph* and Turner. See *Lord Byron: The Complete Poetical Works*, vol. 2, *Childe Harold's Pilgrimage*, ed. Jerome J. McGann (New York: Oxford University Press, 1980). For my previous discussion of these passages, along with the bubble imagery in *Triumph of Life*, see *Disastrous Subjectivities*, 135–6, 153–4.

68 Gage, 186–7. Compare Paulson, 103; Finley, 206–7; and William L. Pressly, "Milton as Turner's Muse in the Conjuring of New Worlds," *British Art Journal* 19 (2018): 51.

69 Finley, 207–8.

70 Pressly, 53.

71 Students of Turner's work are often fascinated with a range of his late watercolours and paintings, which seem to indicate that he was cultivating an aesthetics of the blank space or of the severely attenuated image. Deleuze and Guattari, in the passage from which I quoted above, argue that something astonishing takes place in these works, "in the series Turner does not exhibit, but keeps secret," for here the "canvas is truly broken, sundered by what penetrates it" (*Anti-Oedipus*, 132). But one must exercise caution when interpreting these images. Paintings that feature significant blank spaces in the upper centre of the image merely show that the artist often applied white paint to serve as an undercoating for areas to be painted in later. An apparent analogy between these images and *The Triumph of Life* collapses: while the missing word in Shelley's poem indicates that the poet rejected possibilities immediately available to him, these white areas prepare the ground in the usual way for areas of colour the painter had in mind, helping to shape the colour effect presumably intended for the final image. But one can nevertheless

confirm their reading of Turner in an analysis of *Regulus*, which is neither late, secret, nor incomplete. Other images, apparently given over to nothing more than a beautiful, pale light, in fact contain shadowy marks indicating shapes Turner intended to flesh out in due course, as he had done in a host of prior instances. Nevertheless, as the present argument suggests, one need not resort to these latter paintings to make a strong case for Turner's final stance, for the latter is visible in paintings that by most accounts had achieved a more completed state. The two late paintings I will discuss here, however, give every indication of being complete; neither features exposed undercoating or outlines of shapes to be filled in later. For a cogent discussion of the caution necessary when interpreting the late, unfinished work, see Smiles 226–38.

72 Andrew Wilton, *Turner in his time*, 216.

73 Robinson, 105; D.H. Lawrence, *Phoenix: The Posthumous Papers of D.H. Lawrence*, ed. Edward D. McDonald (New York: Viking, 1936), 474.

74 See Jacques Lacan, "The Mirror Stage as Formative of the *I* Function as Revealed in Psychoanalytic Experience," in *Écrits: The First Complete Edition in English*, trans. Bruce Fink and others (New York: Norton, 2006), 76–7. For a reading of *Sunrise* that touches on these themes, as well as further aspects of Lacan's teaching, see Nicolas Flynn, "The Last Modern Painting," *Oxford Art Journal* 20 (1997): 13–22.

75 On Turner's use of a dragon to symbolize aspects of geology and paleontology, see Finley, 164–7; on the depiction of a possibly extinct crocodile who witnesses the loading of creatures onto the Ark and the coming of the Deluge in *Shade and Darkness: The Evening of the Deluge*, see Finley, 169–72.

76 Costello, 102–3.

Agamben, Giorgio. *The Coming Community*. Translated by Michael Hardt.
    Minneapolis, MN: University of Minnesota Press, 1993.
- *Homo Sacer: Sovereign Power and Bare Life*. Translated by Daniel Heller-Roazen.
    Redwood City, CA: Stanford University Press, 1998.
- *Infancy & History: Essays on the Destruction of Experience*. Translated by Liz Heron.
    New York: Verso, 1993.
- *The Open: Man and Animal*. Translated by Kevin Attell. Redwood City, CA: Stanford
    University Press, 2004.
- *Remnants of Auschwitz: The Witness and the Archive*. Translated by Daniel Heller-
    Roazen. New York: Zone Books, 2002.
Allewaert, Monique. "Toward a Materialist Figuration: A Slight Manifesto." *English
    Language Notes* 51 (2013): 61–77.
Bailey, Anthony. *Standing in the Sun: A Life of J.M.W. Turner*. New York: Harper
    Collins, 1997.
Bari, Shahidha K. *Keats and Philosophy: The Life of Sensations*. New York: Routledge,
    2012.
Barnard, Suzanne and Bruce Fink, eds. *Reading Seminar XX: Lacan's Major Work on
    Love, Knowledge, and Feminine Sexuality*. Albany, NY: SUNY Press, 2002.
Bataille, Georges. *The Accursed Share: An Essay on General Economy*. Vol. I,
    Consumption. Translated by Robert Hurley. New York: Zone, 1988.
- *Visions of Excess: Selected Writings, 1927–1939*. Edited and translated by Allan Stoekl.
    Minneapolis, MN: University of Minnesota Press, 1985.
Baucom, Ian. *Specters of the Atlantic: Finance Capital, Slavery, and the Philosophy of
    History*. Durham, NC: Duke University Press, 2005.
Beaumont, Matthew. "Reason Dazzled: The All-Seeing and the Unseeing in Turner's
    Regulus." *British Art Studies* 15 (2020). https://britishartstudies.ac.uk/issues/issue
    -index/issue-15/turners-regulus.
Bennet, Jane. *Vibrant Matter: A Political Ecology of Things*. Durham, NC: Duke
    University Press, 2010.

Bernstein, Carol L. "Subjectivity as Critique and the Critique of Subjectivity in Keats's *Hyperion*." In *After the Future: Postmodern Times and Places*, edited by Gary Shapiro, 41–52. Albany, NY: SUNY Press, 1990.

Bewell, Alan. "The Political Implication of Keats's Classicist Aesthetics." *Studies in Romanticism* 25 (1986): 220–29.

Blanchot, Maurice. *The Gaze of Orpheus and Other Literary Essays*. Edited by P. Adams Sitney. Translated by Lydia Davis. Barrytown NY: Station Hill Press, 1981.

– *The Infinite Conversation*. Translated by Susan Hanson. Minneapolis, MN: University of Minnesota Press, 1993.

– *The Space of Literature*. Translated by Ann Smock. Lincoln, NB: University of Nebraska Press, 1982.

– *The Step Not Beyond*. Translated by Lycette Nelson. Albany, NY: SUNY Press, 1992.

– *The Unavowable Community*. Translated by Pierre Joris. Barrytown, NY: Station Hill Press, 1988.

– *The Writing of the Disaster*. Translated by Ann Smock. Lincoln, NB: University of Nebraska Press, 1986.

Blumenberg, Hans. "Light as a Metaphor for Truth: At the Preliminary Stage of Philosophical Concept Formation." In *Modernity and the Hegemony of Vision*, edited by David Michael Levin, 30–62. Berkeley, CA: University of California Press, 1993.

Bode, Christoph. "Hyperion, 'The Fall of Hyperion,' and Keats's Poetics." *The Wordsworth Circle* 31 (1999): 31–7.

Böhme, Jakob. *Forty Questions Concerning the Soul*. Translated by John Sparrow. London: Simmons, 1647. Online access via Early English Books Online. https://www.proquest.com/books/xl-questions-concerning-soule-propounded-dr/docview/2264190163/se-2?accountid=9681.

Brassier, Ray. *Nihil Unbound: Enlightenment and Extinction*. New York: Palgrave Macmillan, 2007.

Brice, Ben. *Coleridge and Scepticism*. New York: Oxford University Press, 2007.

Brown, David Blayney, Amy Concannon, and Sam Smiles, eds. *J.M.W. Turner: Painting Set Free*. Los Angeles, CA: J. Paul Gerry Museum, 2014.

Bruns, Gerald L. *Maurice Blanchot and the Refusal of Philosophy*. Baltimore, MD: Johns Hopkins University Press, 1997.

Bryant, Levi. *The Democracy of Objects*. Ann Arbor: Open Humanities Press, 2010.

Büchner, Georg. *The Major Works*. Edited by Matthew Wilson Smith. Translated by Henry J. Schmidt. New York: Norton, 2012.

Burke, Edmund. *A Philosophical Enquiry into the Origin of our Ideas of the Sublime and Beautiful*. New York: Oxford University Press, 1990.

Burwick, Frederick. "Coleridge's 'Limbo' and 'Ne Plus Ultra': The Multeity of Intertextuality." *Nineteenth Century Contexts* 9 (1985): 35–45.

Byron, George Gordon (Lord). *Lord Byron: The Complete Poetical Works*. Vol. 2. *Childe Harold's Pilgrimage*. Edited by Jerome J. McGann. New York: Oxford University Press, 1980.

Caputo, John D. *The Prayers and Tears of Jacques Derrida: Religion Without Religion.* Bloomington, IN: Indiana University Press, 1997.

Castellano, Katey. *The Ecology of British Romantic Conservatism, 1790–1837.* New York: Palgrave Macmillan, 2013.

Caygill, Howard. *Art of Judgment.* Oxford: Basil Blackwell, 1989.

Chiesa, Lorenzo. *The Not-Two: Logic and God in Lacan.* Cambridge, MA: MIT Press, 2016.

Chilcott, Tim. *'A Real World & Doubting Mind': A Critical Study of the Poetry of John Clare.* Hull: Hull University Press, 1985.

Clare, John. *The Later Poems of John Clare, 1837–1864.* General editor Eric Robinson. Vol. I, edited by Robinson and David Powell, associate editor Margaret Grainger. Oxford: Clarendon, 1984.

– *Major Works.* Edited by Eric Robinson and David Powell. New York: Oxford University Press, 1984.

– *Poems of the Middle Period: 1822–1837.* General editor Eric Robinson. Vol. IV, edited by Robinson, David Powell, and P.M.S. Dawson. Oxford: Clarendon Press, 1998.

Clark, David L. "Goya's Scarcity." *Constellations of a Contemporary Romanticism,* edited by Jacques Khalip and Forest Pyle. New York: Fordham University Press, 2016. 88–121.

– "Insult to Injury: Romantic Wartime and the Desecrated Corpse." *European Romantic Review* 30 (2019): 275–85.

– "Schelling's Wartime: Philosophy and Violence in the Age of Napoleon." *European Romantic Review* 19 (2008): 139–48.

Coleridge, Samuel Taylor. *The Complete Poems.* Edited by William Keach. New York: Penguin, 1997.

– *Literary Remains.* Vol. 3. Edited by Henry Nelson Coleridge. 1838. Project Gutenberg, 2003. https://www.gutenberg.org/files/8956/8956-h/8956-h.htm.

– *Marginalia.* Vol 2, Camden to Hutton. Edited by George Whalley. Princeton, NJ: Princeton University Press, 1984.

– *The Notebooks of Samuel Taylor Coleridge.* Edited by Kathleen Coburn. Vol. 3: 1808–1819. *Notes.* Princeton, NJ: Princeton University Press, 1973.

– *The Notebooks of Samuel Taylor Coleridge.* Edited by Kathleen Coburn. Vol. 3: 1808–1819. *Text.* Princeton, NJ: Princeton University Press, 1973.

– *Opus Maximum.* Edited by Thomas McFarland and Nicholas Halmi. Princeton, NJ: Princeton University Press, 2002.

– *Poetical Works, Volume II (Variorum Text).* Part 2. Edited by J.C.C. Mays. Princeton, NJ: Princeton University Press, 2001.

Collings, David. *Disastrous Subjectivities: Romanticism, Modernity, and the Real.* Toronto: University of Toronto Press, 2019.

– *Monstrous Society: Reciprocity, Discipline, and the Political Uncanny, c. 1780–1848.* Bucknell, PA: Bucknell University Press, 2009.

– *The Rubble of Culture: Debris of an Extinct Thought.* London: Open Humanities Press, 2023.

– *Wordsworthian Errancies: The Poetics of Cultural Dismemberment*. Baltimore, MD: Johns Hopkins University Press, 1994.

Comay, Rebecca and Frank Ruda. *The Dash – The Other Side of Absolute Knowing*. Cambridge, MA: MIT Press, 2018.

Copjec, Joan. *Imagine There's No Woman: Ethics and Sublimation*. Cambridge, MA: MIT Press, 2002.

Costello, Leo. *J.M.W. Turner and the Subject of History*. Burlington, VT: Ashgate, 2012.

Crary, Jonathan. "Nineteenth-Century Visual Incapacities." In *Visual Literacy*, edited by James Elkins, 59–76. New York: Routledge, 2008.

– *Techniques of the Observer: On Vision and Modernity in the Nineteenth Century*. Cambridge, MA: MIT Press, 1992.

Deleuze, Gilles and Félix Guattari. *Anti-Oedipus: Capitalism and Schizophrenia*. Translated by Robert Hurley, Mark Seem, and Helen R. Lane. Minneapolis, MN: University of Minnesota Press, 1983.

De Man, Paul. *The Rhetoric of Romanticism*. New York: Columbia University Press, 1984.

Derrida, Jacques. *Cinders*. Translated by Ned Lukacher. Minneapolis, MN: University of Minnesota Press, 2014.

– *Dissemination*. Translated by Barbara Johnson. Chicago: University of Chicago Press, 1981.

– *The Gift of Death*. Second edition, with *Literature in Secret*. Translated by David Wills. Chicago: University of Chicago Press, 2008.

– *Given Time: I. Counterfeit Money*. Translated by Peggy Kamuf. Chicago: University of Chicago Press, 1992.

– *Margins of Philosophy*. Translated by Alan Bass. Chicago: University of Chicago Press, 1982.

– *Of Hospitality: Anne Dufourmantelle Invites Jacques Derrida to Respond*. Translated by Rachel Bowlby. Redwood City, CA: Stanford University Press, 2000.

– *Parages*. Edited by John P. Leavey. Translated by Tom Conley and others. Redwood City, CA: Stanford University Press, 2011.

– *Spectres of Marx: The State of the Debt, the Work of Mourning, & the New International*. Translated by Peggy Kamuf. New York: Routledge, 1994.

– *Writing and Difference*. Translated by Alan Bass. Chicago: University of Chicago Press, 1978.

Dolar, Mladen. *A Voice and Nothing More*. Cambridge, MA: MIT Press, 2006.

Dworkin, Craig. *No Medium*. Cambridge, MA: MIT Press, 2013.

Ellerman, Greg. "Speculative Romanticism." *SubStance* 44 (2015): 154–74.

Evans, Murray. *Sublime Coleridge: The Opus Maximum*. New York: Palgrave Macmillan, 2012.

Faflak, Joel. *Romantic Psychoanalysis: The Burden of the Mystery*. Albany: SUNY Press, 2008.

– "Romantic Psychoanalysis: Keats, Identity, and '(The Fall of) Hyperion.'" In *Lessons of Romanticism: A Critical Companion*, edited by Thomas Pfau and Robert F. Gleckner, 304–27. Durham, NC: Duke University Press, 1998.

Finley, Gerald. *Angel in the Sun: Turner's Vision of History*. Montreal: McGill Queen's University Press, 1999.

Flynn, Nicolas. "The Last Modern Painting." *Oxford Art Journal* 20 (1997): 13–22.

François, Anne-Lise. *Open Secrets: The Literature of Uncounted Experience*. Redwood City, CA: Stanford University Press, 2008.

Gage, John. *Color in Turner: Poetry and Truth*. New York: Praeger, 1969.

Gasché, Rodolphe. *The Idea of Form: Rethinking Kant's Aesthetics*. Redwood City, CA: Stanford University Press, 2003.

Gigante, Denise. "The Endgame of Taste: Keats, Sartre, Beckett." In *Cultures of Taste / Theories of Appetite: Eating Romanticism*, edited by Timothy Morton, 183–201. New York: Palgrave Macmillan, 2004.

Goethe, Johann Wolfgang von. *Scientific Studies*. Edited and translated by Douglas Miller. New York: Suhrkamp Publishers, 1988.

– *The Sorrows of Young Werther*. Translated by Michael Hulse. New York: Penguin, 1989.

Goldstein, Amanda. "Growing Old Together: Lucretian Materialism in Shelley's 'Poetry of Life.'" *Representations* 128 (2014): 60–92.

Goslee, Nancy Moore. *Uriel's Eye: Miltonic Stationing and Statuary in Blake, Keats, and Shelley*. University, AL: University of Alabama Press, 1985.

Gottlieb, Evan. *Romantic Realities: Speculative Realism and British Romanticism*. Edinburgh: Edinburgh University Press, 2016.

Gowring, Lawrence. *Turner: Imagination and Reality*. New York: Musem of Modern Art, 1966.

Grant, Iain Hamilton. "Mining Conditions: A Response to Harman." In *The Speculative Turn: Continental Materialism and Realism*, edited by Levi Bryant, Nick Srnicek and Graham Harman, 41–6. Melbourne: re.press, 2011.

– *Philosophies of Nature after Schelling*. New York: Continuum, 2008.

Gratton, Peter. *Speculative Realism: Problems and Prospects*. New York: Bloomsbury, 2014.

Gurton-Wachter, Lily. *Watchwords: Romanticism and the Poetics of Attention*. Redwood City, CA: Stanford University Press, 2016.

Guyer, Sara. *Reading with John Clare: Biopoetics, Sovereignty, Romanticism*. New York: Fordham, 2015.

– *Romanticism after Auschwitz*. Redwood City, CA: Stanford University Press, 2007.

Hägglund, Martin. *Radical Atheism: Derrida and the Time of Life*. Redwood City, CA: Stanford University Press, 2008.

– "Radical Atheist Materialism: A Critique of Meillassoux." In *The Speculative Turn: Continental Materialism and Realism*, edited by Levi Bryant, Nick Srnicek and Graham Harman, 114–29. Melbourne: re.press, 2011.

Hamilton, James. *Turner and the Scientists*. London: Tate Gallery, 1998.

– "'Earth's humid bubbles': Turner and the New Understanding of Nature 1800–1850." In *Turner and the Elements*, edited by Inés Richter-Musso and Ortrud Wetheider, 52–64.

Harney, Stefano and Fred Moten. *The Undercommons: Fugitive Planning & Black Study*. Brooklyn, NY: Minor Compositions, distributed by Autonomedia, 2013.

Hartman, Geoffrey H. *The Fate of Reading and Other Essays*. Chicago: University of Chicago Press, 1975.

– *The Unremarkable Wordsworth*. Minneapolis, MN: University of Minnesota Press, 1987.

Hazlitt, William. *The Complete Works of William Hazlitt*. Edited by P.P. Howe. Toronto: J.M. Dent, 1930–34.

Heffernan, James A.W. *The Re-Creation of Landscape: A Study of Wordsworth, Coleridge, Constable, and Turner*. Hanover, NH: University Press of New England, 1984.

Hegel, Georg Wilhelm Friedrich. *Aesthetics: Lectures on Fine Art*. Translated by T.M. Knox. Volume I. New York: Clarendon, 1975.

– *Hegel's Science of Logic*. Translated by A.V. Miller. Atlantic Highlands, NJ: Humanities Press International, 1969.

Heidegger, Martin. *Basic Writings*. Edited by David Farrell Krell. New York: Harper & Row, 1977.

– *Being and Time*. Translated by John Macquarrie and Edward Robinson. London: SCM Press, 1962.

– *The Fundamental Problems of Metaphysics: World, Finitude, Solitude*. Translated by William McNeill and Nicholas Walker. Bloomington, IN: Indiana University Press, 1995.

– *What is Philosophy?* London: Vision, 1968.

Hill, Leslie. *Blanchot: Extreme Contemporary*. New York: Routledge, 1997.

Hollier, Denis. "The Dualist Materialism of Georges Bataille." *Yale French Studies* 78 (1990): 124–139.

Huet, Marie-Hélène. *The Culture of Disaster*. Chicago: University of Chicago Press, 2012.

Jackson, Noel. "Coleridge's Criticism of Life." *Coleridge Bulletin* n.s. 37 (2011): 21–34.

Jacobus, Mary. *Romantic Things: A Tree, a Rock, a Cloud*. Chicago: University of Chicago Press, 2012.

Jameson, Fredric. *A Singular Modernity: Essay on the Ontology of the Present*. New York: Verso, 2002.

Jarvis, Simon. *Wordsworth's Philosophic Song*. Cambridge: Cambridge University Press, 2007.

Joris, Pierre. "Translator's Preface." In Blanchot, *The Unavowable Community*, translated by Joris, xi-xxv. Barrytown, NY: Station Hill Press, 1988.

Juengel, Scott J. "Mary Wollstonecraft's Perpetual Disaster." In *Romanticism and Disaster*, edited by Jacques Khalip and David Collings. *Romantic Circles Praxis* 2012. http://www.rc.umd.edu/praxis/disaster/HTML/praxis.2012.juengel.html

Kant, Immanuel. *Critique of the Power of Judgment*. Edited by Paul Guyer. Translated by Guyer and Eric Matthews. Cambridge: Cambridge University Press, 2000.

Kantor, Jamison. "Immortality, Romanticism, and the Limit of the Liberal Imagination." *PMLA* 133 (2018): 508–25.

Keats, John. *The Poems of John Keats*. Edited by Jack Stillinger. Cambridge, MA: Harvard University Press, 1978.

Kessler, Edward. *Coleridge's Metaphors of Being*. Princeton, NJ: Princeton University Press, 1979.

Khalip, Jacques. *Anonymous Life: Romanticism and Dispossession*. Redwood City, CA: Stanford University Press, 2009.

– *Last Things: Disastrous Form from Kant to Hujar*. New York: Fordham University Press, 2018.

Kneller, Jane. "Introduction." Novalis, *Fichte Studies*. Edited by Jane Kneller. Cambridge: Cambridge University Press, 2003.

Koselleck, Reinhart. *Futures Past: On the Semantics of Historical Time*. Translated by Keith Tribe. New York: Columbia University Press, 2004.

Kroeber, Karl. "Romantic Historicism: The Temporal Sublime." In *Images of Romanticism: Verbal and Visual Affinities*, edited by Kroeber and William Walling, 149–65. New Haven, CT: Yale University Press, 1978.

Kucich, Greg. "Keats's literary tradition and the politics of histriographical invention." In *Keats and History*, edited by Nicholas Roe, 238–61.

Lacan, Jacques. "The Mirror Stage as Formative of the *I* Function as Revealed in Psychoanalytic Experience." In *Écrits: The First Complete Edition in English*. Translated by Bruce Fink and others. New York: Norton, 2006. 75–81.

– *The Seminar of Jacques Lacan*. Edited by Jacques-Alain Miller. *Book VII. The Ethics of Psychoanalysis*. Translated by Dennis Porter. New York: Norton, 1992.

– *The Seminar of Jacques Lacan*. Edited by Jacques-Alain Miller. *Book XX. Encore: On Feminine Sexuality, the Limits of Love and Knowledge, 1972–1973*. Translated by Bruce Fink. New York: Norton, 1998.

Lawrence, D.H. *Phoenix: The Posthumous Papers of D.H. Lawrence*. Edited by Edward D. McDonald. New York: Viking, 1936.

Levinas, Emmanuel. *Existence & Existents*. Translated by Alphonso Lingis. Pittsburgh, PA: Duquesne University Press, 1978.

– *Otherwise Than Being: Or Beyond Essence*. Translated by Alphonso Lingis. Pittsburgh, PA: Duquesne University Press, 1998.

– *Totality and Infinity: An Essay on Exteriority*. Translated by Alphonso Lingis. Pittsburgh, PA: Duquesne University Press, 1969.

Levinson, Marjorie. *Wordsworth's Great Period Poems: Four Essays*. Cambridge: Cambridge University Press, 1986.

Lindsay, Jack. "Turner and Poetry." In *The Sunset Ship: The Poems of J.M.W. Turner*, edited by Lindsay, 11–75. Lowestoft, Suffolk: Scorpion Press, 1966.

Lindstrom, Eric. *Romantic Fiat: Demystification and Enchantment in Lyric Poetry*. New York: Palgrave Macmillan, 2011.

Lyotard, Jean-François. *The Inhuman: Reflections on Time*. Translated by Geoffrey Bennington and Rachel Bowlby. Redwood City, CA: Stanford University Press, 1991.

– *Lessons on the Analytic of the Sublime*. Translated by Elizabeth Rottenberg. Redwood City, CA: Stanford University Press, 1994.

Martin, Philip. "The Plains of War: Byron, Turner, and the Bodies of Waterloo." In *Literature as History: Essays in Honour of Peter Widdowson*, edited by Simon Barker and Jo Gill, 80–94. New York: Continuum, 2011.

Mazur, Marc D. *Unread: The (Un)published Texts of Romanticism*. The Electronic Thesis and Dissertation Depository, 2018. Number 5784. https://ir.lib.uwo.ca/etd/5784/.

McCarthy, Anne C. "The Aesthetics of Contingency in the Shelleyan 'Universe of Things,' or 'Mont Blanc' without Mont Blanc." *Studies in Romanticism* 54 (2015): 355–75.

McFarland, Thomas. *Coleridge and the Pantheist Tradition*. Oxford: Clarendon Press, 1969.

Meillassoux, Quentin. *After Finitude: An Essay on the Necessity of Contingency*. Translated by Ray Brassier. New York: Continuum, 2008.

– *Time without Becoming*. Milan: Mimesis International, 2014.

Merleau-Ponty, Maurice. *Phenomenology of Perception*. Translated by Colin Smith. New York: Routledge, 2002.

Mileur, Jean-Pierre. *Vision and Revision: Coleridge's Art of Immanence*. Berkeley, CA: University of California Press, 1982.

Milton, John. *Complete Poems and Major Prose*. Edited by Merritt Y. Hughes. Indianapolis, IN: Odyssey Press, 1957.

Modiano, Raimonda. *Coleridge and the Concept of Nature*. Tallahassee, FL: Florida State University Press, 1985.

Morton, Timothy. *Hyperobjects: Philosophy and Ecology after the End of the World*. Minneapolis, MN: University of Minnesota Press, 2013.

Mulrooney, Jonathan Mulrooney. "How Keats Falls." *Studies in Romanticism* 50 (2011): 251–73.

Nancy, Jean-Luc. *The Inoperative Community*. Translated by Peter Connor and others. Minneapolis, MN: University of Minnesota Press, 1991.

Nelson, B.R. *Forms of Enlightenment in Art*. Cambridge: Open Angle Books, 2010.

Nelson, Lycette. "Introduction." In Blanchot, *The Step Not Beyond*. Albany, NY: SUNY Press, 1992.

Newey, Vincent. "*Hyperion, The Fall of Hyperion*, and Keats's epic ambitions." In *The Cambridge Companion to Keats*, edited by Susan J. Wolfson, 69–85. New York: Cambridge University Press, 2001.

Nietzsche, Friedrich. *The Gay Science With a Prelude in Rhymes and an Appendix of Songs*. Translated by Walter Kaufmann. New York: Vintage, 1974.

Novalis [Friedrich von Hardenburg]. *Fichte Studies*. Edited by Jane Kneller. Cambridge: Cambridge University Press, 2003.

O'Neill, Michael. "*When this warm scribe my hand*': Writing and History in *Hyperion* and *The Fall of Hyperion*." In *Keats and History*, edited by Nicholas Roe, 143–64.

Paley, Morton D. *The Apocalyptic Sublime*. New Haven, CT: Yale University Press, 1986.

– *Coleridge's Later Poetry*. Oxford: Clarendon, 1996.

Paulson, Ronald. *Literary Landscape: Turner and Constable*. New Haven, CT: Yale University Press, 1982.

Pfau, Thomas. *Minding the Modern: Human Agency, Intellectual Traditions, and Responsible Knowledge*. Notre Dame, IN: University of Notre Dame Press, 2013.

– *Romantic Moods: Paranoia, Trauma, and Melancholy, 1790–1840*. Baltimore, MD: Johns Hopkins University Press, 2005.

Phillips, Adam. "The Exposure of John Clare." In *John Clare in Context*, edited by Hugh Haughton, Phillips, and Geoffrey Summerfield, 178–88. Cambridge: Cambridge University Press, 1994.

Pladek, Brittany. "'In sickness not ignoble': Soul-making and the pains of identity in the *Hyperion* Poems." *Studies in Romanticism* 54 (2015): 401–27.

Plotnitsky, Arkady. "Beyond the Inconsumable: The Catastrophic Sublime and the Destruction of Literature in Keats's *The Fall of Hyperion* and Shelley's *The Triumph of Life*." In *Cultures of Taste / Theories of Appetite: Eating Romanticism*, edited by Timothy Morton, 161–80. New York: Palgrave Macmillan, 2004.

Potkay, Adam. "Wordsworth and the Ethics of Things." *PMLA* 123 (2008): 390–404.

Pressly, William L. "Milton as Turner's muse in the conjuring of new worlds." *British Art Journal* 19 (2018): 50–3.

Prickett, Stephen. *Coleridge and Wordsworth: The Poetry of Growth*. Cambridge: Cambridge University Press, 1970.

Pyle, Forest. *Art's Undoing: In the Wake of a Radical Aestheticism*. New York: Fordham University Press, 2014.

Rajan, Balachandra. "The Two *Hyperions*: Compositions and Decompositions." In *Romanticism: A Critical Reader*, edited by Duncan Wu. Oxford: Basil Blackwell, 1995. 263–90.

Rajan, Tilottama. "Coleridge, Wordsworth, and the Textual Abject." *The Wordsworth Circle* 24 (1993): 61–8.

– *Dark Interpreter: The Discourse of Romanticism*. Ithaca, NY: Cornell University Press, 1980.

– *Deconstruction and the Remainders of Phenomenology*. Redwood City, CA: Stanford University Press, 2002.

– "Keats, Poetry, and 'The Absence of the Work.'" *Modern Philology* 95 (1998): 334–51.

– "Mary Shelley's 'Mathilda': Melancholy and the Political Economy of Romanticism. *Studies in the Novel* 26 (1994): 43–68.

Reiman, Donald H. *The Study of Modern Manuscripts: Public, Confidential, and Private*. Baltimore, MD: Johns Hopkins University Press, 1993.

Richter-Musso, Inés. "Fire, Water, Air and Earth: Turner as a Painter of the Elements." In *Turner and the Elements*, edited by Richter-Musso and Ortrud Wetheider, 41–51.

Richter-Musso, Inés and Ortrud Wetheider, editors. *Turner and the Elements*. Munich: Hirmer Verlag, 2011.

Roberts, Hugh. *Shelley and the Chaos of History: A New Politics of Poetry*. University Park, PA: Pennsylvania State University Press, 1997.

Robinson, Jeffrey C. "The Immortality Ode: Lionel Trilling and Helen Vendler." *The Wordsworth Circle* 12 (1981): 64–70.

Robinson, Jeremy. *The Light Eternal: A Study of J.M.W. Turner*. London: Crescent Moon, 1989.

Rohrbach, Emily. *Modernity's Mist: British Romanticism and the Poetics of Anticipation*. New York: Fordham University Press, 2015.

Roe, Nicholas, editor. *Keats and History*. Cambridge: Cambridge University Press, 1995.

Ruskin, John. *The Works of Ruskin*. Edited by E.T. Cook and Alexander Wedderburn. London: George Allen, 1909.

Ryan, Robert. *Keats: The Religious Sense*. Princeton: Princeton University Press, 1976.

Schlutz, Alexander. *Mind's World: Imagination and Subjectivity from Descartes to Romanticism*. Seattle, WA: University of Washington Press, 2009.

Schuster, Aaron. *The Trouble with Pleasure: Deleuze and Psychoanalysis*. Cambridge, MA: MIT Press, 2016.

Senancourt, Étienne Pivert de. *Obermann*. London: William Rider & Son, 1907.

Sharp, Ronald A. *Keats, Skepticism, and the Religion of Beauty*. Athens, GA: University of Georgia Press, 1979.

Shaw, Philip. *Waterloo and the Romantic Imagination*. New York: Palgrave Macmillan, 2002.

Shelley, Percy Bysshe. *The Bodleian Shelley Manuscripts*. Edited by Donald H. Reiman. Volume 1: *Peter Bell the Third* and *The Triumph of Life*. New York: Garland, 1986.

– *Shelley's Poetry and Prose*. Second edition. Edited by Donald H. Reiman and Neil Fraistat. New York: Norton, 2002.

Sherwin, Paul. "Keats's Struggle with Milton in *Hyperion*." *PMLA* 93 (1978): 383–95.

Singer, Kate. *Romantic Vacancy: The Poetics of Gender, Affect, and Radical Speculation*. Albany, NY: SUNY Press, 2019.

Smiles, Sam. *The Late Works of J.M.W. Turner: The Artist and His Critics*. New Haven, CT: Yale University Press, 2020.

Sorger, Thomas. "In the Eye of the Storm: Images of Spacetime in Turner and Poe." *Interdisciplinary Humanities* 28 (2011): 60–72.

Sparrow, Tom. *The End of Phenomenology: Metaphysics and the New Realism*. Edinburgh: Edinburgh University Press, 2014.

Sperry, Stuart M., Jr. "Keats, Milton, and the Fall of Hyperion." *PMLA* 77 (1962): 77–84.

Stainton, Lindsay. *Turner's Venice*. New York: Braziller, 1985.

Taylor, Anya. "Superhuman Silence: Language in Hyperion." *Studies in English Literature, 1500–1900* 19 (1979): 673–87.

Terada, Rei. *Feeling in Theory: Emotion after the "Death of the Subject."* Cambridge, MA: Harvard University Press, 2001.

– "Looking at the Stars Forever." *Studies in Romanticism* 50 (2011): 275–309.

– *Looking Away: Phenomenality and Dissatisfaction, Kant to Adorno*. Cambridge, MA: Harvard University Press, 2009.

Thacker, Eugene. *In the Dust of the Planet*. Vol. 1 of *Horror of Philosophy*. Washington, DC: Zero Books, 2011.

– "Notes on Extinction and Existence." *Configurations* 20 (2012): 137–48.

Townsend, Joyce H. *How Turner Painted: Materials & Techniques*. New York: Thames & Hudson, 2019.

Trott, Nicola. "Keats and the prison house of history." In *Keats and History*, edited by Nicholas Roe, 262–79.

Turner, J.M.W. Turner. *The Sunset Ship: The Poems of J.M.W. Turner*. Edited by Jack Lindsay. Lowestoft, Suffolk: Scorpion Press, 1966.

Vardy, Alan. *John Clare: Politics and Poetry*. New York: Palgrave Macmillan, 2003.

Vaz-Hooper, Onita. "'If dead we cease to be': The Logic of Immortality in Coleridge's 'Human Life.'" *European Romantic Review* 20 (2009): 529–44.

Venning, Barry. "'Water, the Image of the Mind': Turner's Artistic Metaphors." In *Turner and the Elements*, edited by Inés Richter-Musso and Ortrud Wetheider. 74–85.

Vicario, Michael A. *Shelley's Intellectual System and Its Epicurean Background*. New York: Routledge, 2007.

Vendler, Helen. "Lionel Trilling and the Immortality Ode." *Salmagundi* 41 (1978): 66–86.

Washington, Chris. "John Clare and Biopolitics." *European Romantic Review* 25 (2014): 665–82.

Wasserman, Earl R. *Shelley: A Critical Reading*. Baltimore, MD: Johns Hopkins University Press, 1971.

Watkins, Daniel P. *Keats's Poetry and the Politics of the Imagination*. Rutherford, NJ: Fairleigh Dickinson University Press, 1989.

Williams, James. "Deleuze on J.M.W. Turner: Catastrophism in Philosophy?" In *Deleuze and Philosophy: The Difference Engineer*, edited by Keith Ansell Pearson, 233–46. New York: Routledge, 1997.

Wilner, Joshua. *Feeding on Infinity: Readings in the Romantic Rhetoric of Internalization*. Baltimore, MD: Johns Hopkins University Press, 2000.

Wilson, Eric. *Coleridge's Melancholia: An Anatomy of Limbo*. Gainesville, FL: University Press of Florida, 2004.

Wilton, Andrew. *Painting and Poetry: Turner's Verse Book and his Work of 1804–1812*. London: Tate Gallery, 1990.

– *Turner in his time*. London: Thames & Hudson, 2006.

Wolfson, Susan. *The Questioning Presence: Wordsworth, Keats, and the Interrogative Mode in Romantic Poetry*. Ithaca, NY: Cornell University Press, 1986.

Wordsworth, William. *The Prelude, 1798–1799*. Edited by Stephen Parrish. Ithaca, NY: Cornell University Press, 1977.

– *The Ruined Cottage* and *The Pedlar*. Edited by James Butler. Ithaca, NY: Cornell University Press, 1979.

– *William Wordsworth*. Edited by Stephen Gill. Oxford: Oxford University Press, 1984.

Yousef, Nancy. *Isolated Cases: The Anxieties of Autonomy in Enlightenment Philosophy and Romantic Literature*. Ithaca, NY: Cornell University Press, 2004.

Zalasiewicz, Jan and others. "Stratigraphy of the Anthropocene." *Philosophical Transactions of the Royal Society A*, 369 (March 13, 2011): 1036–55.

Žižek, Slavoj. *Interrogating the Real*. Edited by Rex Butler and Scott Stephens. New York: Continuum, 2005.

– *The Parallax View*. Cambridge, MA: MIT Press, 2006.

– *The Sublime Object of Ideology*. New York: Verso, 1989.

– *The Ticklish Subject: The Absent Centre of Political Ontology*. New York: Verso, 1999.

Index